THE LAND OF THE TAMILIANS AND ITS MISSIONS

THE LAND OF THE TAMILIANS AND ITS MISSIONS

E. R. BAIERLEIN

TRANSLATED FROM THE GERMAN BY
J.D.B. GRIBBLE

GYAN

Published by

Gyan Publishing House
5, Ansari Road
Daryaganj, New Delhi-110002
Phone: 011-47034999, 9811692060
E-mail: books@gyanbooks.com

Distribution Network
gyanbooks.com
India, USA, Canada, UK, Australia, France

ISBN : 978-81-212-3679-9 (PB)
First Published, 1875

2nd Impression 2020

Printed at: Gyan Press, Delhi.

The Land of The Tamilians and its Missions
Author: E. R. Baierlein

THE

Land of the Tamulians

AND

Its Missions,

BY THE

Rev. E. R. BAIERLEIN,

Missionary, Evangelical Lutheran Society.

Translated from the German,

BY

J. D. B. GRIBBLE, F.R.A.S., M.A.I.,

Madras Civil Service.

Printed by

HIGGINBOTHAM AND CO.

1875.

TO

LADY HOBART,

IN REMEMBRANCE OF MANY ACTS OF KINDNESS

AND

DEEP INTEREST, SHOWN

IN THE WELFARE OF THE

PEOPLE,

WHICH IT ATTEMPTS TO DESCRIBE,

THIS LITTLE BOOK

IS

RESPECTFULLY DEDICATED.

PREFACE.

A PORTION of this book has already appeared in a German Missionary publication. A considerable portion is here translated from the original manuscript, and the whole has been subjected to the revision of the Author.

The book contains so much that may be new to many readers, and so much that will be of interest to many more, that I do not think an apology is needed for it. I feel, however, that some apology is needed for the many faults and imperfections of the translation.

It has been written and passed through the Press in the intervals of Official work, and had I had more leisure I trust it would have been less imperfect. I hope, however, that the intrinsic worth of the book will atone for the errors of the

TRANSLATOR.

CONTENTS.

PART I.

CHAPTER I.

THE LAND AND ITS PRODUCTS.

CHAPTER II.

PEOPLE AND THEIR LITERATURE.

CHAPTER III.

EXTERNAL APPEARANCE OF THE TAMULIANS AND THEIR DOMESTIC LIFE.

CHAPTER IV.

RELIGION AND WORSHIP.

CHAPTER V.

Temples and Temple-worship.

PART II.

CHAPTER I.

The Mission of the Ancient Church.

CHAPTER II.

Romish Mission.

CHAPTER III.

The Lutheran Mission.

CHAPTER IV.

The English Episcopal Mission.

CHAPTER V.

The Mission of the English and American (Non-Conformist) Churches.

THE LAND OF THE TAMULIANS.

CHAPTER I.

THE LAND AND ITS PRODUCTS.

THE world had already attained a respectable age, before it knew anything of the land of the Tamulians. Then a weak delicate man stepped from a boat on to its shores, and gazed at the country long and wistfully, but no one was ready to open his door to him. This man remained for thirteen years in Tamil land, and when he went home, he left to the country as a remembrance his still youthful but weary body. This was Ziegenbalg, the first Lutheran Missionary to the Tamulians. Since his time this distant land has been brought nearer home, and now the land of the Tamulians is known in every quarter of the globe. And yet the longer we look at it the more we feel that it is very far removed from Europe, and that many imagine things to exist which are not, and that things are not which do exist; but as this country has been for more than a century and a half the scene of German labor, and a subject of German prayers, it is right that we should take a careful view of it.

Our first glance shall be at the country itself, and we find that it is larger than the kingdoms of Bavaria, Wurtemberg, Saxony, and the Saxon dukedoms put together, and contains a population which is about equal to that of the abovementioned countries (about 16 millions). This very respectably sized kingdom is washed on the East by the Bay of Bengal, whilst on the West a range of narrow mountains stretches from its most Southern point towards the North and forms a natural boundary to the West. In the country which borders on Tamil land, Malayalam is spoken in the South-West; Canarese in the centre and Telugoo in the North. The highest peak of these hills is found in the Neilgherries, about 8,000 ft. above the level of the sea and already beyond the Tamil-speaking boundary. Another lofty, though somewhat lower, range is that of the Pulney Hills. These are about 7,000 ft. high and stretch far into Tamil land. They are, however, but scantily cultivated. A third still lower group, or rather an eastern off-shoot of the above range are the Shervaroys about 4,000-5,000 ft. high. These are situated entirely within Tamil land; they are not quite removed from the fever range, and are now tolerably covered with Coffee plantations.

From these mountains, or running between them and rising in countries beyond them, several important rivers flow through the country from the West to the East into the Bay of Bengal. The Palar with its mouth near Sadras, the Poniyar near Cuddalore, the Cauvery, broadest near Trichinopoly, the Vygar in Madura, the Tambrapany in Tinnevelly and many others of lesser note. In the neighbourhood of all these rivers and especially in the low country the land is fruitful to a high degree. For even though the soil itself is not very rich, yet if there is only enough water available the Indian sun is capable, with its heating and drawing power, of producing the richest fruits. On the other hand, the richest soil, without water, becomes burnt up, is changed into dust, or is baked to the hardness of stone, and is full of deep cracks and fissures.

For this reason the former kings of the land did much to retain the water of the rivers; they built great dams of stone across the largest rivers in order to raise the water to a higher level, and from thence to carry it by thousands of channels far away into the fields; they built many large tanks or reservoirs, and dammed up natural hollows, which in the rainy season become lakes from which the country is irrigated.

During the rainy season from October till December, and for a short time afterwards, the rivers are often very broad and full of water. They are, however, never used for navigation because these floods last only for a short time. Thousands of channels draw off the water for the supply of distant fields and reservoirs, so that the rivers become very soon emptied and for the greater part of the year are nothing more than broad, glowing beds of sand. They, therefore, cannot generally be said to be picturesque; they are fringed by no green shadowy banks, and only a shallow rivulet runs through the deep sand, for they have yielded what they possessed to the service and benefit of man. But man is not often able to get as much as he wants from them, and comes back to the empty river beds and digs holes in order to find the necessary water for his cattle.

In the districts well supplied with water, the principal product is rice, and for ever rice, as far as the eye can reach. The land is divided into flat square fields, each with an incline of a few inches so that each of these fields lies higher than the other. The water is then taken from the channels and allowed to run from the topmost to the lowest field, so that all are under water. The fields are ploughed and sown with the water standing on them, and when the young plants are grown about a foot above the water they are taken out, tied in bundles and transplanted into other larger fields, prepared in the same manner. This work is generally done by women who stand in the water like storks, but bent at right angles, and thus plant entire fields with great industry. Far as the eye can stretch for days' journeys together, every field is planted with rice. In good soil with plenty of water, two, and in some places, three crops are raised in the year.

Sugarcane also requires a plentiful water supply and sugar is manufactured in numerous places for the markets of the country and for exportation. In districts which are far removed from rivers and lakes or are so highly situated that water cannot easily be taken to them, the soil is, of course, much less fruitful. Large tracts of country are covered with wild jungles, and the villages are few and far between. In such districts wherever there is cultivation, wells are dug and are pretty close together. These have a long crosspole swinging on a high tree trunk; at one end of the pole there is a long bamboo to the end of which an iron bucket is attached; two men run quickly up and down the crosspole, raising or depressing it by their weight, and supporting themselves by a bamboo rail; a third guides the bamboo and the bucket into and from the well, empties the bucket into a trough formed of a hollow tree or of masonry work, and at the same time chants out how many buckets he has brought up, a fourth individual leads the water thus raised into the fields, and in this way they are able to irrigate several acres of land planted with rice or sugarcane.

Indigo, certain pulses, and other similar grains do not

require regular irrigation. They are sown shortly before or shortly after the rainy season when the ground is well moistened by the monsoon rains. But should the rain be not plentiful enough, or should it not fall at the proper time, the whole crop is lost. Indigo bears three or four cuttings, so that there are generally as many harvests before it is necessary to re-plough and re-sow the ground. There are no barns here for storing, nor any threshing machines or even flails; on the field where the crop has been cut, it is at once threshed out and for this purpose they make use of a small portion of the field slightly elevated above the remainder, and firmly stamped down. The rice is taken in small bundles, it is beaten a few times on the ground, and the remainder is thrown into a heap which is trampled upon by oxen. Therefore the Mosaic law, "Thou shalt not muzzle the ox that trampleth out the corn," has a literal application to India, even in our days.

Cotton of course is also grown, for all the natives dress in cotton clothes, and a large quantity is exported. There are many kinds of cotton, which are grown in different soils. The ordinary indigenous cotton plant is only of one year's growth, and has to be re-planted annually. This is done shortly before the rainy season, and it is generally planted together with other grains (pulses) which are first harvested, and thus give the cotton more room to spread.

The first harvest of cotton is in February or March, and if a little more rain falls there is a second in July or August, which produces about half as much as the first; then the land is manured by sheep being penned upon it, and is afterwards again and again re-ploughed and re-sown.

Another kind of cotton is triennial and requires a less rich soil to mature, besides this there is the Bourbon Cotton plant which has been introduced with success, and experiments are also being made with American and Peruvian Cotton.

The Iron manufactures of the Tamulians are both important and interesting. The mountains are rich in iron ore, and no trouble or skill is required to bring it to the light of day. The ore is simply picked up, broken into pieces, washed clean from the earth and placed in the furnace. It must not, however, be supposed that this furnace is a very costly or permanent structure; it consists merely of a few walls of plaster, which two men can build without any expense in one or two days, and it is erected at the place where the ore has been collected.

The bellows, of which there are two, consist each of an entire goat skin, a man squats down on the ground, takes one in each hand and moves them up and down somewhat quickly, so that an equal and powerful blast is effected. The earthen furnace is filled at the bottom with charcoal, and then ore moistened with water is placed on the top of it; again follow charcoal and ore, and the operation with the two goatskins continues for four hours; the iron is then taken out with tongs, beaten with hammers so as to free it from the dross, and then given to the blacksmiths. The smith throws the iron thus obtained into chauldrons full of charcoal, he blows away with two similar goatskins and then hammers it into bars twelve inches long and one and a half broad. The iron is then ready for manufacture.

This iron is, however, very brittle, the color is red and most of our blacksmiths would probably reject it as useless. But this unpretending material produces the Indian steel, celebrated already in the earliest ages, and from which the swords of Damascus were manufactured, and as in olden times no other steel could be procured anywhere, it is probable that steel from India was used in polishing the granite monuments of Egypt.

The preparation of the steel again, is as simple as that of the iron. Small crucibles of mud mixed with husks of rice are built on the spot. Into these crucibles is thrown a quantity of broken iron with about a quarter of the weight of dry wood of the wild cinnamon bush (cassia auriculata) cut into small pieces, and after adding a few leaves of celandine (asclepia gigantia) the whole is covered up. An earthen cover is put over the mouth of the crucible and smeared with mud so as to render the whole air-tight; a number of such crucibles filled in this way are then placed in a furnace and covered with charcoal. A fire is lit and blown with the self-same goatskins for two or three hours. They then quietly wait until the whole has cooled, after which they proceed to extract the steel from the crucibles.

By the above process, all the unnecessary particles of carbon, which are the cause of brittleness in the iron, are removed and the finest steel is obtained. It is impossible to ascertain how the natives of India have arrived at this simple but profitable way of making steel; but it seems certain that in olden times they were the only persons who understood its preparation and the oldest Persian Poems speak in praise of Indian steel.

Salt is manufactured by a process even more simple than that used in the preparation of steel and iron, and this manufacture, of which the Government has made a monopoly, is one of the most profitable sources of revenue. Barren flats of ground, situated near the sea, are levelled in the same way as rice fields, sub-divided and then flooded with sea water. The Tamil sun soon dries up the scanty moisture, and the result is salt, which covers the fields like a coat of snow. This process is several times repeated during as many days, and then all that is necessary is to pick up the salt and store it in heaps, and it is ready for sale or for transportation into the interior. As may be expected, this salt which has been scraped from off the ground is not particularly clean ; but it is not difficult to clean it, and this task is willingly left to the purchasers. The salt thus manufactured can only be sold to Government from whose officers the dealers purchase it in wholesale quantities. The manufacture by private individuals is strictly forbidden, and the Government pays to the small French Settlement of Pondicherry no less than four lacs of rupees (£40,000 circa) in order to purchase the condition that the French authorities will allow no salt to be manufactured in their territory. This sum would seem to be an enormously high one, were it not remembered that Tamil land alone (without taking into account the four other language divisions of the Presidency) yields a salt revenue of over two millions of rupees (£200,000). The cost of the preparation of salt is so insignificant that the Government receive about 500 Rupees for every thirty rupees expended.

The chief source of the income of the Government, however, is the land revenue, and under this head the 16 millions of Tamulians have to pay over twenty millions of rupees, so that after adding a few more millions on account of the manufacture of spirits, the issue of licenses, &c., it will be found that the rate of each man per head, big and little, is about two rupees.

The most remarkable of the trees, of which on the whole, Tamil land has a bountiful supply, are the mighty banians, the thick shady tamarinds, and long branched mangoes, but the most beautiful as well as the most profitable are the tall graceful cocoanut palms.

Linnæus called the palm tree the prince of the vegetable kingdom. There are many different species of the tree, but in Tamil land the commonest kind is the palmyra, which grows wild in a sandy soil; the favorite species on the other hand is the cocoanut palm which especially loves the sea air. The trunks of the palmyra are made into beams and rafters for the houses, the leaves of both trees are used for roofing purposes, the cocoanut yields the fine oil which is so much used in the country, and is in so great demand in Europe, and from the fibres of the nut, are made all the country ropes and strings as well as the strongest anchor cables, which in this form are also exported to Europe and other quarters of the globe.

In addition, the palmyra yields sugar, and both palm species the so-called palm wine or toddy, which, however, has very little in common with proper wine and is more like a bad kind of whisky; it is strong smelling and highly intoxicating. The Tamil people are moderate and sober, but since the Government has introduced the system of selling the right to manufacture this liquor to the highest bidders, who are accordingly obliged to erect their shops in every hole and corner, drunkenness has increased to a serious extent. Not only the lower castes, but also the middle ones, to whom drunkenness was formerly the greatest disgrace, now drink and get drunk, and even their wives sometimes imitate their example. According to the laws of Manoo the punishment of drunkenness is death, and death by pouring down the throat of the offender the boiling urine of the cow. At present it would almost seem that the only sober class of people are the Shanars, who prepare this liquor. They do not drink, though others of their caste, who follow other sources of living indulge in the habit. Members of the higher castes, especially those who live in the towns drink both wine and brandy.

It is certainly greatly to be regretted that under the English Government the sobriety of the people has so greatly suffered. Under the Mohammedan rule the virtue of sobriety prevailed, and though the palm trees grew equally then as now, they were used only for the manufacture of sugar and oil. The responsibility of the increase of the vice of drunkenness is generally supposed to lie upon the Government alone, which by introducing the system of renting the exclusive manufacture of liquor, has rendered the preparation of spirituous liquor not only legal but universal. But though there is a great deal of truth in this, there is, in my opinion, another factor, who is also, and I maintain even more to blame for the prevalence of drunkenness; I mean example; whilst the lords in the land consume beer, wine and brandy in enormous quantities, it follows that the subjects soon regard drinking as a portion of civilization in the culture of which no one is willing to be left behind. Would that some means could be devised whereby the rapid progress of this vice of drinking might be arrested.

There are many remarkable and beautiful specimens of the banian tree which is generally planted only for the purposes of shade, and which ordinarily grows wild. Near Cuddalore there is a tall handsome tree, which from a distance can be easily distinguished from the others, and to walk round which, 163 paces are required, so large is the extent of ground occupied by the tree and its dropping roots. These air-roots often descend quite straight and perpendicular for a considerable distance, and at once take root even in the hardest soil, the sap then mounts upwards, and in a few years' time these string-like roots become thick trunks. Hundreds of such air-roots hang from the tree, I allude to on every side, the majority, however, never reach the ground for boys are in the habit of playing and swinging on them, and thus break off the ends before they can reach the earth. Thirty-five of them, however, have firmly taken root, and one has already grown to a trunk of 19 ft. in circumference three feet above the ground, whilst the youngest is only one and a half inches in circumference. If care were taken these trees might be trained to occupy an enormous extent of land. As it is, the abovementioned tree is large enough to accommodate under its shade more than a thousand men. It is worthy of remark that the seed of this mighty tree is one of the smallest in the world, smaller even than the mustard seed. And if this diminutive seedlet is borne by the wind or dropped by a bird, and falls upon a building in which there is a crack, however small, the strongest and the mightiest edifice must in time yield to its power. I have seen the strongest vaults split in two or thrown into ruins, solely through the power of this little seed, or on account of a thread-like root which had descended from above and taken root.

It is remarkable how great an attachment this the most independent of trees, for it has so many legs to stand upon, shows towards the palmyra palm. As soon as it scents one in its neighbourhood it seems to resign its independence, it becomes a creeper, and creeps and winds round the palmyra. And soon it throws its arms round the tree on every side, until at last the palmyra is perfectly enveloped by the banian. But above, the palmyra rears its lofty crest, whilst the banian throws its shade round the tree beneath. And so these two trees seem bound together by the most tender ties of love.—As far as its timber is concerned, the banian tree is only fit for firewood.

The fruit of the shady tamarind tree is largely used in the Pharmacopœia, but in this country it forms one of the ingredients of curry, and is eaten daily. The shadow of this tree is thicker than that of any other, but it is considered unhealthy and no one willingly camps under it.

The mango tree has often branches of an extraordinary length, that stretch forth from the trunk at right angles and cover a considerate portion of ground. The shade of this tree is much liked, and its fruits are among the best in India. It is a kind of plum, but of the size of a large apple; it is pleasant but not easy of digestion. Altogether the fruits of Tamil land have been praised above their deserts, and bear no comparison to the fruits of Europe, which one may long for here in vain. The most remarkable fruit is the so-called Jack fruit (Artocarpus integrifolia) which grows on large trees to the size of a big pumpkin; it does not, however, hang from the branches, for they would be far too weak to support the weight, butgrows out from the trunk of the tree. A green prickly shell must first be cut through before you can get at the peculiarly shaped strong smelling fruit. This is of a golden color and is highly prized by the Tamulians who may often be seen carrying a Jack fruit for miles, one fruit forming a man's burden. The fruit is repulsive to the European by reason of its strong smell, nor does he find it easy of digestion.

None of the trees in Tamil land, indeed, are familiar to the European. Every one is strange and unknown. And should he by chance recognize some plant, such as an aloe or a cactus, he sees here as a pernicious weed, growing wild in profuse luxuriance, what in Europe is carefully tended in hot houses and flower-pots. The aloe shoots up into lofty stems, as high sometimes as a palmyra, the tops of which are ornamented by bunches of flowers and blossoms. The aloe is often used as a hedge. It is only the flowers in the gardens of the European residents which appear familiar. These bloom throughout the whole year if they are only irrigated with sufficient water, and are not scorched up by a wind hotter than usual.

The forests of Tamil land are situated on the slopes of the hills and mountains by which it is surrounded. In these forests wild elephants are still found, but with the exception of 'rogues,' which attack men, the slaughter of elephants is now prohibited. For every tiger the Government pays a large reward (Rs. 50) taking in return the skin. Many hundreds of tigers, leopards, and bearskins are handed over to the Government annually, but the race is not yet rooted out, and many a Tamulian to this day finds his grave in a tiger's stomach. It is by no means rare to meet English Officers who have sustained lasting injuries in the sport of tiger-shooting. Not long ago two Officers went out to shoot one, but had not got very far when they came quite unexpectedly across a large royal tiger, which seemed to have been watching them for some time. This sudden appearance was so unpleasant to both these sportsmen that they at once took refuge in a high tree, each thinking only of himself, and endeavouring to get to the top as fast as possible. The tiger made a spring, caught hold of one of the Officers, and dragged him down. When the other at the top of the tree looked round for his friend, he saw to his horror that he was lying on the ground in the claws of the tiger. This at once brought him to his senses and enabled him to recover his presence of mind. After taking a cool, deliberate aim, he fired, killed the tiger and saved his friend. Only a few weeks ago I met a Colonel Y——, whose right arm was entirely disabled and who had to do everything with his left. He was still, however, able to command his Regiment. He had been 33 years in India without going to Europe and yet looked quite strong and well; he belongs, therefore, to the few Europeans who become thoroughly acclimatized. He told us his tiger adventure as follows: "One day I felt an indescribable longing to go out tiger-shooting, a sport with which I was familiar. I therefore took a cooly who carried a spare gun, and rode from the station into the jungle. I tied up my horse on the outskirts of the jungle, into which I walked, accompanied by my cooly. We had only gone a very short distance when we suddenly saw a mighty tiger standing right in front of us. I at once took aim, but before I could pull the trigger the tiger was on me. With his paw he struck me in the back and with his jaws he seized my right elbow, and so down we went to the ground together. I lost my senses, but as my finger was still on the trigger my rifle exploded into the air. This unexpected shot saved my life, the tiger was alarmed and bolted away. I stood up and looked round for my cooly, but he, of course, was nowhere to be seen. So holding my bitten right arm in my left hand I trudged off in the direction of my horse. But I found that my cooly had gone off with the horse, and so in the most intense pain, with a succession of fainting fits I had to make way to the station on foot. Not far from the station I met several officers riding out, for my cooly had spread the alarm that the tiger had eaten me up. For a long time afterwards I hovered between life and death, but at last recovered and then learned to use and to write with my left hand with as much ease as I formerly could with my right."

There are numbers of antelopes on the plains and in the jungles, and they are often caught young and made very tame. They are graceful, affectionate little animals. The opposite are the buffaloes with their enormous horns and stupid faces. They are fond of lying in tanks and pools so that only their noses are visible above the water, whilst their horns and even their eyes are beneath it. Their hides are almost entirely destitute of hair and are of a blackish brown.

An animal with an intelligent face on the other hand is the milk white ox with the hump. It is a graceful beast; it can trot for miles and is an indispensable companion in Tamil land, for the native bred horses are small, whilst the imported ones suffer like their masters from the climate, and cannot stand much exposure. The food of these oxen is a kind of pulse known as gram, which is used also for the horses, and rice straw (for horses grass.)

The most wonderful animal of Tamil land is the long tailed ape. In many districts the trees and the roads are quite full of them, and they run in troops across the road or leap from one tree to the other. Sometimes they are so bold, that they will come to a house and steal away from the fire the gram which is cooking for the horses. If ever I drove or ordered them to be driven away, they never went very far, but assumed a strange wounded look, and then in a short time they were again close by the gram-pot on the fire. The reason of that is, that the Tamulians never do them any harm or indeed deny them anything. In many of the large Pagodas there are hundreds of them, if not thousands. Some of the older members of the tribe present a most venerable appearance. They know also how to maintain their dignity towards the younger members of their race, and frequently bring them to a knowledge of their proper position by a well directed box on the ear. In some places, as in Tiruvanamaly, they become a regular plague. Not only is the large pagoda full of them, but every street and every housetop in the town. Wherever they come they can never be at rest, but must for ever be carrying on their mad gambols. In Tiruvanamaly they have made it their especial diversion to pull off the roofs of the houses. Not only do they tear off the thatch and throw it down into the roads, but they also pull off the tiles and merrily scatter them in the streets. I saw some houses quite uncovered, and it was not exactly safe to walk in the streets where they principally congregated. The inhabitants of the town appear to be perfectly helpless as far as these monkeys are concerned, and the English Engineer told me that he had advised the laying on of a thick coat of lime as the only remedy of saving the tiles. They not only run about in the bazaar, but coolly help themselves to plantains, of which they are very fond, and no one ever dreams of preventing them. Others again are more mischievous in their pranks, and run cleverly behind the women as they come from the market with a basket on their heads full of their purchases; they jump on their backs, pull down the basket, and scatter the contents on the ground, whereupon a host of monkeys small and big, come running up and help themselves to what they like best, securing their plunder, and then running up the nearest tree to enjoy it in safety. And they are allowed to do all this only because of the excessive *gratitude* of the Tamulians. The Hindoos have been reproached with being a thankless people, and true it is that the Tamulians, at all events, have no word in their language to express gratitude, so that it is not in their power to thank even if they were so inclined. But still I am not on that account inclined to regard them as less thankless than other nations. For though, for instance, the Germans know how to express their thanks in so many different forms of speech, still there is a German proverb: "Ingratitude is the world's reward." The

Hindoos, however, and among them the Tamulians, express their gratitude in deeds even towards the monkeys, and that after thousands of years. Their tradition is that when Rama made war against Ravana, the Giant of Ceylon, who had carried away his wife Sita, he was assisted in his expedition by Hanooman, the king of the monkeys, and out of gratitude for this help shown to their favorite deity, the Tamulians to this day allow the mad *descendants* of Hanooman to unroof their houses and to carry on all kinds of fantastic tricks.

Of the other animals the crocodile is especially worthy of mention, which lives in many of the rivers and sometimes reaches a length of over 20 feet. Its diminutives, the lizards, run along the walls of our rooms, and catch the small insects, which no one grudges them, and they are suffered in every house. The fat frogs, however, which at certain times of the year throng into the houses and hop about in numbers in the corners, are not so much liked, though they are never killed. This fate happens generally only to the snakes and the scorpions, which are also partial to the houses. The most dangerous is the spectacled snake, the cobra-di-capella, though the black scorpion cannot be said to be much better, for its sting is also said to be deadly, and even the cobra cannot rob one of more than life. In the case of the cobra death generally follows the bite in about three hours. We killed many about our house, and the last was so savage that I had to shoot it, for none of my people dared to approach it. But the worst destroyers in Tamil land are the white ants. Poor man seems to be quite helpless against these innumerable and untiring enemies, and in vain did the Governor of St. Helena offer a large reward for some means by which they might be destroyed, for they seemed to wish to drive men away altogether, by eating away the beams and the entire wood-work of the houses, so that the buildings tumbled to pieces. In Tamil land also most houses have more or less to suffer from these insects.

One cannot exactly call the land of the Tamulians a beautiful country, but it is in parts very fruitful and is a country richly provided with everything necessary to life. The Tamulian is independent of any other country, on the face of the earth, and requires nothing from Europe or elsewhere, for his country gives him in abundance everything he can wish or can use. A European on the other hand is far more helpless, and whether rich or poor, can scarcely manage to get on without the help of Tamil land or its neighbouring districts. Pepper and other spices have long since been daily necessaries to the European, and the Pepper Coast proper lies on our western frontier Malabar. In addition to this, Europe receives from the superfluities of the Tamulians coffee, sugar, cotton, indigo, oil, &c.

Although not exactly a beautiful, still it is a greatly favored country, where the rulers and the people have undergone great expense to make the residence of their subjects agreeable, and the journeys of travellers pleasant. For the first are provided thousands of channels, large artificial lakes, and magnificent tanks which render the land fruitful, and in addition there are large and splendid temples such as are not to be found anywhere else in India, such as formerly existed in Egypt but which are nowhere else to be found upon earth. In no other country of the world are better provisions made for travellers than in Tamil land. "Entertain gladly" is a motto which is stamped upon scarcely any other country as it is upon this, for one can go but very few miles in any direction without coming across fine hostels (chattrams) to which are attached one and sometimes several courts, and which on the outside afford a welcome shelter under an overhanging roof, supported by pillars which forms a verandah. In many of these chattrams, travellers are gratuitously fed with a meal of rice; in all it is to be purchased for a small sum. These, of course, are built for the people, for Sudras and Brahmins. Pariahs are not allowed to enter them, and for Europeans they are only a make-shift. Near these chattrams, however, there are generally very pretty tanks, often built all round with granite steps, and shady groves where the beasts of burden find shelter, and where Europeans pitch their tents, if there happens to be no bungalow, such as the Government has built in many places for the convenience of European travellers. On the roads one often meets a piece of masonry, built in order that porters and carriers may deposit their burdens upon it, and repose comfortably without stooping down to deposit them on the ground, from whence it would be almost impossible to raise them without help.

In one word—for the Tamulian with his habits of life, there can scarcely be a more comfortable or a cheaper country than the land of the Tamulians. He finds everywhere what he wants, and his wants are not many. The country yields water sufficient for bathing and drinking—a necessity; and shade against the midday sun—a luxury. The cloth he wears protects him at night against the cold, of which, his skin, owing to the constant exposure to the air, is less sensitive than ours. The greatest cold in his country, however, is scarcely as cool as the greatest heat in our land of Germany.

The coolest month in Tamil land is January, and in this month the average temperature is higher than in New York; the average temperature is in July, the hottest month of the year. During the coolest season of the year the thermometer stands between 68° and 80° Fahrenheit, and during the hottest between 80° and 100° in the shade. In many years, however, it rises above 100°, and for days I have had it in my room at 103°, whilst at night the difference of temperature was but trifling. Should a Tamulian possess an extra cloth to wind round his loins, and maybe a mat of reeds, worth from threepence to fourpence, he is ready to travel from one end of his country to the other, and often I envy him this power.

But the country which is "Home, Sweet Home" to the Tamulian is only a strange and foreign place to the European. It is true that many of the difficulties are surmounted in time. With ignorance of the language, many a harrassing misunderstanding disappears, and with a better knowledge of the character of the people comes the conviction, that all is not bad which is opposed to our customs and feelings; and then many things become easier. But one evil continues for the stranger as bad as it was at the commencement, and there are very few who can say that they do not fear it. I mean the pitilessness of the sun and all the consequences which follow. Some are able to contrive matters so, that with much care and management in shunning its rays, they do not especially suffer; but there are not a few on the other hand, who soon either fall victims to it, or have to leave India quickly, whilst others though not actually compelled to do that, are in a continual state of suffering, so that their existence scarcely deserves to be called life.

It is clear that God has not only given the earth to man, but he has also assigned to each people its separate dwelling place in the world; he has fixed beforehand where and how far their several boundaries shall extend, and where they can best prosper. "The Earth is the Lord's and what therein is, so let everything that dwelleth upon the earth praise him."

CHAPTER II.

The People and their Literature.

"God has made of one blood all nations of men to dwell on all the face of the earth," and he has also redeemed them all with one blood, and so at the close of the so-called golden age (which went to pieces near Noah's ark), we see the whole of mankind gathered together in the ark and then spreading themselves abroad from Mount Ararat into all parts of the earth, until the building of the Tower of Babel. This seems to have gone on in one continuous stream; and from that time mankind is divided into three main divisions, which soon afterwards separated into numerous branches, and now and then crossed each other. The Semites probably remained tolerably close to the existing habitations of men, for they loved their tents. The Hamites, however, full of restlessness, wandered chiefly to the South, and founded kingdoms on the banks of the Jordan and the Nile, which countries they named after their family chiefs, Canaan and Mizraim. To be sure, in those days they had no flat noses, protruding lips, and curly hair as the negroes of Africa have at present, who are also, but not they alone, Hamites. The Japhetites on the other hand, with the blessing of "enlargement" resting upon them, soon spread in several directions. Towards the West where they filled Europe under different names as Greeks, Romans, Germans, Slavonians, &c., founding different kingdoms and different languages such as exist to the present day; and towards the East, where they established pleasant dwellings on the banks of the Indus, under the name of Hindoos or Indians. Soon, however, they were attracted by another watershed, far larger and more fertile than that of the Indus, namely, the valley of the Ganges, 1,200 miles long and 600 miles broad. Here they founded their fairest and most powerful empires. When they had filled the Ganges valley with their kingdoms and commenced to spread themselves further to the South, they found another people, less civilized, it is true, but still possessing kingdoms and princes, with whom many a battle had to be fought. For at that time there lived, nay, they live there to the present day, the Dravidians, a *Turanian* race. The Dravidians are divided into different peoples, by different languages, as widely different from each other as German, French and English.

The most important of these Dravidian races is that of the Tamulians. They occupy not only the country, described in the last chapter, but also the North of Ceylon and the South of Travancore, on the western side of the ghauts. There is a Christian congregation of Tamulians at Bombay and at Calcutta; and Tamulians are to be found in Burmah, Pegu, Singapore, and in the Islands of Mauritius, Bourbon and even in the West Indies. It is only a short time ago that I had to send Tamil gospels and tracts to Jamaica. In short, wherever money is to be earned, and wherever there is a lazier and more superstitious people to be shoved aside, there will Tamulians be found, for they are the most enterprizing and movable people in India.* Their numbers according to the last census amount to 16 millions.

In the land of the Tamulians there ruled in olden days many kings, but three dynasties made themselves especially remarkable: the Pandian, Chera, and Chola dynasties. Although the two embassies, from Tamulian kings to the Emperor Augustus, of which Eusebius and Strabo wrote, may not have taken place, or may have been but the making of Alexandrian Greeks, it is quite certain, that firmly founded Tamulian kingdoms existed at that time. For there can be no doubt that when we repeatedly read of οἱ πανδιονς and Μὰδωςα βασίλειον πανδιονις, reference is made to the kings of the Pandian dynasty of Madura; for here in Madura, to this day, one of the finest towns of South India, there existed for centuries a mighty and prosperous empire,

* NOTE.—It is remarkable how the Tamil language gradually spread, with the spread of railways and roads. Take, for instance, the district of Cuddapah. Seventy years ago, Canarese was the predominant language; now it is Telugoo; but since the railway was opened 7 years ago, Tamil is spoken by many thousands near the line of rail. But rare instances are to be found of any foreign language, such as Telugoo, &c., spreading in Tamil land. Telugoo shoves Canarese on one side, and in its turn is displaced by Tamil. 100 years hence the whole of the Madras Presidency may be a Tamil-speaking country.

and the palace of the old Tamulian kings is so remarkable a building that at the present moment the British Government is spending hundreds of thousands of rupees in order to save it from decay and to preserve it to posterity.

In the same way Ptolemy's Αρδεαῖω βασίλειον of the Σώφα refers to the Sora or Chola dynasty of the kingdom of Arcot. The *S* in sora is pronounced sharply, and is also written ch and pronounced Chola. The *r* in Sora is a letter peculiar to the Tamil alphabet, and is sometimes rendered by a *v* and sometimes by an *l*. Sora and Chola are, therefore, the same, and the proper pronunciation is something between the two spellings. The land of the Chola dynasty was named Cholamandalum from which Coramandel is derived.

Similarly καρώρα βασίλειον κηροβοϑρω refers to the Chera (also Kerala) dynasty, the chief town of which was at Caroor (Car = black–oor = town.) The rule of this dynasty extended over Coimbatore as far as Malabar and included some portions of the present kingdom of Mysore, though the boundaries and the capitals did not always remain the same.

The three Tamulian dynasties together with their capitals, were, therefore, well known to the Greeks. Of these, the Pandian dynasty at Madura appears to have been the oldest and the most brilliant. Madura was built by Kala Sakhara over the site of an old lingam said to have been placed there by Indra himself. In a short time there sprung up in this youthful and vigorous royal residence a High School with 48 Academicians and it was here that the Tamil language, in contradistinction to the Sanscrit dialects of the North, was cultivated and developed. In time, however, the Professors began to swim with the stream, until just as the Tamil language was in danger of losing its purity, there came a Pariah Priest and weaver from Mylapoor, not far from the present, then not existing, Madras. This new comer, by name Tiroovalloovan, succeeded in obtaining a hearing for his poem the Kural, written in the purest high Tamil, and in this way effected a kind of revolution in the language. Tiroovalloovan is not the real name of the poet, but is his adopted title of honor, and signifies the holy Priest.

The Hindoos, who are never able to narrate an incident exactly as it happened, and who, in spite of the praise awarded them by the Greeks of being lovers of truth, seem to have fallen into this bad habit in the earliest times, make a very pretty little story out of this incident which they tell as follows:

When Tiroovalloovan came to Madura he proceeded at once to the temple and recited his poem in the presence of the king and of the Academicians, the latter being greatly terrified. These tried to get him into a corner by all kinds of sharp questions, but he answered them immediately in fine verses. Then they said: Listen, O Vallava! the last test rests with this bench of gold; if the bench will accept your book, it is accepted; if it does not, it is rejected! whereupon they spread themselves out and so pushed against each other as not to leave the smallest space remaining. Tiroovalloovan, however, nothing daunted, approached the bench, book in hand, which as soon as he came near, stretched itself out so that he and his book found a place on it. Thereupon the book commenced to swell so enormously that it shoved one Academician after another off the bench until they were all left sprawling on the ground. This was a disgrace that they could not bear, and so they all went and drowned themselves in the fine big tank which is still to be seen in Madura. This probably means that Tiroovalloovan found favor in the eyes of the king, which indeed was the fact, and that his reputation soon surpassed that of all his rivals. The bench of gold means, of course, the good income of the Academicians,

This extraordinary Pariah Priest had also an extraordinary wife. When he returned from Madura and again took up his old trade of weaving, there soon collected round him a number of men who wished to be his disciples, and wanted to make him their guroo or High Priest. One day one of the scholars approached Tiroovalloovan with folded hands and said: "My master! which is the better: Domestic virtue, or the virtue of Penance?" for Tiroovalloovan had praised both. Indian sages, however, are tardy of answer, and are especially not in a hurry to answer a knotty question. Hence the scholar had to repeat the question for many a day and yet to remain without an answer. After many such repetitions he obtained an answer and one in three acts:

Act I.—Wife was drawing water from the well at the time the inquisitive scholar put the question. 'Wife, come here!' The wife let her earthern-pot fall to the bottom of the well and ran to ask what her husband wanted.

Act II.—Tiroovalloovan, eating his breakfast; and as he like all poets is only a poor man, his meal consists of the remains of the rice cooked the evening before, now very much cold and flabby. Enter, inquisitive disciple. Puts usual question. "Wife, this rice is too hot; it burns my mouth!" Hastens the wife, and cools the rice by blowing upon it.

Act III.—Broad daylight. Bright Indian sun. Poet weaving, not verses, but veritable thread to earn his evening meal. Enter, inquisitive scholar. Puts usual question. Poet drops his shuttle. "Wife! bring me a candle to find my shuttle!" Wife at once obeys, and, spite of the sun looking in at the door, brings a dim oil lamp, by the aid of which she finds the shuttle and gives it to her lord and Master. Oil lamp at once throws a ray of light into the inquisitive. "Light (oil) dawns upon me! With so excellent a wife domestic virtue is the better. Without such an one, a hermitage is preferable. Inquisitive retires satisfied, but leaves us in doubt to whom the virtue belongs and an awkward feeling as to whether many of us ought not to have chosen a hermit's life.

This same good wife as she lay dying begged her stern husband to explain what to her was a matter of great mystery, and had puzzled her since the day of her marriage: "My Lord, when for the first time I cooked your rice and placed it before you, you ordered me always to put a jug of water and a needle by your side; why did you order me to do this?" whereupon her loving consort replied: "If, my dear one, a grain of rice should fall to the ground, the needle is to pick it up with, and the water to wash it." Then the wife knew that her husband had never dropped a grain of the rice she had cooked for him and died happy.

Deeply moved, Tiroovalloovan sang: "O loving one, sweeter to me than my daily rice! Wife, who failed not in a single word! Woman, who gently stroking my feet lay down after me to sleep and arose before me! and dost thou leave me? How shall I ever again be able to close my eyes at night?"

Tiroovalloovan had preserved the purity of the language and given a check to the prevalence of Sanscritisms. But soon a still greater evil made its appearance, emanating indeed from the golden bench itself. Tiroovalloovan was a Jain or semi-Buddhist, a kind of Indian rationalist, and did not care very much for the Brahmins and their gods. His poem, however, was of such a nature that all the different sects were attracted by it, and none was exactly hit. Whether by means of Tiroovalloovan or not, we cannot exactly say, but certain it is that about this time Jainism, and, perhaps, even Buddhism effected an entry into Madura, and was professed for the most part by the Academicians themselves. Even King Kuna, who is said to have lived in the 9th century, belonged to this sect, so hated by the Brahmins. Kuna, however, married Dasvani, a princess of the Chola Dynasty, all of whom were zealous Sivaites. Queen Dasvani brought with her to Madura the learned Sivaite, Nyana Samandar, who soon found some adherents amongst the wise men. From that time Jainism commenced to lose ground and was soon doomed to disappear entirely from Madura. King Kuna fell seriously ill, and none of his physicians were able to cure him. At last he bethought himself of an expedient not uncommon among heathen. He summoned the sage Samandar and said to him: "If you can cure me, I will believe that your religion is the right one; I will embrace it and will drive away all opponents." Samandar consented, prepared his herbs and the king was cured. Madura's Academicians were, however, by no means anxious to be turned out and demanded another proof of the orthodoxy of Samandar's doctrine. They would write holy words (mantirams) on palm leaves and would place them in the Vyga river; he was to do the same, and he whose palm leaves should float stream upwards, his religion should be the right one. Perhaps they thought to frighten Samandar by this test, but he agreed to it. Each party threw their leaves into the Vyga, and behold! Samandar's leaf floated up the stream. Then there arose a mighty storm. Those Jains who did not at once make themselves scarce were put to death or at all events hunted out of the country, 8,000 principal men in number. Then the land was quiet and Brahmanism again resumed its ancient sway. At the spot where the palm leaf touched the ground, a temple was built and dedicated to Tiroo Veda Nader—The Lord of the sacred Vedas. Samandar was made High Priest of the temple, and founded an order of celibate priests, the prior of whom was to be always called Nyana Siva Achary, and which order has survived to the present time.

At the end of the 11th century, Madura was burnt down and even the king and his family are said to have perished in the flames. After this misfortune Madura never again attained its former power and magnificence, although long afterwards a Prince of Madura built a hall of pillars which is said to have cost 10 millions of rupees, and which is still in a state of good preservation, and is one of the most splendid of India's buildings. The wars, however, with Mahomedans, which soon followed, never permitted the Tamil kings to regain their former power, until at last the British power came upon the scene and put an end to them both. At the present time there is not a Tamil king remaining with the exception of the shadow Prince of Poodoocottah.

As far as the literature is concerned it is for an Indian language extraordinarily rich and by no means unimportant. The favorite work is that of Tiroovalloovan of whom we have just heard—the Kural—or short lines. It consists of 1,330 verses, each of two lines and sings of the three objects of man. Virtue (denial), Possession, and Love. The rhyme in all Tamil poetry is at the commencement of the verse, and the language is much compressed and not easily to be understood which renders it not very attractive to Europeans. The Kural is one of the earliest examples of Tamil literature which still exist. A few other books of a not much more recent date are to be found in a collection of the so-called minor Poets and are learnt by heart in all Tamil schools, heathen as well as Christian. The language indeed is so high and difficult that each word must first be translated into ordinary Tamil before the children can understand it, but the innate love for such things as well as the intrinsic value of the poetry enables them to overcome all difficulties. The first of these books is attributed to Auviar Tiroovalloovan's sister and commences thus :

Ārăm ssheya virumbû

Be anxious a deed of kindness to show;
Ere eating, your alms your first should bestow;
A benefit shown you, you ne'er should forget;
Nor let sleep a mastery over you get;
Be not idle to-day and idle to-morrow;
Nor yield up entirely your mind to your sorrow;

And so on for a hundred and eight lines. The second book contains eighty verses of which the following are an example :—

In temples to worship in truth is a great good;
What a miser has saved will be spent by a bad man;
Like two eyes to a man are reading and writing:
To the humblest who meets thee speak friendly and kind;
In a land rich with water take up thy abode;
Share all with thy guests; aye, even to Nectar.

The third book of this collection which is said to have been written by a Pandian King of Madura, Adi Vira Rama, supposed to have lived about A.D. 1040, strikes a higher note. The following are a few examples:—

The mighty seed of the sweet juicy fruit of the palm tree
Though nourished and borne high up in the heaven,
Yields when grown to a tree for one man not even
Shadow sufficient:
The diminutive seed of the fruit that grows on the Banian,
Though smaller than even the tiniest fish spawn in water
Gives when grown to a tree—to kings and their four-fold army*
Of riders and footman, of chariots and elephants
Shadow sufficient.

Therefore:

The great 's not always great at all
Nor always little what is small.

Not always children those we bear,
Nor are our kinsman always friends
The married often not a pair.

The wise man knows no joy nor pain.

Another little book sings:

If thou dost a good deed ask not again in the instant,
What good will it bring me, what fruit?
For see how the palm tree gives back at its summit
The water it drank at its foot!

A benefit done to a good man
Lasts for ever, like writing on stone,
A benefit done to the loveless
Like writing on water is vanished and gone.

---

* The armies of ancient Indian kings consisted of foot, horse, chariot and elephants, and were thus four-fold.

As the beautiful lotus attracts the swan in the water,
So wise men are drawn to mix with each other
Like the crows that by offal are drawn and attracted
One fool is sure to be drawn by another.

Till it falls, to the man that e'en fells it
Gives shadow refreshing——— the tree
Till he dies, to the doer of evil
Shows benefits only——— the sage,

Another little book of less antiquity sings :

Like a bubble in water is youth
And wealth like a long rolling wave of the sea
Like a writing on water our body
Yet we worship not, brother ! our God.

Look round upon those who are poorer, more needy than thou
And rejoice in the wealth which is granted to thee;
Look on those who are wiser more learned than thou,
And, then having banished all sense of conceit,
Say, what is my knowledge to theirs ?

The man whose heart is tainted with a blot
Takes that as evil which is done to him as good
Whose heart is free from any guile or spot
Takes what is done for evil as for good.

There are samples of the spirit of these little books which have still so youthful and vigorous a life that they have even found favour in the eyes of the western stranger who has introduced them into his schools.

There is also no lack of Poets who attack rude idolatry and mad pilgrimages to remote spots. The most pungent of these is an unknown one who has disguised himself under the name of Sivavakier. I will again give a few specimens adapted from Dr. Graul's translation.

" O fools ! who wander restless and cry 'tis hard 'tis hard
In towns and lands and deserts to find the highest Lord
Whose all-pervading presence through earth and Heaven swell
Look nearer home, ye fools, within your breasts he dwells.

To *Kasi! Kasi!** criest thou, until thy feet are sore,
When reached, is thy heart's pain less biting than before?
But better tame thyself and bid thy passions flee,
Then gaze within thyself; the true Benares see.

" I read and write and who knows more I pray"
Such are the notes ye asses like to bray;
O worms! who nothing know, can never know
Be wise, your writing madness to the breezes throw.

Brahminical cheat with the close shaved head,
With offerings, Vedas, and sacred thread
Let thy mummeries cease and wisdom learn
Ere in Brightness divine absorption thou'lt earn.

The following may serve as a specimen of Tamil proverbs. They were written by that Tamil Solomon Adi Veera Rama from whom I have already quoted:—

A wise man's beauty is his blameless speech;
A teachers' ....if he practise what he preach;
A rich man's............if he helps his kindred poor;
A king's..................whose righteous sway is just and sure;
A merchant's............to increase his store of gold;
A Statesman's ....who the future can unfold;
A host's..................to see his guests around his board;
A wife's.... ....who never contradicts her lord;
A farmer's..............if his plough can give him bread;
A Mistress' ....if with gold she deck her head;
A Sage's..................to repress conceit and pride;
A Poor man's...........honesty whate'er betide.

We often think, led by a liar's specious tone,
That words of truth within his falsehoods lie,
But, from his awkward stuttering speech alone,
We often think the true man tells a lie.

---

* Note.—It is perhaps needless to remind the reader that Kasi is the Indian name for Benares, to which hundreds of thousands of pilgrims tread annually a weary road from all parts of Hindostan.

Who rides in State for but a mile or more,
May have to walk until his feet are sore ;
Who feasted crowds may beg from door to door ;
Whilst those are princes who have begged before.

In conclusion, I will give a few examples of the warlike poetry of Paraporul, also a translation from Dr. Grant.

(The king goes to battle.)

Like a sea surges up the terrible host
As by wind by its fury now goaded
And the Monarch storms past through the opening ranks
In a chariot with gold overloaded ;
And there flies round the host in its front and its rear,
In circles still growing more narrow,
A flock of black demons, whose wide gaping maws
Will feed on the fallen one's marrow.

(The Queen's sorrow.)

Who once filled the throne lies stretched on the field
And foes of his valour are singing
But "husband! O husband!" exclaims the wife
Of the smile so tender and winning ;
And weeping and moaning she puts next her heart
His wreath all faded and gory ;
And clings to the breast, which pierced by a dart
Is covered with heavenly glory.

(A Hero's death.)

As the lion who roams thro' the forest glade wild,
His eyè with majesty flashing,
Yields his life without murmur when struck by a rock
That comes through the valley down dashing ;
So the hero with sword all dripping with blood
Looks round on the hosts that surround him,
Then flashes his eye, he raises his hand
And falls with his foes all around him.

(Self-sacrifice of the Royal wives.)

And now the great kings of the mighty Sword
On the field stark and cold are all lying
And see! the proud king with the giant-like arm
Where the slain lie the thickest, is dying :

The world too is weeping, and now the sad wives
  Themselves in the flames are all throwing,
But horror ! the death-god is not yet content
  But gloats o'er the death piles still growing.

The oldest works of Tamil literature even the philosophical ones, are all in verse, to which the Tamil language is peculiarly adapted. Even at the present time much Poetry is written and the people feel a preference for it. There is, however, much of importance in Prose also, and at the head of all stands undisputably the Tamil Ramayana, a free rendering of the Sanscrit Poem, and as the Tamulians pride still better than the original.

It is a work of two ponderous volumes, and not a few persons earn their livelihood by travelling about like the ancient troubadours, and singing the Ramayana with explanations to their audiences, for Prose even is sung by the Tamulians. The people do not weary of sitting up till midnight listening to these minstrels and accept, of course, every oriental exaggeration as a positive fact. As an example of the Ramayana, I will give the description of the town Ayodhia by Valmiki :—

" In former days there was a mighty kingdom which was called Kossala, and this country was happy and contented, and full of cattle, of corn, and of riches. In this country, on the banks of the river Sarayu, there was a beautiful town named Ayodhia. All the houses in it were well built and large, and the streets were always watered; there were many richly ornamented temples and costly palaces with domes like the tops of mountains; and there were lovely gardens, full of roots and of flowers, and shady clusters of trees laden with the most delicious fruits, and high above all was the sacred and beautiful chariot of the god. The tanks in this town were beautiful and magnificent beyond description; they were covered with white lotus flowers, and the bees were thirsting for their honey, but the wind blew the lotus flowers away from the bees, like modesty causes the timid bride to retreat before her husband. Ducks and swans swam on the surface of the tanks or dived beneath their clear waters. The kingfisher gazed proudly at his own image reflected in the waves, and snatching at a fish, struck the waters with his wings. The plantain trees round the tanks bent beneath the weight of their fruits like reverential pupils bend before the feet of their master. The whole town was decorated with jewels, so that it seemed a mine of precious stones, and was like Amaravatí, the town of Indra. Everything smelt of flowers and of incense; glittering flags were waving, and there were always to be heard the sweet tones of music, the sharp hammering of arrows, and the holy songs of the Veda hymns. The town was surrounded by a very high wall inlaid with many polished precious stones, outside the walls there was a moat filled with water, deep and uncrossable. The town gates were strongly guarded, and the pillar halls of the gates and the towers were filled with bows and weapons of all kinds. Each quarter of the town was guarded by a mighty hero, as strong as the eight gods who govern the eight ends of the Universe, and as watchful as the many headed snake that guards the entrance to the lower world."

"The town of Ayodhia was full of men, every one of whom was healthy and happy and well fed on the best of rice, and every merchant had his shop full of treasures from all corners of the earth. The Brahmins constantly tended the sacred fire, were deeply read in the Vedas and Vedangas and were all gifted with the most distinguished virtues. They were very noble minded and truthful, zealous, and compassionate like the great Sages, and had their wills and their passions in perfect command. All these Brahmin Sages had three classes of pupils: first, youths who served them as servants do their masters, then students who received from them instruction, and lastly *Brahmacharis* who maintained themselves and their teachers by soliciting alms. The next after the Brahmins were the Kshatryas all of them soldiers and always practising themselves in the use of arms in the presence of the Maharajah. After these came the Vaisyas or merchants who sold all kinds of goods brought from all ends of the earth. Last of all came the Sudras who were always occupied in the worship of the gods and in the service of the Brahmins. Besides these there were also, jewellers and artists, singers and dancers, charioteers, and footmen, potters and smiths, painters and oil-sellers, and vendors of flowers and of betel nut. In this town of well-fed and happy people there was no one who practised a calling which did not belong to his family or caste, or who lived in a common house, or who was without relations. There were no misers, or liars, no thieves or scandalmongers, no cheats or braggarts; no one who was arrogant, malicious or vulgar or who lived at another's expense, and no one who had not a number of children, or who lived less than 1,000 years. The husbands loved their wives only, and the wives were chaste and patient towards their husbands and faithful in the fulfilment of their several duties."

"Every one had a bridal crown, and earrings, necklaces and bracelets. No one was poor or wore ragged clothes; no one was dirty or ate unclean food or neglected the sacrifices, or gave less than Rs. 1,000 (annually ?) to the Brahmins. All the women of Ayodhia were wonderfully beautiful and gifted with wit, sweetness, dignity and every good quality. Their jewels were always bright and sparkling, and their appearance spotless and clean. In the whole of Ayodhia, there was not a man or a woman who was unhappy or discontented, or melancholy, or restless, or frightened, or disobedient towards the king. All were given to truth, practised hospitality and honored (in accordance with their duty) their superiors, their ancestors and the gods; all the four castes were subject to the king. No caste intermarried with another caste, and throughout the whole town there were neither Chandalas* by birth nor as punishment for crimes."

"In the middle of this town was the beautiful and magnificent palace of the great king, surrounded by walls so high that the birds could not fly over them, and so strong that no wild animal could break through them. At each side of the palace walls there was a gate, and over each gate the music of the Mahabat was played every quarter of the day and night, and within the walls and round the palace there were many temples of the gods and filled treasure houses. In the middle of the palace on columns stood the king's throne, with many other pillars around it, and all the pillars and the throne itself were decorated with jewels. The palace was guarded by thousands of warriors, zealous as flames of fire and as vigilant as the lions that guard their caves in the mountains."

"In this palace reigned the mighty king Dasaratha, the king of the Kossala country and of the town of Ayodhia. He was a son of Aya and a descendant of Ikswakus. Dasaratha was very learned in the Vedas and in the Vedangas: he had much prudence and skill and was beloved by his whole people. He was an accomplished chariot-driver, a royal Sage, celebrated in the three worlds, the conqueror

---

* Chandalas are considered lower than pariahs, and are said to have sprung from a Sudra father and a Brahmin mother.

of his enemies; he always loved justice and had always his passions under control. He was like Indra in riches and magnificence, and protected his subjects like another Manu. Satisfying all the wants of his people he proved himself a true father to them, more so than the real father who had begotten them. He took the revenues not for his own use but in order to give them back to his people in greater gifts and charities, like the sun that draws up the salt water of the sea and gives it back to the earth as refreshing rain."

"His ministers were also gifted with every virtue, able to understand his hints and were wise and constant to their beloved king. Dasaratha had eight especial advisers; the first of whom was Sumantra, and his chosen Priest and Instructor were Vasishta and Vamadeva. By the aid of such ministers and Priests, Dasaratha ruled the world virtuously and happily; and seeking by means of his discoverers throughout all the world, as the sun penetrates the world with its rays, the great Dasaratha was not able to discover one person who was at enmity with him: his glory brightened the whole earth." * * *

The Christian literature of the Tamulians is also very important, and probably the richest in India. At the head ranks the translation of the Bible and of 369 Church hymns. There are indeed four different translations of the Bible in Tamil, but none of the last three even approaches in excellence to the good old translation of Fabricius. God had granted him peculiar gifts in this respect, and as he was unmarried, he was not only, like other Missionaries, acquainted with the Tamil language, but it was the language of his ordinary and almost exclusive use. To many English Missionaries his translation is not sufficiently in conformity with the English Bible, and they have accordingly again and again attempted a new translation, but have not been able even to reach the translation of Fabricius, much less to surpass it. They have not been much more fortunate in the translation of hymns, so that our German hymns are used by almost all Tamil Missionaries, although now and then set to English tunes.

The Tamulians are not only a talkative, but a reading people, and men are often found reading where they are little expected. Lately I went to visit an old Muthadar, 83 years of age, who was not able to get up but whom I nevertheless found reading on his bed, and without spectacles, for his eyes had suddenly regained youthful vigour. Instead of the Tamil poet he was reading, I gave him a Gospel which he accepted with pleasure.

There are several Tamil newspapers and an enormous quantity of Tamil tracts, which it is true are not all an ornament to the language. In 1871 alone, 717 different Tamil books, big and little, were printed. The "Christian Vernacular Education Society" printed between 1862 and 1871, 1,088,320 Tamil school-books ; and other works which were printed during these years (but without reckoning the labors of the Bible Society), amount to above 4 million copies. In no other of the twenty languages of India is there anything like the same number of books printed. It is not, therefore, without reason that I have called my dear Tamulians the most moveable and stirring people in India.

CHAPTER III.

External appearance of the Tamulians, and their Domestic Life.

Tamulians on the whole are a dusky race of men, and in color somewhat resemble a handful of roasted coffee beans, with all their various tints from light brown to dark black. They are smaller and weaker built than Europeans, though more graceful in shape. Hair and eyes are always black, and the latter have a peculiar sparkle and a look of calculation.

The men always look intently at the person they are talking to, especially if it is a European with whom they have any business to transact, and they soon find out his strong and his weak points. There is something watchful—dog-like—in the look with which they follow each of his movements, and it is remarkable with what accuracy they are able in a short time to judge their man. The European on the other hand is at considerable disadvantage. He may mix with a Hindoo for years and yet scarcely more than half know him.

Their clothing is admirably chosen and well adapted to the climate. The men wear wound round their loins, a piece of white thin cotton cloth about 6 cubits in length ;

another shorter, but somewhat finer cloth is thrown over the shoulder, and in this way they are thoroughly and sufficiently dressed. Mahomedan influence has induced the majority to add the turban which is generally white, and assumes the most different and the most peculiar forms. Those, however, who have remained untouched by foreign influences either of a remote or a recent date, and especially Brahmins, go about with the head uncovered, the hair being shaved, with the exception amongst Brahmins of a small tuft, and amongst others of a sometimes very considerable pig-tail. This pig-tail always hangs behind except amongst the people of Malabar, who, as is proved by their language were the last to separate from the Tamulians, they carry this tail in front, and thus also enjoy the advantage of seeing it.

The most disagreeable and the most repulsive to a Christian, but an important portion of the dress of a heathen, are the idolatrous marks on the forehead. Three of these marks, two red and one white, thickly plastered on the forehead are the signs of the Vishnavite. The forehead marked with lines of light grey cow-dung ashes—or indeed quite covered with this mixture, shows the Sivaite, who generally finds his forehead too small for the purpose and is, therefore, in the habit of also smearing his chest and arms. These caste marks form part of their ablutions and have to be put on before they can take their meals. To appear in public without these marks would be considered a laxness in observance of religion. The holiest and the most zealous of the Saniyasis—begging priests—not only smear their hair —for they do not shave—and forehead with cow-dung ashes, but also the whole body, and beyond this wear but little else in the shape of clothing.

The women but seldom mark their foreheads, but when they do, they look doubly demoniacal. In other respects the clothing of the Tamil women is most practical, as well adapted to the climate as can be imagined, and can scarcely be surpassed in simplicity. One piece of seamless cloth about 14 cubits in length covers them from the feet to the throat, and allows their arms full freedom for any kind of work. This cloth is generally colored—widows alone dress in pure white—and varies considerably in value, but it is everywhere worn in precisely the same manner, first of all wrapped tightly round the loins and then thrown over the shoulder. Brahmin women only tie their cloths somewhat differently though not so gracefully. The 'delight' of the women (and the pride of the men) consists in jewels, silver rings on the toes and the ankles, gold chains round the neck, bracelets on the arms, and precious stones or pearls round the ears, and in the nose. Even the very poorest cannot get on without ear ornaments and armlets, which in the absence of gold are made of glass.

In conversation the Tamulian adapts himself to the position of the person he addresses. Towards his inferior he is generally rough and of few words. Towards his equal he is natural, that is to say, he speaks as he is disposed, but towards his superior he is extremely polite, if asked how is he, his answer generally is : "Through your favour" or also "Through the grace of God and your honour's favour—I am in good health," or indeed, "your servant is well." He seldom contradicts, even when he thinks exactly the opposite, and always tries to show off his own ignorance and littleness and his superior's greatness and wisdom. If paying a visit, he never goes until he has obtained permission to do so, and he waits quietly and does not feel offended when he is told that he can go. If he is anxious to go and permission has not been offered, he asks politely if he may be allowed to take his leave. Social intercourse with Tamulians is, therefore, pleasant as long as you have nothing unpleasant to say to them. And even at religious discussions they are seldom discourteous, at least as long as they are visitors or visited, and they always reckon a visit as a great honour. When a crowd is addressed it is of course different, no right of hospitality is affected, and when there are many together courage increases, and the wish to push one's self forward is greater.

The Tamulian's house is almost as simple as his clothing. In many of the old towns there is not even a two-storied house, and those of one story are as low as possible, for it is considered decent and proper that the dwellings of the gods should tower high above those of man.

The house of a man of the middle classes is from 30 to 40 ft. square. It has an open verandah towards the street, a door in the middle, but no window. Through the first door you enter a small raised room, which also has no window. Here the master of the house receives his guests, or reposes quietly practising the art of doing and thinking nothing. Through a second door, opposite the first, you reach the inside of the house, and will then remark, that the house is built round an open court, paved but not roofed. In the middle there is a square hollow, where the rain water collects and is drained off. Into this open court the doors of the rooms open. Windows are not needed; where they exist they are an innovation. Towards the south there is an open hall, resting on wooden pillars and open in front. In larger houses there is often a second smaller court and a small garden.

Tables and chairs are not to be found in a Tamulian house, but now-a-days every well-to-do man likes to have a cot, otherwise a rush mat serves as bed, as chair and table. A few earthen and metal pots, round as a cannon ball, and a box for keeping cloths and jewels, form the whole of the house furniture.

When a respectable Tamulian, not exactly of the poorest class, is born, a Brahmin is summoned, who is well versed in Astrological science, and with whose house the family has stood in connexion from the time of their forefathers. The time of the birth is told to the exact minute, and the Brahmin then draws up the horoscope of the child, going into the minutest details of its history. This horoscope is carefully kept and is consulted on occasions of importance.

The sex of the child is of especial importance amongst the Tamulians, as indeed it is amongst all Hindoos, because only the son is competent to perform the funeral ceremonies of the father. A man without a son is amongst the Tamulians a poor man, and has to help himself by adoption, and this of course costs money.

When the child is a few days old a name is given, and generally one of the thousands of names belonging to the gods, for the frequent repetition of the names of the deities is held to be a good act, which consumes sin like fire. The law, therefore, against using the name of God in vain is understood by the Tamulians in an opposite sense. Daughters also frequently bear the names of the goddesses. The ceremony of naming is a very simple one, but still it is a ceremony and as such may not be neglected. If the father hesitates between several names, which as there are so many gods is not seldom the case, he writes down the different names, places a lamp before each and selects the one in front of which the lamp burns the longest.

When the name has been chosen, the priest is summoned, the parents sit down on the ground, the mother takes the child in her arms, and the priest gives to the father a vessel with raw rice, upon which is inscribed the child's name and the star under which it was born. The name of the child is then three times pronounced, an offering is made to the household deity and the ceremony is at an end. The real end, however, consists in the feeding and rewarding of the priest, and in the invitation of as many guests as the means of the father permit. The name thus given remains until death, but before his death the wife may never mention the name of her husband.

When the daughters are from 6 to 8 years old it is time to marry them. The boy is older, but to be in accordance with the wish and the custom of the country, the girl is seldom more than 8 years. The bride should not be taken from a family which neglects its religious duties, which is subject to disease, or which has no sons. In other respects the walk of the bride should be like that of the 'young elephant,' her voice soft and her whole figure blameless. No regard need be paid to her mental qualifications. The ceremonies at a betrothal are many and of different kinds, but all have one result: spending money on the Brahmins. The betrothal consists in the following forms: after many preliminaries the young couple walk three times round an altar on which burns a fire, and then prostrate themselves in honour of "*The unknown god.*" This is a most remarkable instance in the wedding of a Tamulian, that the priest orders him to worship the unknown god (Ariada devanei.) In the land of the Tamulians, as in Greece, the number of idols do not satisfy nor put at rest the craving of the soul, which is longing after the one and only God, and he is unknown! After this, the wife touches fire and water in order to signify her willingness for household service. Then she eats with her husband for the first and the last time in her life; for afterwards he always eats first and she after him. After these ceremonies, familiar conversation commences amongst the guests, and if there happen to be any learned Brahmins present, they recite for the edification of the company some such old sayings as the following:—

Sloth and sickness, woman's worship,
  Contentedness and bashfulness
An overweening love for home
  Are six things, obstacles to greatness.

The sage becomes, although devoid of riches,
An object of respect,
The miser is, although possessed of wealth,
An object of contempt.

Like dust on the feet are riches
Like the rush of a torrent is youth,
Like bubbles in water is life
Like dropping of water is man.

If with firmness of purpose thou keep'st not the laws which alone
Can remove all the bars and open the portals of Heaven,
By the hot fire of sorrow thy mind will be surely consumed
And racked by remorse when the days of old age overtake thee.

Will he, who clothed the swans in white,
And parrots dressed in green,
And decked with fairest colours bright
The peacock's glittering sheen,
Will he refuse the daily food
To one who honours him ?

Hence it happens that a marriage costs a lot of money, so that it often takes a man's whole lifetime to pay off the debts incurred at one. This alone is a reason, at all events, in respectable families, that the tie should not be loosened.

Family life amongst the higher classes is generally quiet and well ordered, and in the attachment and fidelity of the wife to her husband, there is frequently nothing to be desired. In the lower classes matters are, of course, much more lax. Should a quarrel happen, the wife generally manages to get the best of it. She begins by cooking nothing for her husband, and thus touches him in the most sensitive part. For in the land of the Tamulians there are no hotels or dining rooms where men can go and get what they want to eat. If this, however, is not successful, the wife retires into her 'chamber of wrath,' *i. e.*, one of the windowless rooms, puts away all her ornaments, throws herself on the ground and only comes out on the condition that her wishes will be granted. As a general rule these are not exorbitant, and are confined for the most part to a new cloth or a jewel or two. This *ruse* of the woman, however, is by no means a modern one, but has all the authority of age, for we read of it in the Ramayana, where the wife of the noble-minded but weak king Dasarat retires into her 'chamber of wrath' and so obtains the banishment of Rama and the coronation of her own son.

It is not only in the confined family circle that a Tamulian has such close family ties, but it is remarkable how far this circle extends and how many relations it embraces. It frequently happens that an official maintains a perfect host of relatives, widows, &c., who come to him from all sides and take up their abode with him. For their sakes he will incur debts and would rather be ruined than send them away.

This very praiseworthy example of their family attachment, which puts so many a Christian to shame, renders it, however, very difficult for individuals to act according to their own convictions. Individuality is entirely lost and the wish of the many prevails, and in most families even for the preservation of what is wrong and bad. And if by any chance a member of the family becomes convinced of the truth of Christianity, this close relation of the members of the family circle becomes the greatest obstacle to his conversion.

After the marriage, and bringing home of the bride, which takes place only after the bride is of mature age, the young couple *generally* remain in the house of their parents, *i. e.*, the wife remains with her husband in the house of her father-in-law. Even though there may be several sons married, they remain together until the death of the father, when the eldest son steps into his place, and so in course of time separate families are formed. It is only the daughters who, when they marry go over into other houses.

In this way a death is no very great misfortune, if there are grown up sons. It is indeed regarded as a misfortune, but as a necessary one, and is generally accepted with sullen resignation. The beautiful consolation of Rama on the death of his father is still the consolation of the Tamulian. When the news of his father's death reached Rama's place of banishment, and he saw all around him in great grief he spoke as follows :—

In vain weak man for ever strives
　To live as most he would desire,

By Fortune's fancy he is tossed
  First here, then there, on every side;
Unhindered none can ever move
  Towards the object of his life.
And hence it seems unreasonable
  To mourn for those who've passed away.
That which is stored will dwindle down,
  And what is highest raised, will sink,
The closest ties be cut in twain
  And all that lives must one day die.
As every fruit whilst ripening fast
  Draws nearer to its time of fall,
So from his birth does man each day
  Draw ever nearer to his death.
And as the house most firmly built
  Must some day fall in ruins low;
So gradually all men must fade
  Towards old age and day of death.
The night that once has passed away,
  When gone returns again no more,
'Tis passed and vanished like the stream
  That spends itself in ocean wide.
'Tis thus our days must flow away
  And each one with it takes a part
From out our life, just as each ray
  Absorbs at least one water-drop.
Why mournest thou for others dead?
  Mourn for thyself whose time and life
(Where'er thou goest or may stand)
  Is fading slowly, surely, past;
For death goes ever at thy side
  Is seated always at thy hand.
And whereso'er thou wanderest forth,
  Death, constant death, comes with thee home.
The face in wrinkles is drawn up—
  The darkest hair is blanched and white,
And who can keep his zeal and strength
  When age has sapped his vital powers?
We hail the rising of the sun,
  And when it sets our thanks arise,
But seldom do we pause to think
  That our own life may be as short.
How glad is each when joyous spring,
  Returns with beauty ever fresh,

But do we think each season's change
  Brings each man living nearer death ?
Far on the ocean's bosom broad
  There meet two little splints of wood,
One moment they are side by side
  Then drifted by the tide apart.
Thus are our wives, our children too,
  Relations, friends, our wealth and goods ;
They come, and then they float away
  And leave us stricken by their loss.
Like one who stands beside the road
  And tells the wanderers passing by :
Lead on ! I too shall come behind,
  And follow you upon the way !
So each man here must surely know
  That he the path will also tread,
His father trod before. Then why
  Lament o'er that which must take place
And since our life must onwards flow
  Like water that cannot return,
Strive each for his own happiness
  And also for his subjects' good.*

With these beautiful thoughts Rama comforted himself and his friends when the news of his father's death arrived. But if we examine them carefully all these fine words only mean : 'The father is dead and we too shall die. It has always been so, and cannot be altered.' This, however, can only lead to silent resignation and is no consolation. True it is that the wise men of Greece knew of no better consolation :—

" The same career was destined for the growth of earth,
And for that of her children. The life of one will blossom
And of the other fade and then be mown away."

And again :

" We children of a day ; what are we and what not ?
We men are but a shadow's dream†

That is the consolation which one of the philosophers of Greece sent to another on the occasion of his son's death,

* After Professor Holtzman's translation from the Sanscrit.

† Plutarch's Letter of Consolation to Apolonius.

and try as he will, man can never bring it further than this shallow consolation which fails entirely to touch the heart. How much better is Job's consolation, whose time was long prior to that of Rama and the Greek sages:

I know that my Redeemer liveth
And that he shall stand at the latter day upon the earth.

But the Tamulians as such, know nothing of the consolation of the Resurrection. There is, however, a change taking place in the people.

The ceremonies performed at the death of a Tamulian are many more than those performed at a marriage and are continued for years.

The dying man likes best to be laid upon Kusa grass, (a kind of bean straw) for that is considered to be a holy and sin-destroying grass. The relatives all press to pour into the mouth of the dying man a few drops of milk and at the same time call their own names aloud, so that the dying man may remember them in another world and not forget this last act of kindness.

When the death has really occurred, it is the duty of the eldest son to wash the deceased's head and to anoint it with oil, and in this he is aided by his relations. The dead man is then wrapped in a new cloth, is placed on a litter in a half-sitting position, a little ground rice and betel are placed in his mouth, his last food and last refreshment.

After the usual death lament is over, (the duty of the mourning women) the corpse is carried out only a few hours after death, the eldest son leading the way with some fire in a pot and the death music following behind. Only the male relations follow the body, the females remain with the widow in the house of mourning. If it is a person of position who has died, cloths are laid down in the road over which the procession passes. These cloths are quickly picked up and then laid down again in front, so that not many of them are required, and the long white seamless Tamil cloths are well adapted for this purpose. Arrived at the burning place, the corpse is placed on the already-prepared funeral pile with the feet towards the South, so that the dead man's head points towards the North, the direction of the Hindoo Paradise. (The Hindoos having come originally from the North, they imagine their Paradise, where their gods are throned upon icy mountains, to be in that quarter). The eldest son then walks three times round his father's corpse, with a torch in his hand, and a pot of water on his shoulder. He then thrusts the torch into the head-end of the pyre, and lets the pot fall from his shoulder, so that it breaks and the water flows on the ground: for "Like a broken potsherd is the body, and as the water in it, so does our life flow away." The son then bathes in some water near at hand and goes straight home without looking round, so that his father's sin may not come upon his head. Corpse-burners employed for the purpose do what else is required.

On the next day, the son generally goes again to the burning ground, offers a cocoanut to his patron deity as a greeting, collects the ashes of his father in a small earthen pot, in which there is a little milk, and carries it to the nearest river where the pot is buried in the sandy bed. The time of mourning lasts 18 days, during which only one meal a day is eaten, thereupon follows a feast to the relatives, and with that ends the first act of the mourning. But every six or 12 months a memorial feast is celebrated, on which occasion Brahmins are fed and cloths given away.

From thenceforth the widow remains under the protection and the guidance of the eldest son, who not only with reference to her, but also in regard to the whole house, assumes the father's place as the head of the family.

The condition of widows in India has been painted in the most glaring colors. But on the whole we can scarcely say that the widows among the Tamulians are worse off than those of other nations, Europeans not excepted. It is true that Life Insurances and Widows' Funds are unknown things amongst the Tamulians. The widow lives upon what her husband has left, (if he has left anything,) or if she has children, by their labor. In the event of there being neither property nor children, the nearest relative, even though a distant one, provides for and maintains the widow. And if all other resources fail, the widow will go to such an one and make herself useful in domestic duties.

Here, however, as everywhere else, a great deal depends upon the conduct of the individual. Respectable widows are seldom despised, even in Tamil land. Cases of oppression, of course, occur, for it is everywhere to be found in the nature of things that the strong oppress the weak. But it seems to me that even in Tamil land the widows and orphans stand under God's peculiar protection, who in ancient times has declared himself to be "an avenger of the widows and the father of the fatherless," and that, not only for Israel. There is, however, a widowhood amongst the Tamulians of a peculiar kind. When the girl is married at the age of about 8 years, she may be a widow at 9 or 10 years of age, and after the old Hindoo customs, she cannot marry again.* It is here where the real misery of widows is found. But even this now begins to disappear, since influential members of Hindoo society have re-married their widow girls, and though they have had to suffer for it, they will certainly break the way, and be followed in a short time by all reasonable parents.

Even the smallest village has its Headman or Magistrate (Moonsiffdar) who rules like a little king and often oppresses the weak. The other village officials are the Maniyakaran, whose duty it is to collect and remit the Government dues, and the Kanakan, who keeps the accounts and the registers of the different holdings. (These registers consisting for the greater part of palmyra leaves.) These three are Sudras, and are the principal persons in the village. Their posts are hereditary. Not far from every Sudra village, there is a little suburb, not too adjacent, the Chēry, which is inhabited by Pariahs, who cultivate the fields of the Sudras and get little enough for so doing. Among them is a Taliyari (headman) whose duty it is to guard the whole village, to catch the thieves (if he can get them), and to send them in custody to the Police, for which purpose he carries in many villages a spear. His adjutant is the Vettiyan, who also looks after the burial of dead cattle, &c. Their posts are hereditary, and are paid by the grant of a piece of land. With this the official *personnel* of a village is complete.

In larger villages and towns, each division has its Moonsiff, Maniyakaran, Kanakan, Taliyari, and Vettiyan, so that no one has particularly much to do, what the Tamulian

* The consummation in no case takes place until the girl has attained the age of puberty (12 to 13), and though the marriage may be celebrated when the girl is only 6 or 8 years of age, she always remains in her parents' house until this occurs.

especially enjoys. Next comes the village carpenter, who squats down on the ground, seizes a piece of wood between his toes, and works away with chisel and hammer until it is of the required form. If he happens to have a saw, (of which, however, the teeth are set backwards), and an iron plane in addition, he will turn out any piece of furniture that may be wanted. Then comes the smith who also squats on the ground and works in that position. By his side squats the bellows-blower with a goat skin in each hand. The smithy and its tools are easily transported, and the furnace is built in a few minutes. To these must be added the indispensable potter who shapes round pots, big and small, whilst *standing*, by turning the wheel with a bamboo and shaping his clay whilst it is in motion. Nor may the barber be omitted who squats down and shaves the head and face of the customer squatting near him. The washerman fetches his linen from house to house, and carries it to the river or the tank, where he beats it upon a stone until he has knocked the dirt out and some holes in. If the river is too far, he keeps one or more donkeys to carry the wash, but as these animals have to find themselves, they are by no means Egyptian in appearance.

We must not forget the calendar writers, the Astrologers, &c., but these are always Brahmins, and their science is a part of religion, of which we shall speak in the next chapter. Goldsmiths and oilmongers, confectioners and bazaarmen belong of right to this chapter. The goldsmiths, particularly those from Trichinopoly, are capable of turning out the finest work, which is admired even in Europe. The oilmongers yoke one or two oxen to a long beam turning the grinder, which fits into a hollow wooden mortar. The oil is thus pressed, and the operation produces loud organ-like tones which are heard for a long distance. The confectioners exhibit all kinds of tempting dainties, which, however, are only tasty to a Tamulian palate. The bazaarmen sell everything that is required for daily life, and are often to be seen in their little shops, reading or rather singing old books. It is a remarkable and a good feature of the Tamil people, that they are fond of reading. They are especially fond of old stories written in verse, but they are beginning also to have a regard for prose. Would that only what is good come into their hands!

The trades of the Tamulians are just as much hereditary

as their village appointments, and within these clearly defined boundaries there are many ancient families. The smith knows for certain, that his forefathers were smiths at the time of Manu, and the toddy-drawer who, with great dexterity, climbs the tall, graceful, branchless palm tree twice a day, in order to tap the juice at the top, knows with equal certainty that his ancestors were palm climbers even before the days of Rama. Beneath the hot Indian sun, however, forms are easily petrified. The carpenter works often quite near the smith, and sometimes on the same piece of work. He lives also in the same street, but he dare not eat with him nor can their families intermarry, unless there exists some special connection, and yet these two are the nearest akin among the hundreds of divisions which are to be found amongst the Sudras alone. In the same way, though the Brahmins have no hereditary trades, and are generally called by strangers the Priest caste, yet have they many different divisions and castes, none of which will permit table-companionship or intermarriage with the other. The Pariahs have also in the same way a number of sub-divisions.

The Tamil people is, therefore, very divided and cut up, for each man first looks at his neighbour's caste-marks, and asks regarding his caste before he will have anything to do with him. These divisions, however, have not been made without method and plan, and if sin had not stepped in and introduced itself into their forms, so as to have distorted them into caricatures, and to have made their influence bad in every particular, they would be much less objectionable. As it is even the Tamil people afford a proof that sin divides. From the time of the tower of Babel down to our days, sin has divided peoples and families, and introduced dissensions and quarrels into the houses and the hearts of man, and all patching up and bringing together is of no use, and only makes the divisions wider. It is only faith in Christ, which by removing sin instils a new life, unites families and nations and introduces peace into our own hearts. It is true that oaks do not grow so fast as thistles, nor does gold sprout from the ground like mushrooms. Faith builds for eternity and its structure cannot, therefore, be raised in a night.

CHAPTER IV.

Religion and Worship.

The religion of the Tamulians was originally a simple demon-worship, and demons not only of good, but also of evil influence were worshipped and were appeased by offerings. Much of this demon-worship, and often of a very wild and savage character, has lasted to this day, but as the whole life of the Tamulians was altered by the Aryan immigration so also was their religion. The stream of men that poured forth from Central Asia and flooded the whole of the old world styled themselves Aryans or nobles. One branch established the kingdom of the Persians, and another founded Athens and Lacedæmonia,* and then spread themselves under different names and languages over the whole of Europe; another branch wandered towards India and took with it an already well-arranged system of popular government. This race, in introducing to India its social customs, also introduced its religion. Whilst the aboriginal inhabitants were content with worshipping the spirits of deceased individuals, who had distinguished themselves by good or by evil deeds, the Aryans brought with them sacred writings which they called revelations of God. It is true that these sacred writings consisted only of poems dedicated to various deities—natural powers—or of instructions regarding the necessary sacrifices to be made to them; but the Aryans believed and taught that in these poems the deity had revealed itself, and so they had therein an advantage over the half-savage Turanians. As the conquering race, moreover, they had little difficulty in introducing not only their political system, but also their religion, which was so closely connected with it. To understand, therefore, the religion of the Tamulians it will be necessary to glance at the religion of the Aryans as thus introduced. In order to take a clear and comprehensive view of this field it will be necessary to divide this religion into three periods. Religion is the heart and soul of a people, and whoever would know a people must first make himself familiar with its faith. It is in their religion that the mainspring of their outward actions is to be found, and without any knowledge of their religion most of the actions and motives of a people will be either not at all or only half understood.

---

* According to Manu, the *Yavdnas* and *Palavas* (Greeks and Persians) take their descent from the *Ksheytrias* who had lost their caste.

The first and the oldest period of the religion of India is that of the Vedas. In the second, an essence of the Vedas is prepared, and in the third, the husks of the Vedas are dished up. In the first period, the powers of Nature were praised and personified; in the second, the origin and nature of all things was enquired into by the guidance of the Vedas, and the leaves of the Vedas were worked into a powerful abstract or essence; while in the third period, the boiled-out Veda leaves are administered as food, seasoned here and there with a few drops of the essence. I will treat of these three periods in turn, but in anticipation would ask for forgiveness, if in the second period I make more than ordinary demands upon the reader's attention.

First Period.

The first period is the one in which the Vedas were originated and exclusively used. The Vedas are such copious and comprehensive works, that there is, perhaps, scarcely a Brahmin who knows them all intimately, or indeed has read them all through. The oldest and most important is the Rig Veda, containing hymns which were, and which in part still are, used in praise of the gods. The remaining Vedas consist more of directions regarding sacrifices and go very often far into details.

In reading the hymns of the Rig Veda which were, perhaps, sung before the time of Moses, one cannot help being struck with the idea that the composers or compilers had suddenly awoke from a long sleep, and were gazing around them, here and there, without being perfectly masters of their senses. What struck them was always Nature with its various powers and phenomena, and towards Nature they turned with admiration, which breaks forth in hymns, and with worship which found utterance in sacrifice. For in the beginning the minds of the Japhetites (for these are the Aryans) were directed towards the world around them, and this is the reason that they wandered so far from their original dwellings towards the east and the west. The Semites, on the other hand, remained at home or near it, and were more in the habit of casting their looks upwards, of admiring the stars in heaven, and of contemplating and worshipping them. The Hamites, again, stricken by the paternal curse, cast their frightened glances towards the ground, and anything (Fetish) was good enough for them to make into a god. But the Japhetites with the blessing of "enlargement" upon them, went out into the world, and looking around them praised everything that was useful to them, and endeavoured to appease by good words whatever could harm them; and so by the Aryans day and night, fire and water, clouds and wind, even animals and herbs became regarded as objects of worship.

The very first hymn in the Vedas is addressed to fire, (*Agni* or in Tamul akkini): light, brightness, life's warmth, &c.; for in grey antiquity fire was on account of its gladdening and exhilarating influence not only of great importance, but on account of the difficulty in kindling it—by rubbing two sticks together was much more imposing than it ever can be to the match-box race of our days. Therefore, and because the want of fire was calculated to bring the whole household into disorder, the son inherited it from his father, and transmitted it to his children, with earnest cautions to keep it sacred and never to allow it to die out. For, apart from being indispensable for cooking purposes, it was used every day at the sacrifice. The day would have been lost, as if the good genius had forsaken the house when the fire remained unlighted, and the sacrifice omitted, for the offerings were thrown into the fire, which thus became the receiver of the sacrifice and the means by which it was carried to the gods. The ancient Hindus were, therefore, never tired of praising the fire, and of pouring on its flames clarified butter with long handled wooden spoons. The following is an example of the first hymn of the Rig Veda :—

"Agni, I praise, the great High Priest of offering,
"The god-like servant who brings to the gods all our [offerings
"Possessor of riches, of wealth, without limit."

"We near thee, Agni, with reverence in our minds
"Daily at morning and eve."

"Agni, be ever with us as father is with son,
"And for our good be always near."

The second hymn of the Veda is addressed to Vayu, the king of the winds, for this deity with his army—Marats—probably often pressed the Aryans hard, during their long travels over the inclement mountains of India. Fur clothing, as a protection against cold was, perhaps, not then invented. At all events our peace-loving ancestors preferred propitiating the adverse powers to setting them boldly at defiance. It was for this reason that the Greeks named the Black Sea so dreaded for its storms: Pontus Euxinus, the hospitable sea—in order by flattery, to propitiate. And the Tamulians to this day calls the snake whose bite is certain death (cobra-di-capella) Nalla Pâmboo or good snake, in the hope, that pleased at this compliment, the snake will be appeased and do them no harm. Accordingly the Aryans praised the cold winds, gave them a father, Rudra, and a king, Vayu, and addressed themselves first to one and then to the other and sometimes to the winds—Marats—generally. For instance:

" Approach, lovely Vayu, this offering is thine,"
" Drink it and hear our petition."

" The offerers hear the murmurs of Vayu's approval,
" And those who invite thee to drink of the *Soma* juice."

" May the Marats who conquer the whole of the world
" Hear the hymns which are offered by those who would praise them
" And bounteous food on us their adorers bestow."

" The mighty subduers of foes
" The loud sounding chiefs of the clouds
" The Marats all clothed in the rays of the sun
" Are visible now on the heights."

Rig Veda, i, 6, 14.

Wherever the ancient Aryans travelled, and wherever they pitched their tents, they found the vast firmament spread over them. This, therefore, must be a god and was called Indra. But because envious clouds often hid the face of the sky, it was supposed to be engaged in a conflict with them, and, therefore, celebrated as the god of war and awarder of victories. In addtion; from the sky comes the rain and it is, therefore, the distributor of wealth; and because the old Aryans wanted only the satisfaction of their natural wants, and gifts of the earth, Indra was the most highly praised god of the Vedas. They contain a kind of litany addressed to him which I have often read to Brahmins, and to the closing words of which I have quoted in contradistinction, Matthew v, 44-48.

This litany embodies the whole tone of the Vedas, and, therefore, deserves to be given complete :

Mightiest drinker of the Soma juice,
Although we all are unworthy of thee :
Indra whose riches are boundless, O grant us,
Thousands of beautiful cows and of horses.

Handsome and powerful lord of nourishment
Thy favour for ever be with us and therefore,
Indra whose riches are boundless, O grant us,
Thousands of beautiful cows and of horses.

Cast into sleep the two, each other regarding, servants of death.
That they fall into slumber and wake not again,
Indra whose riches are boundless, O grant us,
Thousands of beautiful cows and of horses.

May those who are our enemies slumber,
But our friends, O hero, let them ever be wakeful ;
Indra whose riches are boundless, O grant us,
Thousands of beautiful cows and of horses.

Destroy, O Indra, this ass, our opponent
Whose praises of thee sound harsh and discordant ;
Indra whose riches are boundless, O grant us,
Thousands of beautiful cows and of horses.

And grant that the storm in its crooked course
May alight afar off on the forest,
Indra whose riches are boundless, O grant us,
Thousands of beautiful cows and of horses.

Destroy, thou mighty one, all who despise us,
Visit with death all those who would harm us, and
Indra whose riches are boundless, O grant us,
Thousands of beautiful cows and of horses.

If, however, Indra would not hear even after such fine entreaties as these, it sometimes happened that he had to put up with reproaches, and it is remarkable, that even the tongue of a Hindoo which can praise and flatter better than any other, is still more eloquent when it blames and scolds than when it praises and adores. For example :—

Our prayers and entreaties, O when will they reach thee, O Indra ?
When wilt thou give thy adorers the (means of) maintaining thousands ?
And when will my worship with riches and wealth be rewarded ?
And my ceremonies bear their fruit in subsistence ?

When bringest thou, Indra, the leaders and leaders together ?
And heroes and heroes to give us the victory in battle,
Who can conquer from foes the flocks which yield nourishment three-fold,
And when wilt thou, Indra, bestow on us wealth in abundance ?

When mightiest Indra, when wilt thou deign to bestow
On those who now worship thee, food in sufficience ?
And when can we join to our prayers, our thanksgiving ?
When grantest thou herds in return for our offerings ?

Give then, O Indra, thy worshippers food in abundance,
Herds ever increasing and horses renowned for their strength
Let the pasture increase, and the cows that are easily milked,
And grant they may shine with fat and enjoyment of health.

Our foeman be pleased to despatch the wrong way*
O mightiest Indra ! thou hero, and conqueror of enemies !
O, may I not weary in praising the giver of bounties
O satisfy, Indra, with food the Angiras !

Rig Veda, iv, 7, 3.

Even the night which prepares the way for the sun, must be deified and is called *Varuna*, who is afterwards praised as the god of waters and of healing.

The sun is praised under various titles, but occupies an inferior place to that of the other gods. The moon is also mentioned, but is still less regarded, as also the stars. Time,

* Of death.

on the other hand, is greatly exalted, and much is spoken of its "three steps" the Past, the Present, and the Future. Its representative is Vishnoo, of whom a later period has made so much.

But in spite of all this adoration of the various powers of nature, the hearts of the ancient Hindoos remained unsatisfied, for in spite of all their gods they had no God, but had stopped short with the *Powers* of nature, just as certain men now-a-days pin their faith to the *laws* of nature, fill their heads and mouths with nature, and nature's laws, but refuse to know anything of the *Lord* of Nature or His laws, and, therefore, remain empty in their hearts and restless in their minds. Man was created for and towards God, and, therefore, nothing less than God himself can entirely quiet and satisfy him. The ancient Hindoos, who knew not God, did something in which the ancient Athenians afterwards imitated them, and addressed their praises to unknown gods:

"We will worship the great gods, and worship the small ones,
We will worship the young gods and worship the old ones,
We will worship all gods to the best of our power,
Nor may I forget to worship the gods of old times!"

Rig Veda, 1, 2, 4.

After these extracts there will probably be no one inclined to assert that the Vedas inculcate the doctrine of the one God. There is, indeed, no passage, which says (although the idea exists,) that the sacrifices offered to one god are also meant for the others. The god which is addressed appears for the time being as the greatest and the most powerful, for Hindoos love superlatives. At best can it be said that the Vedas adore Nature itself and from time to time exalt as deities and powers first one and then another of its phenomena.

Their household life was as simple as their religion was childish. The head of each family performed his sacrifice daily, and to the god to whom he was most partial. Soma juice or clarified butter, was the sacrifice, the household hearth was the altar and the flames received the offering. Many offerings, drink-offerings, were sprinkled on the ground, after it had been first strewed with kusa grass. The larger houses had an especial altar for the offerings. Priests were often present, but they were chiefly employed in the singing of hymns, and, on account of their accurate ceremonial knowledge, at the more important festivities. They were rewarded by a share in the repast, the wealthy presented them with clothing and princes with cows.

Besides these daily offerings to imaginary deities, the *manes* of the ancestors had to be remembered. Offerings were made to them not daily, but monthly, and not in the houses, for they were, perhaps, afraid to have the ghosts of the departed in such close neighbourhood, but in distant and lonely spots, in groves or best in the vicinity of a river. The offerings which had been brought were burnt, rice cakes and melted butter were deposited with much ceremony on the ground and the spirits of the departed were then politely invited. No one doubted their coming, and this sacrificial guest-meal was, therefore, held in silence. It is remarkable that similar offerings to the dead, which imply the belief in an ever constant community with deceased relatives, are to be found among every people upon earth. Greeks, Romans, and Germans, Chinese, Hindoos and the Red-Indians, had and have their offerings to the dead, and their guest-meals to the departed; and amongst the Hindoos, this custom has so grown into the minds of the people that even many Christians still practice it secretly.

At special times and occasions, the Hindoos also had animal-sacrifices, and mention is especially often made of the horse-sacrifice. That, however, seems to have been so expensive a sacrifice that even Princes quarrelled regarding the right to perform it. The horse was cut in pieces and cooked, and, as it seems, eaten. But before it was killed, it was held necessary to arrive at a good understanding with it, and at the same time to beg its pardon that it was necessary to kill it, and to give the assurance whilst praising it with many words that it was going the straight way to the gods. The following is a sample:—

"O may we not be blamed by Mitra nor Varuna
Arjunan, Vayu, Rithuskin, nor by the (mighty) Marats,*
If at this sacrifice the virtues we proclaim
Of the divine descended horse."

"O horse, mourn not for this thy glorious form,
Thou goest now the way unto the gods

* Comprising day, night, twilight, the king of the winds, Heaven —the seat of the gods—the winds.

Nor shall the axe within thy body rest,
Nor yet the priest with knife thy limbs deform.

Thy chariot follows thee and men do wait,
Cows go before and fairest maids attend
Claiming thy friendship crowds of demons follow
And e'en the gods will wonder at thy powers.

Thy mane locks are of gold, of iron are thy feet,
And they can move as quick as thought can fly
E'en Indra lags behind, is not so swift as thou
The gods desire to have thy sacrifice.

O may we through this horse much wealth and riches gain,
Herds of cows, of horses, droves, and many a vigorous son,
May through this lusty mare all evil be removed,
And may she on our bodies much power and strength bestow!

Rig. Veda, ii, 3, 6, 7.

Something like this is the oldest religion of the Hindoos, the much praised religion of the Vedas. It seems to be a kind of *Shamaismus* with innumerable hosts of gods, with consciousness of a life after death, and a certain kind of undefined belief in the intercourse of families on this and the other side of the grave; of a one only God, however, who has created and preserves everything, there does not seem to be the slightest trace. Everywhere there is nothing except the expression of the natural man and his earthly feelings, without height or depth.

But the height and the depth which we so much miss was found by *Vayasa*, the collector and compiler of the Vedas who lived about the time of the first Judges. He introduces the second period by condensing these so unpalatable Vedas to an essence or abstract which is worthy of all admiration. We shall be able to understand this a little better by going closer into this in the discussion of the second period.

Second Period.

About the time of the first Judges in Israel, there lived on the banks of the Yamuna a man named Badarayen. He lived a lonely life and troubled himself but little about the world, but by degrees he absorbed into himself the whole knowledge of the world. When he lived there were many hymns of the Vedas scattered here and there; these he undertook to collect and to arrange: on account of this meritorious work, he received the name of Veda Vayasa, the editor and arranger of the Vedas—and is generally known, simply as Vayasa.

Scarcely were the Vedas collected by means of Vayasa, and by others similarly minded, when the remodelling of them commenced, and the minds of all were agitated by endeavouring to find solutions to the most difficult problems of existence.—Whence? Whither? and Wherefore? The various theories which subsequently gave the sages of Greece so much employment, seem all to have originated in India. What Thales and the Ionians taught regarding the eternity of matter, and of matter as the origin of everything that is, all this and much more had been taught by the sages of the Sankhia School—five to six hundred years before them. And though in Greece Democritus was held to be the inventor of the theory of atoms, the learned men of the Nyaya School had inculcated this doctrine long before his time. But neither of these theories was sufficient for the sages of India. They started again from the Vedas, and Vayasa compiled the *Brahma Satras*, (also called *Attar Mimansa*) a theology of the Vedas, or rather an essence of them; and gave to them a zest which has not its equal.

This so-called Vedanta School has attained great celebrity in India and still leads the whole of the national thought. Not only the learned men, but also the lower classes of the people, are so imbued with it, that they regard all things from its point of view, and give their answers in accordance with its spirit, although many of them may, perhaps, never have heard of the name Vedanta. It is, therefore, absolutely necessary to treat of this period in some detail, since otherwise it would be difficult to understand the people, its ways, or its motives of thought.

In reading the Rig Veda, it is almost incomprehensible how Vayasa could have prepared from these so insipid Veda leaves, an essence as powerful as the Vedanta is. We, however, are as far removed from the time and its method of thought, as Vayasa was nearly connected with it, so that we have no right to be surprised that he should have been able to accomplish what to us would seem impossible.

There is especially one Hymn the longest in the Rig Veda, which the Vedanta takes as a foundation. The following are a few examples :—

" I gazed at the lord of mankind with his sons who are seven
The joygiving, beneficent object of our adoration
Who has also one brother, all things with his spirit pervading,
And yet a third brother well nourished with offerings of butter.

Say ! who saw at His birth or perceived the original Being ?
What is the mortal that holds in itself the Immortal ?
From the earth, breath and blood ; but the *Soul*, whence comes it ?
Who can find the sages to wisely answer this question ?

My senses unripe, and not comprehending the meaning,
I grasp to find things, which seem from the gods to be hidden,
What mean the seven threads which the sages have spread
To shut out the Sun which gives to all things their being ?

Ignorant, I, of the wise men I seek for this knowledge,
Myself not a wise man I anxiously ask for this wisdom,
Explain what is that which alone sustains the six spheres,
And preserves in its form the thing which is unborn ?

All the gods take their seats in the highest of Heavens,
In the holy immutable text of the Vedas.
What can he who ignores this, do with the Vedas
Those only who know this, those only are perfect.

They have named him Indra, Mitra, Varuna, Agni,
And he is the heavenly light-winged Garutmat ;
For the priests who are learned give to one many names
When they speak of Agni, Yama, Matariswan.

Who perceives the Lord of the World as the Highest conjoined with the lowly
And the lowly conjoined with the Highest, is wise ;
But who in the world has ever been found to explain
Whence the spirit divine in its strength is engendered ?

This is the garb in which such darkly worded questions are put by those who lived in grey antiquity. Vayasa and his friends applied themselves to find the answers. In attempting this, however, they did not look around them, like those of the Sankya School had done, and who got no further than Materialism, without approaching the divine spirit; nor did they cast their eyes to the ground, as Budha did after them, and who sitting under the shady Banian tree, could not, or else stubbornly, would not, see the heaven above him; who found no peace in an existence that was always commencing and always ending, and so took refuge in an empty Nothing, and taught, that dead emptiness.—Nirvana—was the only thing unalterable and eternal. The Vedantists raised their eyes boldly towards heaven and gazed, and felt in their spirits the eternal spirit—God. Of this absolute spirit the Vedantists mention the following qualities :—" Constancy—Amplitude—Unity—Highest being—Protection—Rest—Truth—Entirety—Absoluteness—Impartiality—Omniscience — Witness—Knowledge—Purity—Purpose—Eternity—Life—Reality—Aether—Brilliance—Self-redemptiom—Penetration"—and as many negative qualities as: " Unmoveable—uudimmed—immortal—unfathomable—spotless— unspeakable—-immaterial—painless—without form—without parts—unborn—endless—without locality—memberless—without commencement—without body—changeless—without duality—without attributes.

Especial stress is laid on this last expression—without attributes,—and this definition is again and again insisted upon. Brahma is *nirguna*. God is without attributes. The Vedanta puts the following proposition : " Is it not as unreasonable to speak of the attributes of a Being without attributes as to talk of a barren mother ?" It proceeds to give the answer : " No wise men are so perfect that we can at once argue with them esoterically. Exoterically we speak of God's attributes, in order to make his Being apparent ; but esoterically we maintain that God is without attributes.

Objection.—But a Being without attributes is incredible. If God has not attributes he does not exist, and you are Nihilists.

Answer.—God *only* exists. He only and nothing else but He.

Question.—What attributes could be assigned to this *advaita* Being?

Answer.—Omnipotence—Omniscience—Justice, &c.

Question.—What is omniscience, &c., if it has no object?

Answer.—The object is the world.

Question.—Is then the world an existence outside God? Is it an object as compared with Him?

God alone is existence (*sat*) without whom nothing can exist. That, however, which exists is Thought (*chit*), and this thought is actual joy (*ananda*); the joy, however, exists only in thought, and *is* Thought. This thought, therefore, which is joy, can only be defined as "Joy—Thought." This it is that exists, and this only. What exists,—this existence,—itself is nothing more than joy thought; existence (*sat*), thought (*chit*), and joy (*ananda*), are, therefore, only three different names of the same thing. For—what exists is only Thought, and is only joy, and this eternal existence, this Joy—Thought, is Brahma—the absolute—as the formula teaches: "Brahma is that which exists, namely, Thought which is Joy—"

or in other words:

"The Real is the Intellectual, and the Intellectual is at the same time the Real. For if Intellectuality were separated from Reality, Reality would become Materiality—where then would be the power that maintains the matter? Reality and Intellectuality in harmonious conjunction constitute Bliss-consciousness."

God, therefore, has no attributes, at least such as the Vedanta terms attributes. Existing Thought, which Thought exists as joy is, however, not an attribute. Something, therefore, does exist. Joy—Thought is what exists—the absolute—Brahma—God.

The conception which the Vedanta has of God, would, however, be very imperfectly understood, if we failed to glance at what the Vedanta teaches regarding the world, and especially regarding man. We will, therefore, first look at the world of the Vedanta. In so doing we must not forget by what means the Vedanta gained its knowledge. The Philosophers of the old western world, regarded the world itself, when enquiring into the nature of all things. The world, therefore, engrossed their looks and their senses, and they became Pantheists. It is true that they manufactured gods, but there were only powers of nature, like Zeus and his brethren, and behind all stood stern Fate, the cold, heartless and unconscious necessity of Nature. Beyond this there was nothing, and nothing, therefore, beyond nature.

The sages of the Vedanta, started in an exactly opposite direction, and reached a point diametrically opposed. They raised their eyes only too boldly towards heaven, and gazed, undaunted, into the sun of the eternal spirit, until, blinded by its glare, they were scarcely able to see the world or even themselves. In a contemplation of the eternal spirit, their minds found a resting-place, and they rested here securely, whilst not only their cousins on the Persian Highlands had remained sticking in dualism, but their own brethren, the sages of the Sankhya, had stopped short with *Prakriti* or *Pradhan* (eternal matter), and those of the Nyaya School were floundering in eternal *anus* (atoms). We are, therefore, bound to be thankful to the Vedanta, that it did not take to the common high road of eternal matter, but dared a bold flight towards the eternal spirit, even though we must lament that the fate of Icarus awaited it.

But to descend to the world :

God is the absolute spirit, perfect, alone, and blissful ! In the second instance He is the causing Principle, and in the fourth instance only, is He the cause of the material world. The world proceeds from the will of God; but God is not merely the effecting cause of the world, not merely the potter who fashions the clay into the jug. Nor is the world a metamorphosis of God, in which the original cause (God) resigns its original form and takes upon itself another (as curdled milk resigns its hitherto-form and takes another.) God remains unchanged, after, as well as before the creation of the world, (or to speak more correctly the world's appearance). But the whole world from Aether to corporeal beings appears in God as in its material cause. In God everything exists, and in God everything ends. Irrespective of God, therefore, nothing else exists. "Since without the clay the jug is not apparent, so, irrespective of God, the world does not exist. Therefore God is not only the *causa efficiens.*"—*Panchadasa,* pir. 13, 1.

The Vedanta endeavours again and again to prove that God is not merely the *causa efficiens*, in the most emphatic language. It is bound to do so, since otherwise its chief doctrine, the *advaita*, would fall to the ground, to which doctrine it clings with a certain fixedness of purpose, and out of love to which it does not shrink from the most enormous consequences.

It therefore calls God, though not without hesitation, and in the fourth instance only, the material cause of the world. The world is the clay out of which the jug is made. But it endeavours at once to temper the bad impression of this consequence, by explaining this clay to be only a semblance and shadow of the eternal spirit, so that we feel how it is grasping after the idea of a *creation ex nihilo*—without being able to find it; a discovery indeed which can only be vouchsafed by God himself.

The Vedanta implies that the Vedas also show God to be the material cause of the world and it says: "A Shastra, such as the Rig Veda, which is gifted with omniscience, can have had its origin in omniscience only." The Bagavadgita not only implies this, but teaches it so emphatically, that one who was ignorant of the reason why the Vedanta parades such expressions, and insists upon God not being the *causa efficiens* merely, would find difficulty in understanding them. The reason, however, is to be found in the contrary doctrine of the Sankya and Nyaya sages, who wished to make of God the mere potter, or manufacturer of the already existing clay, and so to again revive the old story of Dvaita (Dualism).

The passages of the Bagavadgita, to which I have alluded, are the following: "I am the creation and the end of the whole world, and all things depend upon Me, as beads hang upon a string. I am moisture in water, the Light in the sun and moon, adoration in the Vedas, colour in the sky, human nature in men, sweet savour in earth, glory in the fountain of Light. I am the Life in all things, and know: I am the eternal seed of the whole of Nature."—*Bagavadgita*, vii. "The man whose mind is occupied with this contemplation, who regards all things as equal, sees the eternal spirit in all things and all things in the eternal spirit; who sees me in all things, and all things in me;

him will I not forsake, nor shall he forsake me. I am the adoration, I am the offering, I am the invocation, I am the ceremonies performed to the *manes* of ancestors, I am the food (which is offered to them), and I am the sacrifice, and also the fire which consumes the sacrifice. I am the mystic OM : I am the *Rig*, the *Sam*, and the *Yajur* Veda."—*Bagavadgita*, ix.

God, therefore, is everything in everything, and the world is only an appearance, like water in a desert mirage, or in other, and its own words, "As a town may be reflected in a mirror, so should the world be seen in the eternal spirit." "All things effected must be seen in the form of the effecting cause."—*Panchadasa*, xiii, 3. "Even though a man appears reflected in water with his head upside down, we know perfectly well that it is nothing more than an appearance; it does not exist. In the same way when the working (of yonder Sakti) appears, the knowledge that it is a mere reflection will be its destruction. Such a knowledge as this is the highest aim of the Advaita sage."—*Ibid.*

The assertion that the world is nothing more than a mere appearance, is repeatedly made in various similes. For, if the world had an existence of its own, there would again be a dualism which the Vedanta, and rightly, holds in horror. The world of the Vedanta is however not an empty appearance. It is not a *nihilum* but merely an *inanitas* "as God is Reality, Intelligence (Thought) and Bliss, so is the world, unreality, stupidity and pain, and consists only of a name and a form."

"The *Maya* which existed as an undeveloped power before the creation, produced first the modification which is called Aether. God only is existence; all names and all forms took their origin from the creation, and will cease at the end of the world, and God only remains for ever." "The Maya has two attributes: materiality and confusion. Its images are material, but no one can say with reference to them either that they are, or that they are not." All Maya images are, however, "Realities, within the worldly creation. They cannot be defined by philosophical definitions, but to the Vedanta sage they do not exist." "When waking, they *appear*, like an unrolled picture; in deep sleep, however, in a state of trance, in the ecstasy of contemplation, they do not appear, like the picture when folded up."—*Panchadasa*, i, 3.

The world, therefore, is mere appearance, *inanitas, vanitas, avam;* but not so that trees are not wood, gold and silver not metals, or that men and animals have not life. For, "within the worldly creation Maya images are realities." The world, however, is an appearance, because it has no independent, no self-standing existence; because it once was not, because it once will not be, and is, therefore, only in a state of transition. The world is only an image, but an image of God, a revelation of God, or, according to a favorite simile of the Vedanta, a picture more or less unfolded, according to the circumstances of man. The picture consists only of colours, which could form no picture, unless they were painted on canvass. The canvass that bears the picture is God. The fool cannot distinguish between the two; he looks at the picture only and looks no further. The wise man, however, distinguishes both, and knows that the canvass bears the picture, and that without the canvass there could be no painting. "To recognize what is, *as* it is, is an object worthy of man. To hold that which is not, as what is, is unworthy of Him." The canvass *was,* before the painting appeared upon it. The colours may be washed off, but the canvass will still remain what it was before. In other words, "God *was,* as He *is,* before the world began. The world proceeded from His will, but did not alter the being of God. The world will pass away according to God's will, but He will remain unchanged. The Vedanta, therefore, is Vedanta, and not Pantheism, and desires only that men should not remain floundering in the outward appearance of things, like fools, but should recognize that all this is *avam,* and should struggle through this to the eternal spirit, who alone is Reality.

But let us turn our glances from the world towards man. What is man? A great and difficult problem! Above the hall in which this problem is to be discussed the Vedanta inscribes the words, literally: "If thou knowest thyself, no harm can befall thee!" as if it had so learnt the saying from Chilon, the Lacedemonian—or he from the Vedanta.

Those only know themselves, who can distinguish between the body and that which dwells within the body. What then is that which dwells within me? What is my *ego?*

I am the *ego,* says the fool. *I* live and feel, *I* see and hear, my body is my *ego*. But the body which becomes ashes is only a modification of the elements to which it returns, and cannot, therefore, be the *ego*.*

Nor is it, say other fools, but my intellect, my senses, these form my *ego*. But, intellect and senses are temporarily dead in sleep, or in a trance, &c. These, therefore, cannot be the *ego*.

My soul is my *ego*, says the learned man. But what is the soul? Surely not the living soul of life (Jeeva) as those "cheats of the Sankhya pretend." The soul is only a refined appearance of the elements, in contrast to the body which is a gross one.

No! that is not the *ego*. But Isa, the universal soul is the *ego*, say the "cheats of the popular religion." But the whole must be equal to its parts. Isa, however, is a *created* appearance that once was not, and once will not exist. For, "the sacred cow Maya, has two calves: Jeeva and Isa. Both are Maya appearances although spiritual ones. For even the individual soul can, in a dream, create not only bodily, but also spiritual appearances, which, however, are without reality. "Jeeva and Isa make their appearance together with elementary nature, and pass away with it. But above them is the spirit."

In order to know more of Jeeva and Isa, we must consider their attributes, but at the same time must bear in mind that the subjects to be treated of, are in the world, not above it. The attributes of Jeeva (individual soul) are: partial knowledge, partial dominion, &c. The attributes of Isa (universal soul) are omniscience and omnipotence (within the limits of the Maya world). The *works* of Isa are: all the created beings, from the time of the Maya development until the entrance of *Jeeva* into the body. That which happens to the body in its created state,—the whole course of waking and dreaming until its close—is the work of Jeeva. "The fools who pretend that the six inimical feelings, (viz., Lust, Anger, Avarice, Passionate attachment,

---

* Throughout this section, I feel how entirely I have fallen short of the German original, because I have, like others, been able to find no rendering of the *Ich*—at first, I attempted to translate Ich by "I am" but this proved a failure. The Latin *ego* though perhaps better, is still only a dead rendering of the living "Ich." Cannot some Philologian enrich our English language with a new word to convey the idea of the German "Ich?"—*Translator.*

Pride and Envy) originate from Isa, whereas in reality they come from Jeeva, will go to the lowest hell."—*Kaival* ii, 59. For, "even though the whole works of Isa should be destroyed by floods, who could thereby disprove Isa's existence? On the other hand, body, time, and place, might remain, but if the works of Jeeva, if the senses and the passions died, a man would, though living, be saved by wisdom. The blindness of the passions which chains us down in fetters is a work of the living, not of the Lord of the living."—*Kaival*, v, 7.

"Isa and Jeeva are what is understood by the word *Tat* and the word *Twam* (*hoc* and *tu*). Each is in the other as butter is in milk, and are, therefore, one."

"Isa is Brama, Vishnoo, and Siva, who together constitute Creation, Preservation, and Destruction. They know the thoughts of others, and they know everything within the three periods of time." Above these, however, is the spirit.

The spirit, therefore, is neither Jeeva nor Isa, neither the individual nor the universal soul, but it is that which is above the whole Maya world.

"The spirit has none of the attributes of the world, and beyond the spirit there is nothing. Should anything non-spiritual appear, it is a deception, like a mirage of water in the desert."—*Atma Bodha*, 62.

"The *ego* has no attributes; it is without activity, without change, and without form; it is released for ever; it is pure." "Since the *ego* is distinct from the body, it is also free from birth, age, emaciation and decay, &c."—*Atma Bodha*, xxxi, 33.

For, "where there is a thing created, there also is a thing which will pass away. The spirit, in which there is nothing created, that is the *ego*."—*Kaival*, x, 164.

"Like the rock which stands unmoved in the midst, although water floods may rage around it, so the spirit remains always the same, even although names and shapes may change; and this is the spirit which we must recognize as the *ego*."—*Panchadasa*, xiii, 3.

The spirit that says: Beyond me is nothing; everything that I see is an embodiment of myself, like my dream it is a form of the imagination—that is the *ego*."—*Kaival*, 172.

It is, therefore, clear, that not only the unity, but also the oneness of the spirit is inculcated. The recognized truism that equals only can comprehend equals, does not terrify the Vedanta. It jumps boldly at the conclusion: "I comprehend the absolute spirit, and, therefore, I am the absolute spirit," and it says this in so many words.

"Each man's contemplation becomes a birth (*i. e.*, a man becomes that which he meditates upon). Those who contemplate corporeal subjects, become such. He who meditates upon the Highest Being, becomes the Highest Being."—*Kaival*, ii, 85.

This certainly sounds hard, and even harder sounds the formula which is taken from it: *I am the absolute spirit.*

If, however, we look into it closely, it is not altogether nonsense, for:

"The self-knowing remains, and passes not away. It may, therefore, be called *Sat* (existence). It understands the Maya visions: time, place and thing; and it may, therefore, be called *Chit* (Intelligence, Thought). It is transcendental and untouched by these three, and may, therefore, be called Ananda, Joy."—*Panchadasa*, viii, 2.

In the tropics they talk in tropes and in a hyperbolical sense, and these expressions upon which so much stress is laid, are intended only to distinguish distinctly Spirit from Matter. The *ego* is, therefore, the spirit, a portion or reappearance of the absolute Spirit. According to the Vedanta, there is only one independent absolute Being. It is remarkable, however, how the Vedanta, in spite of its anxiety to insist upon the unity, nay, the oneness of God, has yet arrived at a kind of Trinity. I do not allude, of course, to the much hackneyed Trinity of creation, preservation, and destruction, for these are all three conditions of Maya, of appearance, and are summarily treated by the Vedanta. I mean the Sat, Chit, and Ananda (Existence, Thought, Joy) which it is not so very difficult to translate into Father, Son, and Holy Ghost, since Thought expressed, is the *Word;* and Joy is conformable to the Spirit of Joy—free spirit—of Christianity.

Our acknowledgments are due to the Vedanta that it did not, like most other systems of philosophy, lose sight of God in its contemplation of the world, but on the contrary maintained so emphatically, the alone, original and attributeless quality of God, that it treated the world as a reflection of Him (as the moon in water, or a town in a mirror). And when it refuses to let God be the mere *causa efficiens* of the world, we must also agree with it. For God cannot be the *causa efficiens* only, like the goldsmith is of the jewel, or the potter of the jug; for God had no material before Him. The attempt of Leibnitz to solve the difficulty, by taking eternal nomads, and by making God to be the original nomad, only leads back again to the atom theory of Democritus, and to Pantheism. The effectivity of God is different to that of man. We cannot, however, go with the Vedanta when its calls God the *causa materialis;* but it can agree with us, when, instead of *causa materialis,* we call Him *causa materiæ;* and God *must* be called *causa materiæ.*

It is clear that the Vedanta did not quite know what to do with the world, in the same way as the Western sages did not quite know what place to give to God. The sages of the West, looked too exclusively at the world, and, therefore, could not find God. The sages of the Vedanta, looked too exclusively into the bright sun of the Eternal Spirit, until dazzled by its glare they could only distinguish the dim outlines of the world and of themselves as it were in a dream.

The Bible shows us the world as a revelation, or to use the expression of the Vedanta, as an unrolled picture of God, behind which He Himself the Creator is standing. The Bible teaches us by a contemplation of the visible world, to arrive at a knowledge "of that which is invisible, of the eternal power of God." The Vedanta reverses this, and gazes directly at the eternal spirit. It endeavours to *grasp and comprehend* with the understanding (a part of man) what can only be *believed* by the heart, (the combination of man's every part.) Like the creation of the world, the Almighty power of God is an article of faith, not of science. "Through faith we understand that the worlds were framed by the word of God, so that things which are seen were not made of things which do appear." Not, therefore, from a substratum of eternal matter, not from atoms or nomads, nor yet from the Maya, as a peculiar power of the eternal spirit; but from His Almighty power, according to His will, and by His word.

There still remains, however, a difficult question with reference to man, namely, his redemption. For even the Vedanta speaks of a redemption, and recognizes that it is indispensable. And here again we shall find many things with which we can agree, for the Vedanta treats man far more worthily than the naturalists and simialists of the present day. The Vedanta recognizes clearly that the inward being of man belongs neither to the coarser or finer elementary matter, and that it is not to be confounded either with the body or with the senses. It recognizes that man is of divine descent, and, had its professors perceived that the spirit of man is a breath from the mouth of God, they would probably have rested content with that, and would not have arrived at the preposterous conclusion that the spirit of man is itself a part of the eternal Spirit, which deduction, however, the Vedanta attempts to modify by the simile of the reflection of the moon in water.

The spirit of man is banished and confined to a body, which is without reality. But since appearances deceive, so is man in a constant, deceptive unhappy condition, he is full of folly, which leads to hell, and the way thither is broad and easy enough. And the Vedanta has but little pity for this state of things, and resembles in this respect our old and new philosophers. "What happiness awaits the fool?" asks the scholar in *Panchadasa*, xii, 1, and the teacher answers coldly: "Let him, on account of his sins and his virtues, incur a hundred thousand births." A few cyphers more or less are as immaterial to the sages of India as to those of Europe. But the scholar, in whom activity of mind, (which since it is an occupation of a portion only of man is apt to make him one-sided,) has not yet hardened his heart, asks again: "But shall he be thus rejected?" Should he not be shown all possible good?" The stern philosopher answers: "What is the use of crying, Oh! and Ah! Before all things, it is first necessary to examine whether a man is an externally or internally inclined fool; and our instruction must be regulated by this. The former we refer to religious ceremonies, to the latter we teach wisdom on his way to self-bliss."—*Panchadasa,* iv, 3; for: "To teach foolish spirits before they are ripe for it is only to produce an excess of disappointment. The seed will not germinate in their spirit."—*Iden,* i, 11.

Those who do works, are, therefore, left to their works,

until they are tired of them and pine for something better. That which is better, is the knowledge of the nature of things, or, dissected, the answers to the questions: "What is the *ego* in the body? What is the spirit? What is matter? What are the ties by which spirit and matter are united? What is redemption?"—*Kaival*, ii, 63.

These are the difficult questions that have to be answered. "When wishing to identify the persons of those who have disguised themselves; if we try to understand their disguised nature, their qualities or their marks, their true being will not be known though we may see them run, jump or stand on their heads, or perform ever so many similar works. And so it is with the wisdom which the Vedas have offered disguised in flowery words and similes, which, leading to the knowledge of Brahma, can only be obtained by search. Without this you may know the holy writings by-heart and may bestow alms, perform penances, prayers, ceremonies and sacrifices; self-knowledge will not come through any of these."—*Kaival*, ii, 66—67.

Without self-knowledge there is, however, no redemption.

The *Talabakar Upanishad*, (3, 5, 15) affords us a glance at these difficulties; it says:

"The eye cannot see Him, nor language or the reason grasp Him. We know Him not and understand Him not; how can we then explain Him? He is apart from the known, and raised superior to the unknown. He can be seen by no eye, but has fashioned the eye in order to regard Him. To him who regards Him as incomprehensible, He is comprehensible; but the man who thinks Him comprehensible knows Him not."

A teacher is regarded as indispensable; but both teacher and pupil must be no ordinary men. The pupil must long ago have subdued the world, must have neither fear of, nor love for, the world; must regard neither joy nor pain; money and goods must have been long worthless to him, before he is worthy, or in a condition to receive the teacher's instruction. For: "the wicked, the passionate and those of restless mind, will not reach the Almighty through a mere knowledge of him."—*Katha-upan*, ii, 6.

It is, however, so difficult for the teacher, to handle the subject worthily and to make it comprehensible, that even the gods are afraid of the task. Here is an example from the *Katha Upanishad* (1, 2, 3). The pious pupil Nachiketa came to Yama (the god of death and justice) and begged him to impart to him instruction. But Yama answers terrified: "Ask for long life, for sons and grandchildren, elephants, herds of cattle, and horses, gold and dominion upon earth. Be the Lord of a mighty kingdom, O Nachiketa! and I will grant every desire which may arise in thy breast, but ask me not to solve the difficult question regarding the existence and nature of God." Nachiketa answers: "O Yama, such delights as these only weaken man's powers; and even the age of the world is but short. No man can be made content with worldly possession; why should man, subject to death and disease, delight himself in beauty and in love, when he knows that by approaching heavenly things, he can gain a higher knowledge? give me, therefore, O Yama, the solution of my doubts with reference to the existence and nature of God."

The Upanishads give many other detailed instructions regarding the acquisition of knowledge, and add: "The way to the knowledge of God is difficult, and as hard as a road on the edge of a razor."

Redemption by means of the Vedanta is, therefore, only attainable by very few, and the road to God which it teaches even narrower than that of Christianity. It is especially no royal road, no free path, in which all may walk, but only the path of a school, through which few can pass. For this way is full of steep steps. They are as follows :—

I.—The knowledge that appearances of the senses are faulty.

II.—Disgust with such things.

III.—A ceasing to strive after them.

IV.—Subjugation of the spirit, until all things, even Brahma's heaven, are regarded but as a stalk of straw.

In this way a man is prepared to be a pupil of wisdom. Pupils not so constituted are not worthy of instruction. The actual pupils must then, of course, climb other steps of which the following are the principal :—

1. To hear proper instruction.

2. Reflection over its words.

3. Spiritual contemplation of their meaning.

Then follows:

4. The turning away from all appearances.

After which,

5. The sore of the bad self does not again break out.

"From which follows that whereas formerly the body was firmly regarded as the *ego* now the absolute spirit is recognized as the *ego*."—*Panchadas*, i, 12.

This is the difficult road of the sage of the Vedanta; but now that he has at last reached his destination what has he found? He has discovered that God is the absolute spirit and the only existence. He has discovered the world to be a mere empty appearance "as of a town in a mirror." Inside the world there is reality as the reality of hunger, of pain, &c., may convince every one. But the world, as a whole, is simply an appearance, with no lasting existence and of no real worth. And finally, he has discovered that he himself has been banished into this world, this inanitas,—as water is confined in a jug. No death can break this jug, for one birth follows another, until at last the *upadi*, the modality, passes away. And this can only happen through knowledge of the one existence, and through being able to distinguish from it what is merely appearance. And then?

And then, "When one of these jugs breaks, the moon which has been reflected in its water, joins again the original moon; the individual soul returns to the unity of the original self."—*Kaival*, ii, 39.

That is all. The jug breaks and the water returns to the well from which it was drawn.

That is redemption.

"Thus the life-released gain release from the body, by being absorbed into the nature of knowledge which like Ether remains eternally undisturbed."—*Kaival*, i, 93.

So after a long and weary road no father's house, no father's arms, no brother's heart, no communion of saints in light. Nothing but the cold joy of the drop of water which falls from the bucket, and again reaches the depth of the well.

But yet the joy at this discovery was very great. Democritus did nothing, but laugh after he had discovered the nature of all things to be in atomic existence; Tandava threw his cloth in the air, and did nothing but dance when he discovered the nature of things to be in himself, and exclaimed: "To whom can I explain the joy ineffable which has come to me? It arose within me, it bubbled forth, it spread over the whole universe, it swelled high and higher and became eternal. Hence I adore the flowery feet of the teacher, the Lord, who has entrusted to me the secret of Vedanta wisdom."—*Kaival,* ii, 177.

"But many have an abundance of this knowledge and have still not attained joy and freedom from care;" is a query which the Vedanta makes to itself and then answers: "because their contemplation rested upon a superficial understanding, which has been unable to grasp the spirit of the holy writings and make it its own." "But when the sore of the evil self has passed away, the desires, which still arise in consequence of former transgressions are no longer of harm;" and as regards the difference between the wise man and the fool: "a man (is known) as a learned or an ignorant man, not by his outward form but by his knowledge of the Vedas. And in the same way a sage in whom the sore of his evil self has passed away, is not known by his outward fortunes, but thereby, that in activity or in passivity he has neither disgust nor longing." —*Panchadas,* i, 11.

The life-released, reposes with his *ego* in the Absolute, but his body is still in, and subject to the Maya world, and, therefore, for convenience sake, he does as others do around him, namely, when with fools he performs acts of ceremony, and when among sages he abuses all ceremonial. "For though activity is of no use to the sage, inactivity is also of no use."—*Panchadas,* ii, 9.

Sin does not seem to be mentioned in the Vedanta, though, Ignorance, Folly, Passions, Evil-longings, &c., are, and these resolve themselves afterwards into Lust, Anger, Avarice, Pride, Envy, &c., and are innate in the natures of all men. The Vedanta rightly attributes the seat of the disease to selfishness, to the "Sore of the evil self." Works are of no avail towards redemption from this selfishness or rather self-love; and without redemption there is no bliss. Union with God is the only thing that leads to this redemption, and is itself redemption. The evil self, the Passions, all tend to hinder this union for "only when all passions which have their seat in the heart, are torn out by the roots is the life-released one ready."—*Panchadas,* i, 11.

And now for the difficulties:

The Vedanta attempts to prove that it is possible to root out from the heart all passions, but at the same time it always feels afresh that this rooting out is contrary to experience. But yet it attempts the task again and again, for it feels that with these passions there can be no redemption.

This entire rooting out is either possible or it is impossible. If it is impossible the Vedanta has lost all, and its redemption is an illusion. But even were it possible the stain of guilt which was contracted at the time when these passions were still in force, would still remain.

There is, therefore, a stain of guilt and indeed a double one. The capital sin from the time when the passions reigned, and a continually increasing interest of sin from the time when the passions were subdued but not yet rooted out.

The Passions "anger," "hatred," "envy," &c., are, however nowhere, and never, mere ignorance, as may be seen in the transgressions between man and man, but they are also and essentially *wrongs.* As ignorance, therefore, can only be purged by knowledge, so can wrong only be purged by righteousness, (Isaiah, i, 27). This justice has, however, a double demand upon man: as regards the Past, the justly earned punishment for *committed* wrong, and as regards the future the duty of *avoiding* all wrong.

The Vedantist cannot meet either the one or the other of this double demand of justice. For, as regards the first only he would be compelled to go to prison from whence he could never emerge even to commence to meet the second. And, therefore, for the Vedantist there is no approach to God, and his union with God is an illusion.

This double justice is only possible in Christ, for He, as regards the Past, has borne the punishment for us: and as regards the Future, He has for us met the demands of Justice, and He works in us towards the uprooting of the passions, in other words he kills the desire to sin.

Conclusion.—The highest aim of man is union with God. This the Vedanta rightly teaches, though clumsily, because mathematically; but to the Vedantist it is impossible. To the Christian only is it possible.

Period 3.

What the wise men of the Vedanta produced is still the possession of the people. Sankya and Nyaya Professors are to be met with; but they scarcely know what they are. In the north of India they are possibly more numerous; but in the land of the Tamulians, the more earnest Vedantists kept the superficial materialists and atomists for the most part back.

But though greatly esteemed by the people, the high-soaring Vedanta could never become a popular religion. The people require something human and are not content with an Absolute Spirit. The reason of this probably is that man, as he is, feels that he has nothing in common with the Absolute Spirit. The holiness of God must always appear to sinful man as a "devouring fire," and this is the reason that the Mahomedan only becomes excited regarding his Prophet, Allah leaves him unmoved. And that is the reason that the Church of the Middle Ages, when it transformed the loving Saviour of mankind into an angry Judge, turned to Mary and the Saints. In the same way the people in India discovered that they could not draw near to a heartless and unsympathetic Absolute Spirit, and that they could not approach Him, even though the way had been less difficult than "over the edge of a razor." They wished and longed for individuals to whom they could draw near with offerings, as in their country each superior is approached with a present on the occasion of a formal visit, even though it be only the ordinary walnut-sized lime.

The Brahmins, however, knew how to give the people what they wanted, and in a short time there arose a perfect forest of numberless gods and legends of gods.

It is not my intention to lead the reader into this Indian jungle. There are many roads leading into it, but the way out is uncertain. For, like an actual jungle, each road, when it gets to the middle, branches off into narrow paths going towards all the quarters of the globe, with every possible winding and turning, so that it requires a skilled mind to find the way out, and then, perhaps, the only good derived is a bad head-ache. In other words, each Swami (god) appears under so many different names, and so many different stories are told of him under each name that it is most difficult to preserve the golden thread, if golden thread there be. The people does not feel it to be a reproach that it has as many as three hundred and thirty millions of gods, but seems the rather to be proud of the possession of so much wealth.

It is often said regarding the present popular religion, that it has no connection with its holy writings, the Vedas. But this is only partly true.

It is, indeed, true that at the time of the Vedas, there were no stone or metal gods, at all events, not during the first period. We have, however, remarked above how the Vedas idolize all things around them, that is, deify them, though they do not reduce them to graven images. I have not space here to show the many instances in which in the Vedas, things visible are addressed and extolled. I will, however, quote one short passage in which the snakes are addressed:

The Heaven is your Father and the Earth is your Mother,
Soma, your brother, Aditi, your sister, O serpents
Unseen but all seeing remain in your holes, and hiding,
Enjoy and amuse yourselves there in your fashion.

Rig Veda, ii, 5, 12.

In the same way everything that can be of benefit or that can harm, is adored and praised; grass, on account of its powers of healing; the partridge, on account of its powers of prescience; food, on account of its powers of satisfying, &c. We cannot, therefore, deny that even the wildest idolatry of the present day has to a certain degree a foundation in the Vedas. The sages of the Vedanta pressed the Veda leaves and extracted from them an essence which in many respects is worthy of admiration. But this food was too meagre for the "enthusiasts of popular religion." They, therefore, helped themselves to the dry squeezed husks of the Vedas and manufactured for themselves a mess, namely, the present idol-worship, which as far as accommodating itself to the country and customs of the people is concerned has not got its equal.

Buddhism, which, although banished from India, has left a mighty impression behind, aided, though without wishing to do so, the idol-worship to reach the power and influence it has obtained. In Tamil land, the already existing demon-worship assisted in giving idolatry a peculiar coloring. When an adoration of natural powers becomes diverted into an adoration of individualities, it almost always take the form of a worshipping of departed spirits of man, which, as demons, influence the people that serve them and keep them back from a knowledge of truth. For, in the light of truth, these shadowy forms cannot stand, but as long as the darkness of ignorance about God lasts, these evil spirits "reign in the darkness of this world." The Greeks made to themselves gods of Tubalcain and Jubal, the sons of Lamech and called them Vulcan and Apollo; and in the same way, the people of India took to themselves two king's sons, Rama and Krishna and made of them gods even to this day. The Greeks went further and took from out of their own times the old soothsayer, Trophonius, and dedicated a shrine unto him, in order to hear him even after death, and accordingly oracles were heard as wished for from his shrine. In the same way, the Tamulians dived into the present and made idols out of well known deceased men, and provided these images with temples and temple worship.

A few years ago, there was in Cuddalore a great dispute amongst hundreds of Brahmins regarding their idols. The Collector, as Magistrate of the district, had to decide this dispute, and decided it in favor of the majority who were able to cry the loudest. The following are the facts of the case: About four hundred years ago there lived at Srirungam, near Trichinopoly, a pious Guroo by name Desigan. These Guroos are a kind of bishops in the country. Their rank is hereditary in the family, though they themselves do not marry. Whenever they travel, they do so with great pomp, riding on elephants and followed by horses and by carriages.

Wherever they come, each disciple of their creed, if an official, pays them as tribute one whole month's pay, and the other inhabitants according to the best of their ability. They remain in each place a few days, hold a kind of confirmation, give large banquets, and, perhaps, never again visit the place in their lives. The sole doctrine which such a Guroo teaches, seems to be "continue thus," which when preached on the occasion of presentations of gifts has a very obvious meaning. Desigan was such a Guroo, and as he was a very holy man, at least according to what the Hindoos consider holy, he was held in high honor. When he died, a few of his disciples made a golden image of him and worshipped it. After a time, this pleased others also, upon which, the gold figure of Desigan began to be carried about in procession like other gods, and the country people flocked in as they always do when there is something to stare at. This was only done by the Vadakalei or northern branch of Vishnoo Brahmins. The southern branch of the Vishnoo Brahmins called Tenkalei, who are distinguished from the others by a mark from the forehead down to the middle of the nose, had, however, also a celebrated Guroo, who was Desigan's cotemporary, and was called Manuwalawamuni. They wished to honor their Guroo in the same way as their neighbours had done theirs, and, therefore, made another little golden image, but smaller, (for their numbers were fewer) carried it round in procession and built for it a temple. This, however, the numerous opponents, the Vadakalei, would not allow, and hence a dispute arose in the town. As the Tenkalei were in the minority, they, of course, were in the wrong, at which they were so enraged that they almost would have become Christians. They were, however, priests who had to live by their religion, and who get pickings at births, marriages and death feasts, public festivals, &c., sufficient to give them the means of living, and hence, they first of all wisely enquired, whether as in their religion they could gain enough from Christianity to support wife and children.

In this way the gods of Tamil land grow more numerous from day to day since the people continue to worship the spirits of departed men, and of demons, to make idols of them and to build them temples. And the "principalities and powers" "the evil spirits under heaven," "the rulers of the darkness of this world," take advantage of this worship, and thus become actual powers which influence men that worship them, which check, drive and plague them, and prevent them as long as possible from arriving at a knowledge of the truth. For their dominion is only in the darkness of this world which can be banished, not indeed by any lamp of human invention, but by the Light from above. When this darkness disappears, then the influence of these shadow-powers will, of course, cease. Where and in what degree this darkness and ignorance of God prevails there and in such proportion do these evil powers have dominion? And this explains the so-frequent appearance of the actual lives of these dead idols.

Vishnoo and Siva are the principal of the gods of Tamil land. Vishnoo, mentioned casually already in the Vedas, appears to have represented Time, and his often mentioned "three steps," probably mean both the rising, meridian and setting of the sun, as well as the Past, the Present and the Future. In after times, of course, wives were assigned to him, and he was allowed many changes of form. These Avatars, however, have been so often described, and have so little in them that I shall probably be excused if I omit to reproduce them here. Vishnoo is called by many different names, and is said to have appeared in all kinds of places, which form as many excuses for festivals, to which the country people flock from all sides, and by which something respectable always comes into the hands of the Brahmins. To describe each in detail, would be a very fruitless task. Vishnoo's adherents besides, are for the most part to be found in the north of India.

In the south of India, and, therefore, in Tamil land also, Siva is the god chiefly worshipped, and the largest Pagodas are erected in his honor. In the worship of Siva, however, as much of the original Dravidian demon-worship has been absorbed, as the Brahmins found suitable to their plans, and many of the elements of the Kako-demons are to be found in Siva, and in the destructive qualities attributed to him and to his spouse Kali. Siva has one thousand and eight different names, and is, therefore, worshipped in as many different forms and ways. Amongst this number, however, are to be found several Tamil kings, who in virtue of their own deeds or their bards words, have been stamped as incarnations of Siva and are worshipped as such. Siva, like Vishnoo has, of course, long domestic histories, but no object can be served in furbishing them up; they are useless as far as instruction is concerned, valueless for edification and too hacknied for mere amusement.

The followers of Vishnoo carry the distinguishing mark of their god on the forehead, painted in glaring red and white lines, which sign is often to be found on their house doors. The Sivaites, on the other hand, smear themselves on the forehead, breast and arms with cow-dung ashes, and thus give themselves sometimes a really demoniacal appearance. Between these two sects, there are many disputes which sometimes end in blows. In former days, such occurrences were more frequent than now. Their disputes consist in the question which god is the greater, and which is the original one? Now, one often hears the opinion that Vishnoo and Siva are one, and that all worship offered to any one of the gods, is intended for the supreme God and is agreeable to Him. The picture-servers and Mary and Saints-worshippers say just the same and from the same reason. God the Lord, however, pronounced himself most emphatically against this doctrine, when men commenced to worship Him (not *strange* gods) by means of images, for, he destroyed the Aaronitish image-worshippers. And when, afterwards, Jeroboam again brought into Israel this image-worship, he and his whole race were rooted out. It will surely be allowed that the Lord of Heaven has the same right, as every master upon earth to order how his servants are to serve Him, and to allow them no opinions of their own upon the subject. And when He orders us to worship Him in spirit and in truth, not only do we not require any images, but we have no right to make use of them.

The worship of all these idols is of one kind; they are anointed with oil and sometimes milk is poured over them. With each motion of the hand, every one of which is prescribed, prayers are utterred, which consist for the most part of flattering praises or requests, and which have often nothing whatsoever in common with the present necessity. The principal matter here also is naturally trust in these gods, whereby a bond of union is formed between the idol-worshippers and the demons which are represented by, and are not far removed from the idols worshipped.

For an idol image is only the husk, or the body for the Schedim, (the "Devils," Deut. xxxii, 17) who, hidden behind it, received the proffered worship. And, therefore, the doctrine of the Brahmins that after certain prayers and ceremonies, the god takes possession of the idol, which till then had been nothing more than stone or metal, and that after certain other acts the god leaves the idol, should not be rejected as a simple lie.

I should, however, be doing these idol-worshippers an injustice, if I did not expressly say that among them there are many pious and earnest minds. These do not remain floundering in the quagmire of idolatry, but regard it as a mere outward husk, and reject it indeed in words, but still as far as their actual daily life is concerned they cannot disconnect themselves from it, for the whole life of the people is entwined with it. Minds of this kind rely in spirit on the truth and the good which the Vedanta has brought to light. They seek to grasp God as the most perfect Being; as the most perfect Intelligence; and as the most perfect Bliss ("Sat," "Chit," "Ananda,") and endeavour to find union with Him by the path of self-contemplation. Although I know some such individuals, I cannot describe them better than Tayumanaver, one of themselves has described them in a poem full of tenderness and longing for God, and which reminds one of the 42nd Psalm. The following is taken from Dr. Graul's translation in the "Indische Sinnpflanzen."

1. *The road to the Supreme Being.*

Thou standest at the summit of all the glorious earth,
Thou rulest and pervadest the world from ere its birth.
O Supremest Being!

And can the pious man find out no way to Thee
Who melting into love with tears approaches Thee.
O Supremest Being!

Already on the way is he who takes as guide,
An earnest loving heart and self-discernment tried.
O Supremest Being!

Who'd gaze at heaven first climbs the mountain height,
Self-contemplations wing towards Thee aim their flight.
O Supremest Being!

The union of the soul with the Supreme Being.

Thou throned above the Æther's pinnacle, O Lord,
'Tis thou who art the Spirit and thou who art the Word!
O Supremest Being!

Untouched thyself, the mind of him thou gently moveth
Who pondering, bewildered, the word and spirit loseth.
O Supremest Being!

Things heavenly thou showest unto the wondering sight,
Reflected in a mirror, thou mountain of delight.
O Supremest Being!

He dies, O Lord Supreme, who loves Thee to perfection,
And slumbering ever rests in blissful contemplation.
O Supremest Being!

The object thou of love, of every heartfelt pleasure
Of souls that prize alike the potsherd and the treasure.
O Supremest Being!

The poet's conversion.

A madness there possessed me, to kill the 'Self and Mine'
In need I wandered helpless, seeking help divine.
O Supremest Being!

My pride became then softened, and touched by Thee above
To water ran my bones, and I dissolved in love.
O Supremest Being!

O Thou of all the weary and heavy laden, Rest,
Henceforth thy name by me for ever shall be blest.
O Supremest Being!

Grant, thirsty, I may plunge in thy fresh stream of bliss
Or else o'erwhelmed I sink, within the deep abyss.
O Supremest Being!

A taste of bliss.

Knowing all my thoughts, for ever and again
Thou comest to refresh me, thou grace bestowing rain.
O Supremest Being!

Thou Nectar never cloying, thou stream of heavenly bliss,
O thou the good that dwells, in perfect loneliness.
O Supremest Being!

All things pervadeth Thou, O sweetest honey dew!
My inward self-possessing Thou sweetnest through and through. O Supremest Being!

My coral Thou, my pearl, my mine of purest gold,
My beam of brightness, Spirit light, my priceless wealth untold. O Supremest Being!

My eye, my thought, my tree, my heavenly stream,
Thou art my Aether-ray, my joy and wonder dream.
O Supremest Being!

Complaint over inward barrenness.

Lost in myself, my spirit lies here helpless
Like dried up wood—and Thou wilt leave me sapless
O Supremest Being!

O sea of bliss may I not plunge in Thee,
Nor quench the thirst, which now destroyeth me?
O Supremest Being!

When will my sorrow cease, my fountain spring,
And flow again with joy, my Prince and King.
O Supremest Being!

Why turn thy face away? all that I knew,
To get a closer view of Thee away I threw.
O Supremest Being!

My tears of grief, my soul seem to destroy,
When wilt Thou change them Lord to tears of joy?
O Supremest Being!

To Thee in silent worship I ever cling and twine,
And like an orphan child I long and pine.
O Supremest Being!

Though free and joyful I myself may boast,
I still must ever wander in a dreary waste.
O Supremest Being!

Like to a stalk of straw in whirlwinds blown and tossed,
So is thy wretched slave within this desert lost.
O Supremest Being!

But earthly powers and kings are nought of worth to me,
If they not humbly raise their hands in prayer to Thee.
O Supremest Being!

The cow bestows upon its helpless offspring love,
Show me, O gracious mother, thy pity from above.
O Supremest Being!

However guilty I, whatever wrong I do,
I ask Thee, mother-like, thy pitying love to show.
O Supremest Being!

One would think that minds so constituted, would at once turn to Christianity. But no! everything must await its time and its fulness. But we may well say of them that they are not far from the kingdom of God.

Besides the idol-worship, countenanced by the Brahmins, there are again other idols and worship which they themselves reject as devil-worship. These are the last remains of the religion of the aboriginal inhabitants of the country, the Turanians. Almost every hamlet has its village and boundary devil who, as they are not always in the best of humours, have to be propitiated with worship and sacrifices to keep them in a good temper. This species of Kakodemons are fond of blood, and of flesh still quivering with life: cocks and goats are the ordinary sacrifices, and in another place I have related how these are conducted.

From the above, which however leaves much to be said, it will be clearly seen how necessary it is to pray and to work, that "The heathen may turn from darkness unto Light, and from the dominion of Satan unto God."

CHAPTER V.

Temples and Temple-Worship.

All nations in the world who have permanent dwelling-places of their own are in the habit of building dwellings—temples—for their gods, and take often a pride in making these temples as big and as handsome as possible. Doubtless, a beautiful and noble feeling is the cause of this, but nevertheless, what Stephen exclaimed before the gorgeous Temple of Herod in Jerusalem, is true: "The most

High dwells not in temples made with hands." For, as Solomon says: "Behold the heaven of heavens cannot contain Thee, how much less this house, that I have built." And, as the Lord Himself says: "Heaven is my Throne, and earth is my footstool, what house will ye build Me, or what is the place of My rest? Hath not my Hand made all these things?" This knowledge, however, the heathen do not possess; they believe that their gods really live in their temples, and as these gods have only limited attributes, of such a nature that other deities can exist by their side, this their belief is not so unnatural.

The large temples of the East are not wholly roofed-buildings like those of the West, but they also enclose large open spaces, in the same way as all the better houses in the Orient do. On festival days, thousands collect in these open spaces. Thousands also find lodging in the spacious halls of columns, which are often two-storied. The temples of Solomon and of Herod, the mightiest temples of Egypt, and the temples in the land of the Tamulians, are alike in this respect.

It may, perhaps, sound strange that I should class the temple of Solomon and those of Egypt together with the temples of the Tamulians, but, in truth, they belong to each other. For the temples of the Tamulians are not only by far the largest temples in India, but are besides the largest temples in the world. Solomon's temple was about 300 feet square with many open spaces in the middle. Herod's temple which also enclosed a large outer court for the heathen, was 500 feet long and as many broad. The large Mosque in Mecca is, it is true, 650 feet long and 400 feet broad, but the interior for the greater part is an open space. The great temples of Egypt were also partly open in the middle, and the largest at Carnac encloses a space 1,200 feet by 360, and contains, therefore, 532,000 square feet. These are or were the largest temples of the old world. They are, however, all by far exceeded in size by the temples of the Tamulians. The temple at Chellumbrum, in the Cuddalore district, although not the largest in Tamil land, is four times as large as Herod's temple and more than double the size of the largest of the temples of Egypt. It is according to my own repeated measurements above one thousand feet in length, and the same quantity in breadth, so that it contains more than one million square feet.

Temples in all other parts of the world must yield to such as these in size. It is true, that the temples of Egypt make a grander impression with their pillars of such enormous height and thickness; but the impression which the Egyptians sought to create by colossal size, the Tamulians have endeavoured to convey by massiveness; for instance, although the greatest column hall of Egypt, that of Carnac, contained 138 pillars; the Pilgrims' hall at Chellumbrum alone contains as many as 930 granite columns. Besides this largest hall, the flat roof of which is also of granite, this temple contains others similar, and one in which the carving is very fine and delicate. From the outside, this, like all other Tamil temples, shows only a smooth high wall with lofty towers 150 feet high, which cover the entrances on each of the four sides. In these towers are granite stones in one block 40 feet in length. Thousands of figures of the gods cover them from top to bottom. These are for the most part made of plaster, but so good was the workmanship and the materials that they have lasted hundreds of years. Greek æsthetics are, of course, not to be found here, but the Orientals have æsthetics of their own; and what to us, cold Westerns appear to be only brainless grotesques, is to the Indian a book easy of comprehension and affords him delightful glimpses into his world of deities; for these gods all live to the Tamulian, and he lives for them. Fifteen years ago, the finest hall of columns in Chellumbrum was lying neglected in ruins, and many of the beautiful pillars lay shattered on the ground. Then there came a poor old man, who said: I will rebuild this hall! and he kept his word; for it is now, and has been for some time, perfect and complete. But how was this done? In this way. The old man travelled all over the country with bare feet, bare head and bare body, with only a narrow strip of old cloth round his loins. In his hand he always carried a bag containing the holy ashes with which the Sivaite smears his forehead and breast. The offerings he received, he placed in this bag, and in return, he gave a little of his ashes. And so he wandered about until he had collected a considerable sum, and then he commenced to build. Ash-bag in hand I saw him superintending the building, and from the bag, paid many a gold piece, and when the money was finished, he started again on a begging expedition and collected more. In this way he obtained many thousand Rupees, and at last completed the restoration of the hall, which is said to be finer now than it was before.

Inside, all round the high walls, are halls with pillars, generally two-storied, which are capable of containing many thousand pilgrims. The fine square tank also, the four slopes to which are ornamented by steps of granite, is built round with pillars and halls. The wants of the festival guests are, therefore, well provided for. By the side of the tank are the dwellings of the gods, who love the darkness. Their worshippers remain standing at a respectful distance or prostrate themselves lengthways on the ground in the most profound adoration. This position is called Sashtângam or 'six members,' for in it the forehead, the breast, the two knees and the two elbows must touch the ground. Only the ministering priests enter at certain times in order to oil and to adorn the god with flowers. Loud music—or what is intended for such,—the firing of cannons, &c., forms part of the ceremony.

The whole building conveys a mighty, though not elevating impression, and there is no one but must wonder at the multitude of pillars, at the masses of granite in the midst of rice fields far from any quarries, at the hugeness of the whole building and at the wonderful industry which has been bestowed upon it.

The land of the Tamulians has not a few such temples, and no other race in India has such large ones. Even in this same Cuddalore district there is another temple of almost equal size and celebrity, which is visited at the time of its festival by from 150 to 200 thousand people. It is the temple of Tiroovanamalai, and is very remarkably built in three divisions, of which the first forms the outer court and the third the holy of holies. The priests allowed me to enter the first without objection, they did not seem to like it when I passed into the second, and protested in screams as I was about to step into the third. The entrance to each division is by a flight of broad granite steps; then comes the tower which is built over the entrance—halls for pilgrims to rest in—called the 'thousand pillared,' though there are always several missing out of the 10th hundred—are in each division. The whole is 1,200 feet long and 700 broad.

Besides these two, the largest temples are at Trivallore, Conjeveram, Tanjore, Srirangam, Madura, &c.

The largest of all is that at Srirangam, built upon an Island of the Cauvery of great fertility, and not far from Trichinopoly. It is surrounded by seven walls; the outer of which is nearly a mile each way in extent, so that the whole Pagoda is nearly four miles in circumference. The space between each of the seven walls is about 350 feet broad. In the middle of each wall over the entrance gate, is a tower. The southern outermost tower has stones built in it 30 feet in length, and 6 feet broad, and is a splendid though unfinished work. The building, as a whole, may be called a temple town rather than a temple. Here the Brahmins lived in security and fed upon the fat of the land. But even they were not permitted to find a Paradise upon earth, as they discovered during the wars of the last century. When an army supported by the French invested this Pagoda, (for these mighty buildings are easily turned into fortresses,) the Brahmins got into the utmost terror, and an old man mounted the outer entrance tower and conjured the besiegers by all that was holy not to desecrate this sacred place. But when his entreaties were of no avail and the enemies effected their entrance, he threw himself down from the tower and lay a shattered mass at their feet. But even this act of self-immolation was of no avail,—the days of the ancient Greeks had passed away,—the invaders stepped heedlessly over his body and the fortified temple was carried. Why cannot religion keep itself clear of politics?

Now-a-days the Brahmins allow any one to pass through the first six gates without molestation. No one, however, is permitted to pass through the seventh which shuts in their holy of holies. Enormous treasures are said to be hidden within it, and amongst others an image of Vishnoo of pure gold which they sometimes exhibit to the curious. As, however, he is so big and heavy they bring him out piecemeal, and after having exhibited his head, his arms, and his trunk, take him carefully back into the holy place. He is worshipped only at certain seasons. When a party is made up under the guidance of a local Official, the Brahmins are in the habit of bringing out boxes of jewels and treasure. I have seen the dresses and ornaments of the gods of precious stones set in pure gold. Though the stones are large, they are mostly uncut, and the majority are flawed. The stone carving is partly fretted and is executed with great art. The whole is a veritable jungle of stone and masonry.

The Pagoda at Tanjore is not so large, but is fortified with a deep ditch and a rampart. The entrance towers are not remarkable, but in the middle there is a tower with 14 divisions. Each side of this tower measures 82 feet, and the heights above is 200 feet. One peculiarity of this tower is that it covers the most holy, whereas in most Pagodas the towers cover only the entrance. In front of this tower is a long building. The light enters only by the door of this building, and so there is plenty of the darkness so much enjoyed by the Hindoo gods. As I mounted the steps and made for the entrance of the interior, the guardians ran away in terror to call the Brahmins, all of whom it so happened were absent. I could, therefore, proceed unhindered. I walked on quietly, for I did not wish to excite any tumult, but even in the interior I found no living men, nothing but dead gods; at the end was a kind of altar, in the middle of which was an idol well smeared with oil, and around a number of lamps. The whole was not unlike a Roman Catholic altar, and there is no doubt that Rome in her ceremonies has learnt something from the heathen. For, when in the 4th century idolatry in Italy was forbidden by law, and the unconverted heathen flocked to the Churches, the already worldly-wise Church of Rome commenced to change the simple Christian worship into a gorgeous ceremonial. The worship of God was altered so as to be popular, but ceased for ever to be a worship of God in Spirit and in Truth. And this evil has in the course of centuries grown greater, so that it is intelligible how, when the first Portuguese had found the long way to India round the Cape of Good Hope and landed on her shores, they should have at first imagined heathen idolatry to be Christian worship. They went straight into a Pagoda, and as everything seemed the same as in their Churches at home, they fell on their knees before the idols, whom they took to be Saints, and offered prayers to them. And only one of them arose in doubt and exclaimed, "If these are devils, I am not to be supposed to have worshipped them."

As I emerged from the darkness, a Brahmin hurried breathlessly up, struck his hands together above his head and exclaimed "but it is forbidden to enter here!" I answered quietly, "If you had only told me that before, should I have entered? The man remained silent, but I walked quietly out before a commotion commenced.

I will not, however, weary the reader with a description

of each temple, they are in their fashion all alike: high walls round them, heavy towers built over the entrances, broad at the summit and covered from top to bottom with figures, thousand columned halls for pilgrims, and here and there the dwellings of the separate gods. The whole always makes a striking impression, striking, but at the same time heavy and ponderous and far from elevating. Impressive, but not pleasing, as is the impression created by the beautiful ruins on the Acropolis at Athens. The impression is more like that caused by the Colisseum at Rome. In both cases it is the massiveness which is imposing, but not pleasing.

After these largest temples, there is a large number of ordinarily sized ones, of which, however, many are about as large as that of Herod at Jerusalem. Small temples, down to simple shrines cover the country without number. In the towns and villages there is scarcely a street without a temple big or small, and it is held to be impious to live in a street without a temple. But even in places where men do not dwell are to be found temples and gods without end; on the tops of hills, in the debris on the plains, by tanks, by rivers, by the side of roads and indeed everywhere.

The land of the Tamulians is, therefore, extraordinarily rich in temples, and it is a matter of surprise that so small a people (estimated in numbers at 12, but according to the last census 16 millions) should have been able to expend so much energy, so great diligence and such enormous sums of money on their temples. Even rock temples, that is to say, temples hewn into and out of the living rock are to be found in Tamil land. Mahabalipuram, known also as the seven Pagodas, not far from Sadras, is celebrated. Here it would seem that a whole race of stone masons, have worked for an entire generation, or rather carried on mad games apparently without object or purpose. Here also is a rock, covered with grotesque figures of gods, with reference to which it is narrated that Göethe said—

> I fain would live in India's land,
> Were not the masons so mighty a band.

The whole question of temple-building is a very peculiar one. It is a sign of a certain height of religious know-

---

NOTE.—In Indien möcht ich selber leben
Hätt es nur keine Steinmetzen gegeben.

ledge; but it is a height from which the path leads down hill. Even Solomon's temple is no exception to this. How soon was it desecrated! And the large Churches of Christendom, which were built beyond the actual requirements, how little have they been houses of God for worshipping Him in Spirit and in Truth. How many sellers, usurers and money-changers are to be found in them, who deserve to be driven out with a scourge of ropes! Not only in St. Peter's at Rome, but also in the marvellous Cathedral at Milan, and in the Cathedral at Cologne one may hear the voice of the Lord as He spoke through the prophet Amos: "Take thou away from me the noise of thy songs; for I will not hear the melody of thy viols. I hate, I despise your feast days, and I will not smell in your solemn assemblies!"—if but those who have ears chose to listen. Most of these buildings have proceeded from a spirit like that of Nimrod, by which the people, or some Nimrod among them, have wished to make for themselves a name, and an honour, whilst at the same time God the Lord has to furnish the name and the pretext, and the worship in these temples consists of a medley of ceremonies learnt partly from Jews but mostly from heathens. Ceremonial service has everywhere something striking and tempting about it. Man enjoys a feeling of content and of self-satisfaction, after having performed certain acts held to be duties. And if at times the inward hollowness is felt and the inward voice heard, man endeavours with still more such externals and husks to fill the one, and to silence the other. So men attain a certain drilling, and may even cast out many a devil, only that it will be done by the very Beelzebub of his own Self. At best a well grown *wild* olive tree will be produced; the new man in Christ does not grow in this soil of self-selected works, performances and drillings.

Even the Tamulians reckon ceremonial service as the lowest step in their worship. A higher step is the service of love towards men by which all wealth and goods are placed at the disposal of fellowmen, and the highest step of all, is the alienation of the thoughts from all things worldly, so that "gold and straw are of equal value," and through contemplation Self becomes absorbed in God. How much truth there is in this, and how much nearer is it to the eternal truth than the wearying service of dead saints be they called Rama, Krishna, Januarius, Xaverius, or whatever else you please!

The temples of India are not of great antiquity, and in the land of the Tamulians there are scarcely any older than 800 years. All Japhet's children began to build temples late in life. It is true that the Greeks introduced the passion for temple-building into Europe from Egypt, from whence they borrowed most of their culture, and the Romans were infected by it from them. But when the Germanic races began to take a part in history, they held it "to be unworthy of the greatness of the Heavenly Beings to represent them by images of a man, or to shut them up inside walls," as Tacitus tells us, and it was the same with their brethren in India. The Vedas know nothing of temples and idols or of periodical festivals. Each man and each woman served god or the gods in his or her own house, and offered prayers or sacrifice—for women also offered sacrifice—according to the prescribed form, but without the interference of priests or of any other self-made mediator. What need had such a people of temples? Each place was equally suitable for them to offer their prayers to the unseen gods, and the sun, which in India rises almost all the year round with an equal brightness, was for them the mighty clock which reminded them of their religious duties. As Rama says :—

"When rises the sun we praise and adore Thee,
When at evening it sets with prayers we implore Thee."

For this worship no temples were needed, and at this period there was in India great modesty and propriety of habit. Human writings contain no higher examples of virtue, than those which Valmiki ascribes to Rama and Sita.

But there is nothing for man so hard to bear as days of prosperity, and it is the same with a nation. The prosperity of India led to presumption, and presumption to devastating wars which are reproduced in the Mahabharat. The ancient royal families together with the whole race of Kshetriyas destroyed each other and perished. With them fell India's virtue, and the simple religion of the Vedas passed away. Every state of society was dissolved. Gross lawlessness was the natural result. And whilst the Kshetriyas, who hitherto had been the rulers, were effecting each others destruction, the Vaisyas, the tradesmen and manufacturers, had ample opportunities of gaining great wealth. Wealth quickly gained, leads to luxury and dissolute living; and when in course of time the vacant thrones were ascended by these new made men, the prophecy of Proverbs 30, v. 21, 22, was fulfilled: "When a servant reigneth the earth is disquieted."

Barbarian splendour and luxurious living was the order of the day with these new Kings, and the Brahmins who were almost the only persons left with any learning, became cowardly flatterers, and endeavoured to recover their former influence by intrigues, or else withdrew themselves into the woods, and lived together in lonely hermitages. Krishna is the representative of the period of the Princes of low birth, a period of luxury and laxity of manners.

The re-action was not long in setting in. It did not emanate from the Brahmins, for they had become either cowardly flatterers, or else haughty recluses. The re-action against luxury commenced in the luxurious and pampered courts. Sakya, the son of the King of Kapila Vasta, afterwards known as *Buddha*, was the leader of the re-action. In the midst of the pleasures of a court-life, he became disgusted with them, and the inevitability of age, sickness and death made so deep an impression on him, that, overcome by this "world's dolor," he left his father's palace, and strove to gain wisdom in a secluded Brahmin hermitage in the forest. With the Brahmins, however, he failed to find the wisdom he sought for, and accordingly he removed, followed by a few disciples, to a hermitage of his own. At length after many a severe conflict, he attained that knowledge in the presence of which, Space and Time, creation and dissolution, dwindle into nothing. He now perceived the connecting links of the causes of existence, and their negation, and with this knowledge he attained perfect wisdom, Buddhi, and became himself *Buddha*. Regarding his new knowledge, he puts to himself the following questions and then answers them :—

Question.—What is the cause of this world's dolor: age, sickness and death?

Answer.—Birth.

Question.—What is the cause of Birth?

Answer.—Love of the world and of existence.

Question.—What is the cause of this love of the world and of existence?

Answer.—Sensual longing.

Question.—What is the cause of sensual longing?

Answer.—Ignorance.

When Ignorance is dispelled, the world's dolor comes to an end, and age, sickness and death cease. But this ignorance is not mere stupidity, it consists therein that man believes things temporal to be eternal, and, therefore, what actually is not, to be reality.

This ignorance is a hereditary sin, and propagates itself from one birth to another, clouds man's understanding and perverts his will. It first shows itself in pleasure and desire, it then seeks everywhere satisfaction, and thus engenders love of the world, love of life, desire of existence, &c. These then are the impulses which lead to ever-continuing consciousness of existence, with its world's dolor of age, sickness, and death. It is this clinging to existence which after death drives the spirit to other forms of existence, *i. e.*, to migration of the Soul. For it is the soul which through its desire, clings to existence after the dissolution of the body. By reason of this desire, the soul is driven to new forms of existence in the cycles of time, and the bearing of the soul in the lately deceased body determines the form of its next body, whether that of a man of higher or of lower caste, or even of an animal. The highest and last aim, therefore, of all spiritual life and strife, *is the* CONQUEST OF THIS LOVE OF EXISTENCE.

The means of effecting this is the Thiana or spiritual contemplation, but it must be strenuously supported by outward means. For this reason, a man should forsake the world, "take up his abode among the roots of the trees" and eat only what others leave or what is freely offered him. This doctrine Sakkya taught, and also carried into practice, for the Prince Kapila Vasta wandered about with a pot in his hand, and ate only what was placed in the pot without his asking. In this way he soon collected a large number of followers, and especially of beggars, for begging is one of the most favorite virtues of India. From Brahmins down to Pariahs, everybody ran about with pot in hand and ate what was given him. But it was impossible for everybody to give up his occupation or trade and go about begging with a pot, since then there would have been none left to fill the pots. Buddha, therefore, founded a second class of disciples who were permitted to remain in their occupation, but to whom it was properly inculcated, "that all family life and all household cares had only this one object; spending alms." He abolished all systems of castes, and taught "my doctrine is like heaven, where there is room for all; for men and for women, for boys and for girls, for rich and for poor. As all rivers lose their names when their waters join those of the Ganges, so do the adherents of Buddha cease to be Brahmins, Kshetriyas, Vaisyas, or Sudras."

The aim of Buddha's doctrine is entire unconcernedness towards existence. When there is no longer any more inclination and longing for life, the separate life ceases, and the soul is absorbed in Nirvana, *i. e.*, in eternal emptiness, in the eternal nothing. Such is the unconsoling doctrine of Buddhism. To it the greatest evil is life, and, therefore, greatest good is the destruction of life.

Buddha, therefore, went a step further than the Brahminical Vedantists. These taught as he did, that ignorance is the root of the error in which the soul becomes identified with the *manas* (mind), whereas the *manas* is only an organ of the soul. By reason of this identification, it arises that the soul feels drawn towards many things, and is repelled by many others, and it is the longing that causes pleasure and the aversion that causes pain. From this longing or aversion, arise good or evil works which entail either reward or punishment. Good deeds, then, aid as much as evil ones towards the fettering of the soul; for "it is impossible to escape the fruits of works." This separate existence must, therefore, continue in order that the fruits of the works, good or evil, may be received. True knowledge breaks the magic ring of ignorance and sets the soul free, so that it can return to its original source. The Vedantists say that this source is an absolute Being; Buddha maintains that this source is an absolute nothing—and so their ways separate. Every composition is dissolved, and all that remains is absolute Being—says the Vedanta:—every composition is dissolved and every being passes away, and there remains but an absolute Nothing—says Buddha.

Buddhism had rapid and enormous success and many kings embraced it. But this success of Buddhism which endeavoured to put an end to age, to sickness and to death, was the cause of the ruin of its followers. They soon found the roots of the trees uncomfortable dwellings, and they built themselves large cloisters fitted up with all the wealth of the land, where they found it much more comfortable to renounce the world than at the roots of trees. The Prince of Kapila Vasta forsook his father's palace and sought out the desert, in order the better to be able to contemplate that which is nothing. His disciples built palace like cloisters in order by doing nothing to become better able to serve that which is nothing. Split into eighteen different sects they disputed about that which is nothing, and so their days were numbered. Brahminism awoke to a new life; numerous puranas celebrated the heroes of Indian antiquity, the people began to love them anew, and arose and drove the lazy Buddhists out of the country. Their religious buildings, however, were turned into temples to the deified heroes of former times and also to the images of pure imagination. *This was the manner in which the temples of India took their commencement.*

In such large temples there is naturally a very complicated worship. The idols are anointed morning and evening, and in some temples also at noon. This is generally done with melted butter and sometimes with milk. It is not all Brahmins who do this, but there are especial Poojaries amongst them to whom this duty is assigned. Before worship the priest is bound to bathe, and during it, to repeat the prescribed prayers (mantrams). No mistakes may be made, and after his bath, the priest may not come in contact with even a breath of air that has been wafted past the lower castes or Europeans. Then is formed a regular procession of Indian musicians, who, in truth, understand how to make a heathenish noise, and of *devadasar* who have to dance before the idol. The anointing takes place amidst many ceremonies which it were tedious and objectless to describe. After the oiling, the idol is generally crowned with flowers or flowers are scattered in front of it. Of course, the gods have sometimes to be washed, as it is the smell in their neighbourhood is not the most savoury.

Besides this daily worship, there are a number of festivals. Generally there are 18 in the year, excluding the more especial ones which celebrate certain events supposed to have occurred on the spot. On such occasion as these, the country people flock to the feasts in thousands.

On certain especial occasions, the principal god is carried round the best streets of the town. For this purpose there are peculiar waggons or cars, built exactly like one of the temple towers and covered from top to bottom with carvings and figures of gods. Some of these cars are from 50 to 60 feet high. They move on solid wheels without spokes. Long ropes are attached to the front, and hundreds of people catch hold of and pull at these. The Pariahs from the neighbouring villages are driven in for this service if they do not come of their own free will. As the streets are often soft and sandy, the car does not get very far in one day, nor is this desired, in order that this species of enjoyment may last all the longer. The Brahmins stand above and urge on the people, whose excitement is also stimulated by repeated shots. In former days, those especially excited used to throw themselves beneath the wheels and allow themselves to be crushed beneath them. This is no longer allowed, but accidents are still of frequent occurrence amongst these excited crowds. Only a few years ago at Chellumbrum, a man was crushed to death, and a Brahmin had both of his legs broken, so that he afterwards died. Christianity which has obtained a footing in many of the villages surrounding Chellumbrum, already begins to affect these cars, for the Pariahs are no longer willing to be made to pull.

The cars may only be pulled by men, not by animals, and so they have been obliged to make smaller cars which are easier moved. Of course, the Brahmins try to conceal from the people the real reason, but there are many earnest minds among them who are able to recognize it, and who will openly admit that their religion is going down hill. The temples of India and the worship in them have had their time and their age of prosperity. That has now passed away never to return. As much wealth is connected with these temples, they will, of course, still last a long time, as dead trees remain a long time standing, until at last they fall, unless they are previously hewn down. A Charlemagne would convert India to Christianity by means of the sword. A Constantine would put an end to idolatry by an edict, and change the mighty temples into Christian Churches. An Evangelical Mission, however, cannot use such means, and must, therefore, be content to put up with these small days, and wait for the coming of the time of the Lord. What Christian Missions have as yet done in Tamil land we will now endeavour to put before the reader.

PART II.

THE MISSIONS IN THE LAND OF THE TAMULIANS.

CHAPTER I.

The Mission of the Ancient Church.

The last command which our Lord gave to His disciples upon earth was "to go forth into all the world and to preach the Gospel to every creature." And with this command was coupled the promise that He would be with them until the end of the world. In obedience to this command, and supported by the promise, as by a pilgrim's staff, His disciples went forth into all the world and proclaimed the Gospel tidings to every creature that could and would hear it. But they did not go into all the world at once, for everything has its time. Even after the outpouring of the Holy Ghost the Apostles did not at once set out, but first of all preached the Gospel to the Jews in order to collect out of them the spiritual Israel. And even when the elders of the people hardened themselves, stoned Stephen, and persecuted the whole congregation, so that they were compelled to scatter over the country, even then the Apostles did not leave Jerusalem until they became convinced that the people shared the blindness of their elders, and that the Israel of the New Testament had already been gathered from out of the Jews. From that time the Apostles gradually forsook Jerusalem and Judea, and travelled into all the world. John followed the Apostle Paul to Asia Minor and remained in Ephesus. Peter came to Babylon; Bartholemeus went to Armenia; Thaddeus to Persia and Thomas is reported to have gone over to India, into the land of the Tamulians. Some nine miles south of Madras, is a Hill named St. Thomas' Mount where pierced by a spear the Apostle is said to have found a Martyr's death; and not far from there, is a village called St. Thomé where his grave is shown. And thousands of Christians are still existing, who ascribe their origin to the Apostle Thomas, after whom they are also called Thomas Christians, or Suriani, Syrian Christians. For in former times, India was not so far distant as it is now. When the centre of Christendom was in and around Palestine, the messengers of the Gospel were so much nearer to India. Indian life and manners were more familiar to them than they are to us, stiff western races. And so already at the end of the second century, St. Pantaenus left his influential Professor's Chair at Alexandria in order to minister to the Christians in India, for together with the pride of the Stoics he had also thrown aside contempt for inferiors, and in return had learnt at the feet of the Lord humility and heartfelt piety. In the fourth century, one Theophilus, called the "Indian," worked in Southern India; and in the Island of Ceylon where he found old established Christians. And the monkish merchant or merchant monk, Cosmos, who, from his journey to India, received the name of Indicopleustes, relates of the year 535, that he certainly found Christians in Ceylon and in Malabar (South India) who at Kaliana had a Bishop who had come from Persia. In addition to the sea journey to India there was formerly a land route *viâ* Persia. The Nestorians were for some time zealous propagators of Christianity, Central Asia was dotted over with Christian communities and willing messengers started from Balk and from Samarcand toward the South and South East. Even the cold Northern races found India early, and in the 9th century, Alfred the Great is said to have despatched an embassy under Sighelm, Bishop of Shireburn, to the grave of St. Thomas' in the land of the Tamulians. This embassy is said to have arrived at its place of destination, to have worshipped at the grave of the Apostle and to have then returned provided with precious stones and articles of merchandize.

When the Portuguese had settled in India, they soon came in contact with these Thomas Christians, and were welcomed by them with great joy. But this joy was only of short duration and was soon changed to bitter pain, for instead of improving their deficiency in the knowledge of Christ, the Portuguese endeavoured by every art, by kindness and by oppression to win them over to the Pope. The Bishop of these Thomas Christians, Mar Gabriel gave to the Dutch at the commencement of the eighteenth century a long account of their circumstances from which I will only extract the following: "Fifty-five years after the birth of the Messiah, the Apostle Thomas came to Mylapore (near Madras) on the Coromandel Coast and preached the Gospel. From thence he came to Malabar, preached the Gospel, collected congregations in several places, and fixed their Pastors. He then returned to the Coromandel Coast, where he was stabbed by a heathen with a spear, and thus ended his life. After some time all the Pastors whom St. Thomas had appointed died off, and a false doctrine arose which was followed by many. Only 160 families remained true. But in 745, there arrived from Bagdad Christians and Priests who settled down in Malabar. King Peroomal, to whom the new arrivals addressed themselves, received them kindly and gave them land in order to build shops and Churches. He also bestowed upon them many marks of honor, and the right to trade throughout the whole country as long as the sun and moon should shine, as may be read to this day on tablets of copper. Thus, the Christians lived happy and prosperous, and the Christian Patriarch of the East sent them many shepherds and teachers from Bagdad, Nineveh and Jerusalem. After the Portuguese had come to Malabar, the Patriarch sent four more Bishops, Mar Mardina, Mar Jacob, Mar Thoma, and Jene Allay, who ruled the Christians and built many Churches. After their death, there came to Malabar about the year 1550, another Mar Abraham. But the Portuguese resolved that no more teachers should be allowed to come, and guarded all the roads by which the Syrian Priests could come. When now the Christians had no instructors, the Portuguese spent much trouble in endeavouring to draw them over. But when they could not succeed they gave the King of Cochin 30,000 Ducats, and with his assistance persecuted the Christians for three years, until they could bear it no longer and reconciled themselves with the Portuguese. From that time the Syrian customs were changed, and the Priests were forbidden to marry. That lasted for fifty-five years. Then there came to Mylapore a Priest named Mar Matti, sent by the Patriarch from Syria. Him the Portuguese seized and threw into the sea. Then the Christians gathered together and swore that they would have nothing more to do with the Portuguese."

Menezes, Archbishop of Goa, made the greatest exertions to induce these Christians to submit to Rome. He travelled through the various Christian districts and distributed many alms in order to effect a beginning. He was backed up by his purchased heathen help and was accompanied by a troop of Portuguese soldiers, but he did not use them for open force. Wherever he came, he found the Churches empty and the people but little inclined even to listen to him. In the meantime his progress, his retinue and his alms attracted always fresh crowds. In his Sermons he was in the habit of instructing the Christians thus: He who does not enter the sheepfold by the door is a thief and a murderer. The door, however, is the Pope at Rome, and as the Patriarch at Babylon has not been inducted into his See by the Pope, therefore, he is a thief and a murderer, &c. When the Christians laid before him their old documents to prove to him that they had always stood in connection with the Patriarch of Babylon, he tore the documents before their eyes. This so irritated the Christians that they would fain have torn him also. But the Priests knew his power and restrained the people, hoping to get more by stratagem and delay than by open force. Neither side, therefore, was wanting in deception and cunning, and this makes the struggle a very painful one.

At last they agreed to hold a meeting of the Syrian Priests and to arrive at some conclusion. The Archdeacon, for there was no Bishop, a number of Priests and many armed Christians under two leaders appeared at the Conference. The Archdeacon first asked Menezes if he had not stigmatized their Patriarch as a heretic. Before I answer that question, exclaimed Menezes, first tell me whether you believe the Gospel of St. John. We would rather die than deny its truth, the Christians cried. Very good, said Menezes, but the Gospel of St. John teaches that the Word became flesh and dwelt among us, but all Nestorians, to which sect the Patriarch of Babylon belongs, teach that the Word did not *become* flesh but dwelt in Christ as in a temple. To this Christians knew not what to reply, but insisted that Menezes should only conduct himself among them as a stranger and as a guest, and not as a master and a superior, that he should make no Ecclesiastical arrangements, and that least of all should he introduce unknown practices and ceremonies. Thereupon everything was adjourned to the next Conference. The Archdeacon sent a circular to all Christians warning them expressly to have nothing to do with Menezes since he wished not only to bring them under the dominion of Rome, but also to make them subjects of Portugal. This, however, by no means prevented Menezes from continuing his visits to the Christian villages or from appointing and ordaining Priests, &c., just as if he had been the recognized Bishop of the Syrian Christians. His money, his influence, and the pomp of his progress, of course, helped him to adherents, and even villages began to go over to him and to recognize him as their rightful superior.

These results of the Bishop of Goa excited the greatest apprehensions on the part of the Archdeacon and of the Syrian Christians. A Syrian Bishop there was not, and had there even been one, what could he in his poverty and helplessness have done against the rich and crafty Portuguese? The helplessness of his situation so excited the poor Archdeacon that at last he wrote to Menezes that if he did not leave off disquieting his Christians and perverting his congregations, he would collect the Christians who still remained faithful and assassinate him. Thereupon, Menezes excommunicated him as an enemy of the Pope, and summoned him to appear before the Judgment Seat of God in order to give account of the many souls which through his fault remained in error and were ruined. When the poor Archdeacon received this letter, he fell into a swoon, and soon afterwards declared that he was willing to submit to Rome.

On the 20th June 1599, a Synod was summoned, at which the Archdeacon and 53 Priests appeared. Menezes came with a large following of civilians and military men, in the midst of whom was the Governor of Cochin accompanied by a Military escort. The Sessions were, of course, held without any disturbance, and the poor Syrians agreed to everything that was proposed to them. They recognized the Pope and denounced the Patriarch of Babylon. One thing only they would not agree to. They would not pray in Latin. It is true that of Syriac they understood no more than they did of Latin, but they insisted upon their Liturgy remaining Syriac whatever else was altered. And Menezes allowed them this rag of independance, the rather that wrapped it in it, they might the less feel their complete subjection.

The Bishop of Goa after much trouble and expense on his part and grief and heart-burning on the other part, had, therefore, at last effected his purpose and the Syrians became Romish. Those Priests who would not put away their wives were dismissed, most of the Syrian books were burnt, and in their place others with prayers to Mary and the Saints were introduced, and then the glorious work was complete. About the heathen around Menezes did not trouble himself. They might go to hell as fast as they liked. The Christians too might remain as ignorant as ever, but one thing they must do, they must learn how to pray to Mary and the Saints. Whether they knew more than before of Christ was not the Bishop's matter, but what he insisted upon was that they should know the Pope and know him as their master and on this depended their salvation.

But this triumph lasted no longer than did the power of the Portuguese. And when after 50 years, this power was broken, the work on which Menezes had spent so much care also fell to the ground. By far the majority of the congregations returned to their old customs, and all that remained of the Bishop's laborious work was a lasting disquiet and dissatisfaction. It is true, that they now received fresh Bishops from Antioch, but the Christians were so split up that even the Bishops could not restore order; and this because they had come not solely to feed their flocks, but also to increase the importance of the Patriarch and to collect for him money. As in this latter object they did not succeed, the Patriarch sent other Bishops after them to manage matters better, so that in 1848, the Patriarch of Antioch had five Bishops amongst the Thomas Christians each of whom was engaged in excommunicating the others!

The Dutch seem to have troubled their heads very little about these Christians. They banished the Portuguese, occupied their Settlements, and took from them all the profitable commerce of India, and with that they were satisfied. But they protected the Christians from the crippling and Christianity-destroying influence of the Jesuits. But when in their turn the Dutch had to yield and the English stepped into their place, they soon began to cast glances at the Thomas Christians. They, however, commenced their work in love as Christians should, and only endeavoured to instil life into the dead bones of the Christians, they did not seek to win them over to their Church and customs. And this is a duty which all Evangelical Christians owe to this ancient Church.

The English found still 55 Churches that had nothing in common with Rome, but which recognized the Patriarch of Antioch as their head. Their Bishop, Mar Dionysius, was a good natured, amiable man who desired the good of his flock, but as he did not know how to bring this about himself he was only too willing to let others effect it for him. From 1816, English Missionaries laboured among the Thomas Christians. They built a High School to which two Professors of Syriac and others for the Hebrew, Latin and English languages were appointed. The heathen Queen gave several thousand Rupees for this purpose, and in addition sufficient ground to erect the necessary buildings. Lower schools were erected in different places, and before long there were 900 scholars studying under the Missionaries. The Bible was translated and printed and willingly read by the Priests unchecked by the Bishop. Everything remained in this hopeful state as long as Mar Dionysius and the old Missionaries lived. But after them came a new race and a new spirit that also wished to be something. The new Missionaries were by no means pleased with the certainly somewhat peculiar customs of the Thomas Christians, and would willingly have altered them. Unfortunately for them, however, they had not the smallest power to do so. It is true, that as before, they could preach the crucified Christ in the Churches and teach Him in the schools, but this did not seem to them to be enough, especially as between all this the Priests taught erroneous doctrines. One of their most favorite errors was the doctrine of the efficacy of the prayers of the Priests for the deceased. And this error was the more cherished because it gained for the Priests considerable profits, since the departed could be helped by the prayers of the *Priests* only. The doctrine regarding the Sacraments was also faulty, though in this respect the Missionaries, perhaps, erred as much on one side as the Thomas Christians did on the other. The new Bishop too was no longer so friendly as the old one had been. He still suffered the Missionaries, but he showed little interest in their work and no gratitude for their trouble. Besides he was no longer alone, and rival

Bishops detracted from his importance. The position of the Missionaries and the Bishop was, therefore, by no means an easy one; and when added to all this, the pious but impulsive Bishop Wilson wished to extend his mandate over the Thomas Christians also, they declared that they could only recognize the Patriarch at Antioch as their Head. Upon this the Missionaries withdrew and collected into congregations those of the Thomas Christians who adhered to them just as they would any other Converts. This, of course, put an end to all side by side working, and now the Thomas Christians contained not only a Romish but also an Anglican fraction. When in addition to this, it is remembered that they were by no means agreed among themselves, the only wonder is that they did not entirely disappear. This, however, has not happened for they continue to this day. It only remains for us now to cast a short glance at that fraction which has remained true to its old customs, and whose Bishops still come from Syria.

The real Thomas Christians have still many Churches, and mostly roomy buildings capable of containing thousands of worshippers. The Churches are all built after one style, and are long and narrow. The entrance is low, for those who enter should bring humility with them. There is a roomy chancel for the many Priests who represent almost every time and stage of life. Not a few are ordained as mere boys, and not seldom from the sole reason that the poor Bishop is in want of the ordination fees. There are a number of crosses about the Church, but no images. In front of the altar a lamp is always burning. The altar place is raised a few steps above the chancel, and together with the high altar is separated from the rest of the Church by a curtain. In front of the curtain on the right and the left, stands an altar called a throne. Such are their Churches; of decoration there is but little.

The Bishop wears a long red robe like all Syrian Bishops, and on occasions of State he adds to it a yellow over-robe. The Priests at their ordination have to bind themselves to the Nicene Creed, they are dressed in white and wear their beards as long as they will grow. Each Parochas—Pastor—at the head of a Church is aided by four lay elders with whom he forms a sort of Church council, reproves transgressors, imposes fines, and even excommunicates. The lay elders must have resided for 12 years within the Parish before they can be elected to the post. The Liturgy is very long, and though the people do not understand one word of it, they regard it with great affection, for they believe that our Lord Himself and His Apostles spoke Syriac. The eldest of the Priests chaunts the Liturgy in a loud voice, and the remaining Priests pray in a subdued tone. The congregation, however, pray silently in their own language. The song of praise of the Angels: Glory to God in the Highest, on earth peace and good will towards man, is sung by all the Priests aloud, and at the same time they grasp with both hands the right hand of the eldest Priest. They then stretch out their hands to the nearest standing men of the congregation and cry, Peace! and these in their turn hold out their hands to the men near them with the same ejaculation, and then they break up. The women sit apart from the men. The Bible is read out, but there is seldom any exposition of it. After the close of the Service, the eldest Priest goes to the Church door and administers his blessing to each member of the congregation as he passes out. This blessing is withheld from persons living in open sin, and this withholdal is keenly felt.

On Sundays, the Thomas Christians have two Services like all others, but on the high feast days, they have three, at morning, evening and midnight. At such times the men kiss the hands of the Priests and promise obedience. During Advent and Lent they have fasts.

During the celebration of the Last Supper, the Priests place the Cup to the East and the Paton to the West of the altar. Two other plates stand by, on the one a spoon, and on the other a sponge, with which the Priest wipes his fingers. The bread to be given to the communicants is baked *during the Service,* it is of maize, and is made into round flat cakes. Several crosses are stamped upon these cakes which also serve to facilitate the breaking. At the consecration, the Priest raises the bread, whereupon drums and cymbals are struck up from among the congregation. The curtain falls, and the Priests remain in the altar space unseen by the congregation. After silent prayer, the curtain is drawn up, and the officiating Priest steps forward. He holds the bread in his right and the cup in his left hand, and sings a hymn. After having thus shown the elements to the people, he again turns to the altar and himself receives the Sacrament, during which the music again strikes up. After silent prayer, the Priest administers the Sacrament to the people, by breaking the bread and dipping it in the wine. Whilst receiving it, the communicants hold before them a white cloth. The Holy Supper is celebrated three times during the year. A piece of the bread is preserved from each celebration, and is mixed with the dough from which the bread used at the next celebration is made. In this way they imagine that they still have the same bread which our Lord once distributed to his disciples.

At Easter is celebrated a Love feast in connection with the Sacrament. This consists of cakes and of plantains, and is held not in the Church, but in an open space near the Church. The Christians seat themselves in rows on the ground, the Priest blesses the gifts and distributes them to the sitters who eat them in silence. The elders walk up and down and see that all receive an equal quantity.

Around the Church are the graves of the Christians, but influential members of the congregation are fond of being buried within the Church. The Bishop is buried in front of the altar in a sitting position. The corpse is arrayed in full robes, &c., has a wooden cross hanging on the breast, another cross in the right hand and a shepherd's crook in the left. The nearest mourners shut themselves up for a week, the week of mourning, and after this, invite their friends and neighbours to a meal. At this meal, a relation gives to the chief mourner a new turban, whereupon the time of mourning ceases.

The Thomas Christians are, in general, of a light complexion and show to advantage by the side of the neighbouring heathen. One remarkable trait about them is that they despise eating with heathens, (whilst generally it is the heathen who will not eat with Christians) and that they have strong caste feelings is shown by the Rev. H. Baker, (C.M.S.) in his reports from Cottayam. When, for instance, at the instigation of the Missionary a few Christians of low caste entered the Church of some Thomas Christians who had joined the English Church, these latter felt themselves so uncomfortable, that they actually jumped out of the windows and ran away. This happened in 1867, and is only one of the many instances of English Missionaries meddling in caste matters. For a Mission without caste exists only in the heads of a few people in Europe.

Intercourse among the Thomas Christians is somewhat ceremonious, but by no means artificial. They bare their heads before persons of a higher rank (which Hindoos do not do) and hold the right hand before the mouth when speaking to a superior; (this is a common practice among Tamulians to prevent the breath from proceeding unrestrained and to defile the person of the superior). The women also generally show to advantage by the side of the heathen. Cultivation is the chief employment of the Thomas Christians, but they also carry on all kinds of trades. They make elegant fans which are sometimes finished up by the Priests. Their pertinacious hold on Christianity does them honor, though, unfortunately, they have lost both the will and the spirit to proclaim it to the heathen.

I have not been able to omit the primitive Church of Southern India, although its present place of residence is beyond the present boundaries of the land of the Tamulians. For the separation of Malabar from the Tamil country, is of recent date; even our first Missionaries call Tamil land Malabar, and the language,—even now not very much different—Malabarish. But then the Thomas Christians were spread much more over Southern India and the place from which they started was, as we have seen, Mylapore near Madras. The Romish admixtures and oppressions as narrated above have probably spoilt the Church for ever, from being the starting point of an Indian Mission. Like all the ancient Churches of the East it has become petrified amidst its formulas. But as it is, it forms an interesting and instructive ruin from ancient times. May the light now thrown upon it from Protestant Missions bring life and salvation to the whole body in general and to many souls in particular.

CHAPTER II.

The Romish Mission.

The old road by sea to India lay through the Red Sea. It was through the Red Sea that Solomon's ships sailed and brought him "Gold, Ivory, and precious Stones" from Ophir. Commerce with India continued to turn Merchants into Princes as is proved by Venice and Genoa. By the fall of Constantinople, however, and after it in consequence of the increasing influence and power of the Turks, this road to India was to Christian Merchants gradually made more impracticable, and at last entirely closed. Columbus sought a road to India when he sailed to the West, though he only discovered America. And though this new country attracted much attention the longing after India remained unappeased. For it is with truth that a German Philosopher has called India a land of longing, of fantasy, and of speculation. But in order to perfect the picture, the definition of an Englishman should be added, who calls it a land where everything dies and only death lives.

The Portuguese chiefly undertook to discover a new Sea route to India, and they no longer sailed West but South along the coast of Africa. But when they reached the Southernmost point of Africa they encountered such mighty storms that they called this Cape the Cape of Storms, and returned. For, there, during ten months in the year, strong winds blow continually from one quarter, unchecked and unbroken by any land, so that the waves turn not only into mountains, but into mountain ranges, to navigate the deep gorges of which, other vessels are required and another science to what the Navigators of old possessed. But necessity is the mother of invention, and even these difficulties were overcome. "Call it not the Cape of Storms, but the Cape of Good Hope," exclaimed the King of Portugal, and again sent forth his Sea Heroes. This time they were more successful, passed the Southern point of Africa in safety and in May of 1498, actually arrived in India. They landed on the Western Coast of Southern India and dropped anchor before Calicut in Malabar. Thus, was the sea route to India discovered which has had results of such importance to the whole country. The sailors were beside themselves with joy and gratitude at last to have reached the long-sought-for and desired land; and as they wished to offer their thanks to God, they ran straight into a temple. Here, in the dark back ground, they found an altar, and an image upon it and lamps burning on both sides; just as in the Churches which they had left behind them. Without hesitation they threw themselves on their knees and offered up their prayers. But after they had stood up, one of the sailors became somewhat doubtful, and pointing at the images exclaimed : "But if these are by any chance devils, I have not offered my prayers to them!" Such similarity is there between the idolatry of India and that of the Papists.

When the Portuguese started to find India, they had not come without Priests. Vasco de Gama had taken two Monks on board, but one had died at sea and the other died during the same year. But already in September 1500, there arrived eight lay brothers and eight Monks. They at once courageously commenced Missionary work, and had, in a short time, converted one Brahmin and some Nairs. In the meantime, the Portuguese firmly established themselves on the Coast of Malabar and drove out the Mahomedans with great cruelty. In 1570, Albuquerque took Goa and made it the seat of the Government and Missionary enterprize. Albuquerque, however, had continued fights to carry on against the Mahomedans, and foresaw that for generations to come it would take more soldiers than Portugal would be able to supply, and he, therefore, resolved to draw his recruits from India. He managed that in this manner, he married his soldiers to native girls and the children of these marriages were educated in Military schools. It is true, that neither the Portuguese soldiers, the girls, nor their parents, regarded these marriages with any degree of liking, but Albuquerque knew how to make them palatable. He killed or banished the Mahomedans, confiscated their possessions of lands and houses, and gave them as dowries to these marriages. This had the desired effect. In a short time, hundreds and thousands of such marriages were celebrated, and as the girls were compelled to embrace Christianity before the marriages were celebrated or the dowries bestowed, Goa was soon filled with Christians. They were Christians, however, by name only and by form, and these were allowed to resemble heathenish forms as much as possible. Goa was now soon raised to a Bishopric, and the operations of the Franciscans were now confined, not only to the Western, but also began to spread to the Eastern Coast, as far as Mylapore near Madras and Negapatam, South of Tranquebar, both situated in the Tamil country. As the Mahomedans had treated the lower castes as slaves, the Portuguese were regarded in the light of liberators, and on one occasion as many as 20,000 Maravars alone presented themselves for baptism. They were baptized, but as there were by no means sufficient Priests for so large a number, and as those that there were did not display any remarkable zeal, the Maravars merely conformed to the Christian ceremonies and stitching them like new rags on their old garments of heathenism which remained as they had been before. The savour of this new spreading Christianity was, therefore, by no means a sweet one, and we are bound to thank the Hindoos that they called what they saw, not Christianity, but the Feringhee religion. It was the religion of the Portuguese in India full of meanness, greed and cruelty, flaunting itself in processions of flags and crosses and in the carrying about of wooden and gilded images, instead of stone ones smeared with oil; of the meek and humble spirit in Christ, there were but few traces to be found either among the Portuguese who had come to the country or among those who had been born there.

King John III of Portugal protected the mission among his subjects in a really royal manner and we are bound to mention it to his honor. Whilst the first ten Jesuits were yet in Rome, he begged for six for his service. The self-denial and the energy of this new brotherhood seemed to the King to be peculiarly adapted to the difficult work of a mission among the heathen, and he could scarcely foresee what evil results would spring from such small beginnings. At first, however, he only received two of the brethren, Rodrigues and François Xavier. To the first was entrusted the newly founded Missionary Establishment at Coimbra, which the King had so richly endowed that before long 100 scholars received in it instruction and food, and in a short time this number was doubled. Besides this school, the King founded another in Goa for the education of country-born Priests and Catechists, and this again was so generously endowed that the establishment of Priests, Teachers, &c., numbered above 100 persons, and there were in addition sufficient funds to maintain a large number of Students amounting in a short time to 500. Thus richly did the King sow and it is not to be wondered at that a rich harvest followed. In 1743, J. C. Visher, a Dutch Chaplain, reports that half the population of Goa consisted of clericals, and that these were far more numerous than even the soldiers, for every ship brought out a number of Monks of various orders from Europe, whilst in addition, many of the Natives were ordained in Goa from whence they spread over the whole country.

The second of the ten first Jesuits whom the King received was François Xavier. Upon him the King placed great hopes, and having entrusted him with many powers and caused him to be invested with the authority of the Church, he despatched him to India. It had come to the notice of the King, that with the increase of the number of Christians, there had been no increase in piety. Xavier, however, was quite the man to undertake a difficult task. His only misfortune was that he was a Jesuit. When friends endeavoured to dissuade him from attempting a long journey to a savage people in an unhealthy climate, Xavier replied: "If the money and spices of the country can tempt Merchants to disregard all dangers, shall Missionaries be less heroic? shall not the unhappy people learn the blessings of Redemption? Their character may be barbarous, but though they were much worse, still God, who can out of the stones raise up children to Abraham, can soften their hearts! And if I am only able to win one soul to life, I would still consider myself rewarded for all the troubles and the dangers with which you seek to terrify me." Thus minded, Xavier started forth, and implored God not to spare him troubles and sorrows. He left unused the cabin and its conveniences which the King had ordered to be fitted out for him, and willingly shared with the soldiers and the sailors their hard fare. At the same time he endeavoured with zealous fire to introduce godly fear and order among his wild companions. On the 6th May 1542, he landed in Goa, and labored there for five months, endeavouring to introduce order and to reform the depraved customs. Priests and laymen bowed before this spirit, or retreated timidly out of his way, and even thus acknowledged his superiority.

After these preparatory labors, Xavier commenced his journeys and his work among the heathen. He travelled at first along the Coast towards the South, and there found thousands of fishermen who, it is true, had been baptized, but who had nevertheless remained in the deepest ignorance. He set faithfully to work with them, but after his own fashion. Of the language he understood but very little, but he had learnt by heart the Ten Commandments, the Creed, the Lord's Prayer, and Ave Maria, and what he had learnt, he now endeavoured to teach. A number of soldiers accompanied him to protect, and some Priests to assist. His entry with this retinue soon attracted the curious of the village, and by ringing a little bell, he soon collected others. With those already baptized, he commenced his instruction by saying that there was only one God and that He was Triune, and then he repeated the Lord's Prayer. His hearers all repeated it with incredible joy. Then followed Ave Maria, and after that the Creed. At each Article, he asked them if they believed that, "and they exclaimed with loud cries, and with their hands folded over their breasts, that they believed it firmly. He then told them that all who firmly believed these Articles were good Christians. Then followed the Ten Commandments, and he told them "that the Christian law was contained in these maxims, that he who obeyed them faithfully was a good Christian, for whom eternal life was in store; but on the other hand, that he who broke one of these Commandments, was a bad Christian, who, if he did not repent of his sins, would be eternally damned," of a Redeemer there was nowhere any trace! His name is mentioned between the Articles of the Creed in one or other of these forms, sometimes by both following one after the other: "O Jesu, Thou Son of the living God, grant that we may perfectly believe this Article of the Creed, and that Thou mayest grant this, we offer to Thee, the following prayer of which Thou art the Author: Our Father, &c., and: Holy Mary, Mother of our Lord Jesus Christ, obtain for us from thy beloved Son that we may believe this Article without any doubt. Ave Maria, &c." Poor Saviour! who can give nothing out of love, but must do so either in return for a Pater noster, or in consequence of Mary's intercession! And what good was there of a Redeemer when the Ten Commandments are nothing more than 'Christian law' and nothing is said of their being a mirror to the soul for the convincing of sin. For where the law does not work in us a knowledge of sin and thus become our Schoolmaster to bring us to Christ, that we might be justified by faith: Gal. iii, 124, it is natural that one should not know what to do with the Lamb of God that takes the sins of the world.

Such was the nature of Xavier's work, and he soon prevailed upon thousands, so that they gave their consent with 'loud cries' and allowed themselves to be baptized. According to his own report, he baptized in Travancore in one month 10,000 until "in consequence of the exertion in baptizing, his hands became utterly exhausted." As he had not sufficient Priests to leave behind for the instruction of the converts, he chose out of each village the best man and placed him over the rest as an elder, with instructions to collect the congregation every Sunday, and to repeat what had been already learnt. And so he travelled through the Coast villages and baptized probably some 200,000 persons, mostly of the fisherman's caste. The poor Apostle Peter is quite thrown into the back ground in sight of such activity, and even the Apostle Paul cannot boast of such missionary success as this. Xavier baptized his hundred-thousands within three years.

But after three years even he was weary of these results. He forsook India and went to the Molucca Islands. Two years afterwards, 1549, he returned to India, but his pleasure in the work as well as his hope had vanished. At the commencement of his Missionary labors, he had written: "On Sundays, I collect together in the Chapel the men and the women, the little boys and the little girls, and they all come with incredible joy and the warmest longing to hear the word of God." And only five years afterwards he wrote to Loyola: "The whole race of Hindoos is barbarous and will listen to nothing that does not suit its barbarous customs. Regarding the knowledge of what is god-like and virtuous it cares but little. Most of them are bad, virtue is odious to them; they are incredibly versatile and inconstant, and believe in little or nothing. So far has sin and deceit become with them a habitude." At last, however, he despairs entirely and writes: "The natives are, on account of the magnitude of their sins, quite unfitted to receive the Gospel." In this belief, or rather unbelief, he left India and went to Japan. Returned from thence, he prepared for a voyage to China, and had indeed started for that country, intending to enter it in disguise, when he met his death on the Island Sancian. Xavier's great self-denial and self-sacrifice which he displayed from the commencement of his work, must always excite admiration, and may shame many another Missionary. His precipitate zeal, however, and impatience, leaving his false doctrine and practice out of the question, should also serve as a warning. In a blind over-estimation of his own powers, he often venturously implored God to impose upon him more adversities, and yet, when only a slight adversity of duty was laid upon him, and he did not at once see great results of his superficial activity, he was unable to bear it, he trembled and fled.

Like Xavier, the remaining Jesuits in India also began to despair, and fancied their powers might be employed with more advantage in some other field. Laynes, their general, however, would not hear of this and earnestly ordered them to remain in India, and the good King of Portugal, by no means despaired of Missionary work in India, or allowed his zeal to flag. He caused most of the Churches, cloisters and schools, to be built at his own expense and the Missionaries were supported by him in every way. And as far as the new Converts were concerned, he behaved towards them as a generous Prince and Father. He ordered the Governors to provide the native Christians with appointments according to their capabilities. From the rest, he removed all taxation and other burdens, and those who were persecuted by the heathen and left destitute, he caused to be fed at his expense. He ordered the heathen throughout his dominions to cease all public idolatry, but they were not to be forced to believe. It is true that all these orders were not strictly obeyed, but John III of Portugal is a shining example to Christian Kings who have heathen subjects. Nor was the blessing wanting; for even after the departure and death of the hasty Xavier, the work so spread and increased, that whole districts and thousands of inhabitants embraced Christianity, so that the words of the Apostle were here fulfilled: "He who sows abundantly, shall reap abundantly." That the harvest turned out as it did was, however, not the fault of the King, and amidst all the chaff there was probably some good grain also. The next generation might well have been better, if only the shepherds had been the right people.

The very opposite of this activity, which concentrated so much power in a small space, we find at Madura one of the most important towns in the land of the Tamulians. In 1595, already, a station had been formed at Madura and after the manner now become usual and therefore with the same results. There were a few Christians in and around Madura, and to them Pater Fernandez was sent. He was sent alone and left there alone. He was in all probability by no means idle, for no complaint of the kind is to be found. He even built a Church and succeeded in keeping his people together. But during eleven years (from 1595 to 1606) he is reported not to have baptized a single heathen, and it is not known whether after that time (for he remained there a long time) he baptized any. His littleness disappeared entirely amid the multitudes of heathen, and produced no fruit—because he made no impression. But even at the present day the same happens as then occurred in Madura. A weakling is sent alone to a distant post, and then we wonder that we do not soon see fruits, and are surprised if we do not receive every quarter, reports that so many souls have been converted! But he who sows meagrely shall reap meagrely. Yes! if only every Missionary were a man full of spirit and power! But each period of time produces only a few great men.* They are not to be manufactured in Universities or Mission Colleges. A number of second-rate or ordinary men, if combined, are able to make an impression, and show some results, as little lights, when there are enough of them, are able to light up a large space. But when mediocrity is sent alone, it is like a single rushlight in a large chamber. It can with difficulty be seen, but it cannot enlighten. Pater Fernandez was a rushlight burning in big Madura, and that is the reason that Madura remained so dark, and nothing stirred.

Then there appeared in Madura a man who was certainly no mediocrity. This was Robert de Nobili, a relation of Cardinal Bellarmin. Robert was richly provided with all that which afterwards rendered the Jesuit order so hated throughont Europe, and which was lashed by Pascal in so masterly a manner, namely, a wanton mock of truth and propriety, and the employment of the worst means to arrive at the desired end. It was his misfortune that he was a Jesuit, for true to the system in which he had been reared he behaved exactly like a Jesuit. To the Hindoos he wished to become a Hindoo. This was a great and a good thought, but which by a Jesuit could only be carried out Jesuitically. For to become to the Hindoos a Hindoo, is

* One of the favorite sayings of the great Austrian Minister, Von Kannitz, known as the 'Driver of the State Coach of Europe,' was that 'it took 50 years for a country to produce a great man.' There is a great semblance of truth in this remark, and if a glance is thrown back at the histories of most countries, it will be seen how rarely great men are contemporaneous, and how frequently a period of about 50 years elapses between them.

easier said than done. To the Pariahs many a one has become a Pariah, and now and then a weak attempt has been made to become a Sudra to the Sudras. Robert was the first one to try to become a Brahmin to the Brahmins, and after him no one has made the attempt. When a European first lands in the country, the first thing he does is to surround himself with the unfortunately indispensable evil of Pariah servants, which at once makes him as good as unapproachable to Brahmins. In this way the higher classes who, under any circumstances, are less accessible than the lower ones, are pushed back from the very commencement.

Should, however, the higher classes be won over, they must be treated differently to savages. To the latter we can offer something perfected and can educate them to it, but the former, with a civilization of thousands of years, can scarcely be approached with cut and dried outward forms that have sprung up in foreign soil. They must be given Christianity pure and simple, but not the outward forms of the Church as they have been formed in Europe. It is natural that the most unfitted for this work is the Church of Rome with its dead formalisms. That Church only is fitted for this work, which declares plainly that "*It is sufficient* for the true unity of the Christian Church that the Gospel is preached therein, according to its pure intent and meaning, and that the Sacraments are administered in conformity with the word of God. And it is not necessary for the unity of the Christian Church, that uniform ceremonies instituted by men should be everywhere observed." Robert de Nobili seems to have understood this great "It is sufficient" of the Augustana, at all events, he saw the impracticability of forcing upon a people artificial forms peculiar to the habits and cultivation of a foreign race. He, therefore, attempted to solve the difficult problem of offering to a people of high civilization Christianity without the matured forms of the Church which had developed on a foreign soil. He wished to leave to the Tamulians their outward forms of civilization, and only endeavoured to instil into them a Christian life. This was a great undertaking such as only a great man could undertake. De Nobili was as Romanist, however, already unfitted to this work, and as Jesuit, he could naturally only produce a caricature of Christianity, an abortion of his own great ideas.

He commenced, however, with all necessary caution. After having thought out his plan he laid it before the Provincial of the Jesuits by whom it was sanctioned. Not contented with this, he laid it before the Archbishop of Goa, who also gave to it his sanction. Thereupon, he went to Madura and commenced his work. It is not, therefore, just to attribute to him the whole blame, to his whole order; yes, to his whole Church is due a large share.

Arrived in Madura, he kept himself entirely aloof from Pater Fernandez and his Christians. He lived and clothed himself like a Brahmin, and gave himself out to be a Western Brahmin. His food consisted of the customary vegetable fare of the Brahmins, of milk and of clarified butter. No meat, or fish or even an egg crossed his lips. Abstinence from such things is not only not a sin, but when it is practised from love towards a people and has as its object the salvation of their souls it becomes right and good. But to attempt to prove by this abstinence what is not true, is a sin. And this is the sin that Robert committed. His clothing consisted of a seamless piece of cotton, wound round his loins and another of similar quality thrown over his shoulders. Ordinary Brahmins wear a very clean and perfectly white cloth, but such as have renounced the pleasures of this life, the ascetics *(Saniasi)* choose a pale yellow color, so that from afar off it may be seen how holy they are. Robert de Nobili chose this pale yellow color. Over his shoulder and breast he wore the Brahmins' thread, the distinguishing mark of the twice born. He, however, took three gold threads signifying the Trinity, and two other silver ones in addition to signify the two natures of Christ. At the end of the thread, hung a small crucifix which, however, as the end of a Brahmin's thread always is, was hidden in his waist-cloth. This was the way the Western Brahmin lived and dressed. He was surrounded only by Brahmins, he went silently every morning to his ablutions, for even in the land of the Tamulians, silence constitutes a Philosopher, or causes him to be thought one, otherwise, however, he shut himself up closely, and studied with an iron will Tamil, Telugoo and Sanscrit.

It followed, of course, that in a short time the news of the Western Brahmin caused some excitement. Many came to see him, but only seldom was any one admitted. And those who were fortunate enough to be presented to him could not find words enough to express either the wonderful knowledge or the kind condescension of the Western Brahmin. His mysterious conduct only excited a greater wish for his acquaintance, so that the King of Madura wished to see him. De Nobili, however, remained unmoved in his solitude and would not go to visit the King. This contempt, for the favor of the mighty Prince was the highest test of his sanctity—who could any longer entertain any doubts regarding it? One day a young Guroo (a Brahmin of the greatest influence and with many disciples) came to see his Western colleague and saint, mounted on an elephant and followed by a large retinue. He was wisely admitted, and de Nobili allowed him such glances into the depths of his philosophical and mathematical knowledge that he came again and again, greedy to hear more. Soon he, who himself had so many disciples, declared himself to be a disciple of de Nobili. Now, de Nobili commenced cautiously to enter into religious matters, and in these also the Guroo was convinced, and at last baptized. Through him there soon came other Brahmins for instruction and baptism; and some of the higher Sudras were also admitted to the Font. De Nobili now cautiously commenced to put forward the assertion that he was in possession of the fourth Veda, the Esur Veda. This Esur Veda had been compiled by de Nobili himself and was a very skilful imitation of the old Vedas. Of course, he had introduced Christian principles, and brought them into such connection, that by exposition, still more could be got out of them. In this way he did not seem to have produced anything new, but only something elucidating and leading to a proper comprehension of the whole. This Esur Veda, however, gave the Brahmins of Madura much trouble. The learned men were by no means of one mind, and could not bring themselves either to reject it unanimously, or to receive it as genuine. They, therefore, had recourse to an oath, and de Nobili was to state upon oath whether this was in reality the Esur Veda or not. The poor Brahmins did not yet know what a Jesuitical oath meant! De Nobili, however, did not hesitate to swear before a large assembly that he had received this Esur Veda from Brahma. This sounds almost incredible, but this wicked lie has even in our days been called by a learned Cardinal (Wiseman), "one of the many ways in which modern science has confuted objections to Christianity." In this way the Jesuitical system of doing evil that good may come, and telling lies to spread of truth, darkens the understanding and blinds the spirit.

This lie about the Esur Veda gave de Nobili a firm footing. His work now began to spread rapidly. He himself commenced to go out, and even made journeys in the neighbourhood of Madura. Everywhere where he came had his fame preceded him; he was the great sage, the wonderful Brahmin of the West, the possessor and the explainer of the Esur Veda. In this way he gained many adherents, always from the higher castes, from the lower ones, he always kept aloof. For two and forty years he lived and worked in Madura in this manner, and is said to have baptized some 100,000 Tamulians. Idolatry, such as the worship of the popular idols, he rejected on the authority of the Vedas, but the ordinary processions, &c., he left untouched. Even the towering cars of the gods were dragged about as before by crowds of men, the only difference being that the summits were decorated with a statue of the Virgin or of some Saint. In ordinary life, there was no difference to be seen between the heathen and his followers. At the rising of the sun, both hastened to the rivers or the tanks in order to perform their sacred ablutions, both marked their foreheads with sacred ashes and both remained in perfect friendship, for the former opposition from the heathen had ceased. His system commenced in deception, and strengthened by perjury bid fair to be victorious.

But he had to contend against opposition, and that from an entirely unexpected quarter. Almost contemptible seemed the cloud that arose on his Missionary horizon, and yet it was destined to overshadow his whole work even during his lifetime. It was the resultless Pater Fernandez, who, perhaps, not without envy, raised his voice against de Nobili from the very commencement. He complained against him to the elders in Goa, and from thence, from the place where his plan of work had been sanctioned, he received an order to relinquish all new methods, and to carry on the Missionary work according to old established custom. De Nobili had, it is true, sworn unconditional obedience like all Jesuits, but had no idea of showing it. He knew how to get support in Rome, and there it was decided that he should be allowed to go on in his own way until the matter had been thoroughly examined. In this way he might have been left in quiet for his friends had no intention of making an enquiry. But his enemies had, and Franciscans, Dominicans and members of other orders could not refrain from giving Jesuitism, which rightly had been so hated from the commencement a blow. Accordingly, after an enquiry that lasted for thirteen years, and which was accompanied by many disputes, matters came so far that the Pope gave a decision, and a wonderful decision it was, for it was necessary to prove both sides right. New converts might continue to bathe, decided the Pope, because that was conducive to cleanliness. They might also continue to wear the hair lock, because this was a mark of position and nobility. They might continue to wear the Brahminical thread, but it was not to be put on in heathen temples (which probably had never been done) but Romish Priests should invest them with it, it should be sprinkled with holy water, an appropriate prayer should be recited, and then it would be all correct. And as regards the Siva ashes (ashes of cow-dung) the Christians were not to use them any longer for these were a veritable abomination; but, they might continue to smear their foreheads with ashes, only they must be ashes of sandalwood for that was an ornament, &c., &c. With such a judgment did the Pope in Rome decide the thirteen years' dispute between the Missionaries in Tamil land. It can easily be understood that with this nothing was settled, and that the quarrel soon broke out again, and did not cease until it had ruined de Nobili's work, and had driven the Jesuits from India.

In 1648, de Nobili retired from the Mission, for he was feeble with age and almost blind. He left Madura, the scene of so much self-sacrifice to a false system, and of so great a lie—withdrew to Mylapore, and there spent his last years in quiet. As long as he remained in Madura, his work seems to have kept tolerably well together, but five years after his departure and while he was still living in Mylapore it had entirely collapsed. In the neighbourhood there were still a number of his followers left, but in Madura, itself only about 200 souls remained, and this after 42 years' work with such self-denial and such great talents!

Robert de Nobili like François Xavier was a remarkable man, and far above mediocrity. In the centuries that have passed since their time, the Romish Mission in India has had no Missionary to compare with them. They were both filled with glowing zeal for the Mission, they both willingly endured every hardship, and staked their lives on their work. Both had mighty results and both lived long enough to despair of their work. The work of neither could stand the fire test, for they built with the wood, straw and stubble of human ideas and wisdom, and built too upon rotten foundations. What might not such men have done, if they had only been true disciples of Christ instead of the Pope and of Loyola! But as they themselves despaired of the work which they had built upon quick-sand, they have perhaps found the Rock where alone the soul can rest. May they both have found this peace with their Lord!

Besides the Jesuits, the Franciscans, the Dominicans, the Augustines, the Carmelites, the Oratorians, the Capucins, and many other orders all worked in South India! and as none of them showed any lack of inward jealousy and outward quarrelling, they gave the Popes plenty of trouble, and compelled them again and again to decide what had already been decided by new decisions, and to issue fresh mandates which were as little obeyed as the previous ones had been. In this way, the old Portuguese Mission, with so many resources and so many powers, was inwardly tumbling to pieces and outwardly crippled. It had peace only when in 1759 the Jesuits were driven out of India,—since they had been previously driven out of Portugal. The Portuguese Mission, however, was never able to gain any vital energy.

In the meantime, French Priests had settled in Pondicherry, and soon turned it into a Goa of Tamil land. The power which the Portuguese had displayed on the West Coast, now began to be shown by the French on the Eastern Coast, and their chief town was Pondicherry, situated between Cuddalore and Madras. As they were so powerful, the Pope raised Pondicherry to a Bishopric. This, however, was in contravention of the rights of Portugal. Former Popes had declared the Archbishop at Goa to be the Primate of the Indian Church and with him the Crown of Portugal enjoyed the right of nominating the Suffragan Bishops. But as the power of the Portuguese had now passed away, the Popes appointed as Bishops whomever they liked, and placed them where they wished, without troubling their heads about the rights of the Portuguese Crown or of the Primate at Goa. And this action gave rise to a dispute regarding the privileges of the Pope and those of the King of Portugal which lasted for a hundred years, and when the Jesuit again came to India, new quarrels soon broke out. They conducted themselves not only as the only orthodox Priests, and declared the Priests at Goa and their Archbishop to be Schismatics, but they also claimed as their own all Church property, &c., together with the congregations, and were sometimes able by the use of stratagem or force to get them into their possession. Then again, there arose evil quarrels in Tamil land which came before the English Law Courts. But it is not my intention to enter into details of these, for during this period, there are no Missionary results. The Portuguese always lost more ground, for the more crafty Jesuits and Capucins succeeded in shouldering them out of the way.

At present the Romish Church has four Bishops in the Tamil country, and besides these there are the Portuguese who are under the Archbishop of Goa, and who have a Vicar-General at Mylapore near Madras. The Goa Priests are, for the most part, of mixed race and many are very dark, almost black. They are always losing more ground and their possessions are continually passing over into the more powerful, and more crafty hands of the new Bishops and Priests who are partly Frenchmen, partly Irishmen.

From the *Madras Catholic Directory* of 1870, printed "*Permissu Superiorum*," I extract the following information:

The Diocese of Madras has 57 Priests and in Tamil land (for it also extends into Telugoo land) 31,030 Christians, including the Vicar-General at Mylapore and his flocks. As regards the Missionary work of these 57 Priests, in the year under report, they baptized altogether 167 heathen, big and little. In addition they also baptized 16 Protestants. These 16 Protestants are paraded in the report, as if for show, and it is expressly remarked that they were re-baptized. Regarding how many of their people went over to the Protestants, the report says nothing. If, however, 31,000 Christians let alone 57 Priests, Professors, Teachers and Nuns were not able to make a greater impression upon the heathen than that 167 souls should join then during the year, it is clear that in spite of Episcopal pomp and Episcopal authority neither the inward light nor the outward power can be very strong. And in previous years the results were not larger. Throughout the last 29 years, the whole of the Priests of the Diocese of Madras baptized only 4,612 heathens. I mention this especially because the results of the Roman Mission are often referred to as if they were important as compared with the Protestant Missions. From their own Report of 1870, however, and from those of the previous 29 years, the exact opposite is proved. And if it is necessary to quote figures against figures, the Lutheran Mission has, during the last 20 years with the numbers of its Missionaries varying between six and sixteen, (with of late years a few ordained natives) baptized more than 1,000 more heathens than the whole of the 57 Romish Priests during 29 years. The number of heathens baptized by the Lutheran Mission in the last 20 years amounts to 5,721 souls.

The Diocese of Pondicherry, including the Christians belonging to Goa, numbers 1,29,844 souls, to whom, however, the French and half-caste population of Pondicherry must be reckoned. In this Diocese are 118 Churches and 82 Chapels ; it has two Seminaries for Priests, several Convents, &c., and 77 Priests, and yet all these together, in spite of the considerable interest which the French Government at Pondicherry always shows for Christianity, were able to baptize only 632 heathens and 88 Protestants. Of the many Nuns which Pondicherry possesses, there are four and a Novice at Tranquebar. And these four Nuns and Novice teach two Boarders, two Orphans, and thirty Day-Scholars. The Boarders would seem to be the Orphans, but under any circumstances the work is not surprising.

The Bishopric of Coimbatore has 20 Priests and some 18,000 Catholics. These 20 Priests having, during the last five years, baptized only 398 heathens.

The Jesuits, on the other hand, are much stronger in the Diocese of Madura. There they have again 1,69,500 Christians with 163 Churches and 469 Chapels, with 68 Priests in the field. In the year under report, these 68 Priests baptized only 463 heathens and Protestants. They display;

however, a far greater activity in their own (the Jesuitical) department. They baptize little children of heathen parents when they are *in extremis,* and without the consent or the knowledge of the parents. When the child of Tamulians has fallen sick and they know not what to do, they are willing that anything should be done if only the child can be saved. And they are especially fond of having a mantram or prayer formula, repeated over it, no matter by whom, or to whom addressed. In this way the Romish Priests are called in, and on such occasions they do, as one of them himself reports. They rub a little Eau-de-cologne on the head of the child, and the parents think that to be medicine. Unperceived they then change the bottle, and pour a few drops of pure water on the child's head, and at the same time pronounce the Latin baptismal formula, instead of a mantram, and the child has been baptized without anybody knowing anything about it. This is not done occasionally, as an exceptional case by some feeble and eccentric Priest; no; it is their regular and one of their principal practices amongst the heathens. In the year under report, there were no fewer than 2,986 of such secret baptisms of children. And this is printed '*Permissu Superiorum!*'

Such is the condition of the Roman Mission in the Tamil country, and when we remember that it has behind it the labors of 350 years, powerfully backed up by the political influence of Portugal and of France, and with so many resources of Priests, Monks and Nuns, we can scarcely call the results great. At all events, when compared to it, the Protestant Missions with their much fewer years of work, have no cause to be ashamed. The work done by the 222 Roman Priests in the Tamil country is scarcely sufficient to make good the losses caused by death, emigration, and those who have joined the different Protestant Missions. It can, therefore, be understood that the despair of François Xavier is to be found amongst the Romish Priests of the present day. They perform their duties, and make use of their customary serpent-like cunning, but otherwise they work without hope. And their results during the last 29 years (for the *Catholic Directory* glances so far back) are by no means encouraging. Could it be accurately examined, it would probably be discovered that during the last 30 years the Roman Christians in the Tamil country have rather fallen off than increased in numbers.

It has often been said in reproach of these Roman Christians that they are as bad or even worse than heathens. Sweeping assertions like this, made sometimes from superficial observation, and sometimes from prejudice are worth nothing. On the whole too it is not correct. I have frequently had to do with them, and it has occasionally happened, that during one year, I have instructed and received into our Church as many as the 77 Priests of the Pondicherry Diocese boast that they have re-baptized from out of the Protestants. Naturally I had to instruct them just as if they were heathens, for the most of them were very ignorant. As a matter of fact, they have almost always given me less pleasure than heathen converts. They generally settled in villages, which I could seldom visit, and by no means easily accustomed themselves to good order; for as they had been accustomed to go to their distant Church only once in a year or years, it was difficult to get them to come to Service every Sunday to which, however, the heathen converts allow themselves to be much more easily persuaded. And besides, they had many heathen customs, which it was very difficult to make them shake off. It is almost incredible how much the Priests favor their superstitions at their festivals, especially at that of the Virgin; they openly try to excel the heathens in the matter of lamps, lights, shooting and carrying of images. The miracle-working pictures, of course, play an important part in such festivals. Not far from Virdachellum, there is a little Church in the jungle where no Christians live. A Priest lives there, a dark one, one of the Portuguese. The Church contains a Mada (= mother), an image of the Virgin which is a great favorite with the heathen. When the child of one of the neighbouring heathens is sick, or one of their cattle, or they themselves get into trouble, they vow some thing to the Mada if she will help them. And for this purpose there exists a Church and a Priest. When asked how he could live there alone, since there were no Christians and the heathens would not hear of being converted, the Priest replied with a shrug of shoulders, "The Church has its income here; the Church has its income."

The Roman Christians are almost without exception from the old Portuguese time. I have only very seldom met new converts from out of the heathen, and with them the case stood as follows: the Priests had protected the people and paid their debts and had thus become their creditors.

This debt was, of course, not demanded, but a bond had been executed for it which bound them to the Priest. Were we to do the same, a considerable number of converts would join us; but we have not the means nor the will to employ such means as these. The only good and honest means by which to bring the heathens to Christ, (not to bind them to Priest) is to preach to them the Gospel of the cross without disguising from them that they too, if they declare for Christ, will have to suffer cross and sorrow. For in India, also by the Hindoos, must the cross be borne after Christ whether it be in one way or another even by the most humble that turn to Him. But the effect of bearing the cross is not grief and woe, but praise and thanks from those who well accustom themselves to it. May the Romish Priests and Christians not rest content with placing the cross in every corner of their Churches only, and making the sign of it on their breasts and foreheads. The cross must come nearer home to us, and must strike deeper in us than that, if it is to carry out its redeeming work.

CHAPTER III.

The Lutheran Mission.

"*Behold I am with you every day until the end of the world.*"

In the preceding pages we have glanced at the Primitive and the Romish Church Missions in the land of the Tamulians, and now in chronological order we arrive at the Lutheran Mission. The words quoted at the head of this chapter form the proper motto for this Mission, for it no longer has a country which it can call its own or Princes to protect it. But it has the Lord, and with Him it has enough. For He, the Lord Jesus Christ, has never been separated from his servants in the Mission, but has always been their Trust, their Blessing, Salvation and Peace—yes:

With Mother's hands He guides His own
Nor leaves them helpless or alone
Give to our God the honor.

We must needs linger somewhat longer with this Mission, and must visit together some of the different stations, and see how gradually they have from time to time sprung up here and there. To start with, we have to do with the Lutheran Missions in the country which formerly belonged to the Danes, Tranquebar and Poriar.

Tranquebar belongs to the former kingdom and present district of Tanjore, and is situated on the Bay of Bengal in a fruitful but not beautiful plain. The power of the Portuguese had lasted in South India for over 100 years, and had been continually growing more obnoxious. And this was particularly the case when that sinister tyrant of Spain, Philip II, became also King of Portugal. His favorite Institution, the Inquisition was now planted in India and succeeded so well in Goa that afterwards the whole of its Institutions were burnt. Enough is already known of its inhuman mode of conduct and need not be related here; when Portugal's power began to decline, the Dutch came upon the scene and began to snatch from them their possessions one by one. And they were not much more tender-handed in dealing with the Portuguese than these had previously been with the Mahomedans. In the same way as the Dutch pushed the Portuguese aside, there also arrived other nations; the Danes, the French and the English. Some might call it an accident that the Danes ever came to the Tamil country, but we Christians know that our God rules the world, and that even an Augustus had to set the whole of Palestine in motion in order that one poor family might be induced to journey from Nazareth to Bethlehem at the appointed time. In the same way the Danes had to come to Tranquebar, in order that the poor Tamulians might have the pure Gospel preached to them. For without that, unless Tranquebar had become the property of a Lutheran Prince there would at that time have been no Lutheran Mission station, and, therefore, a Danish Ship Captain, Roelant Crape had to get his ship wrecked on these shores, and to save himself on land. His people escaped also, but they seem to have been a wild lot, for they were all murdered. Roelant Crape, however, sought an audience with the King of Tanjore, and succeeded in obtaining it. The King received the shipwrecked man in a friendly manner and allowed himself to be talked over and made the Danes a present of Tranquebar, so that they might trade with his kingdom. Thus, it was that in the year 1620, Tranquebar became Danish, and they built a Fort there and fortified the town.

The Danes traded with the Tamulians, but did not bring them the Pearl without price. And 100 years passed before they came so far. The Portuguese did things differently for as we have seen they at once brought out eight Clergymen and eight Monks and sent always others to follow; King John III, acting always like a father towards his brown subjects. But in the year 1704, when a German, Dr. Lütkens, became the King's Court-preacher, Frederic IV, expressed a wish to send out preachers of the Gospel to his unknown subjects in India. Denmark, however, had merchants and sailors in plenty who were quite ready to go to India; but messengers of faith she had none. Lütkens, therefore, turned towards Germany, and soon found two young men "who feared the Lord and were of a mind to go to the heathen." Their names are known as Ziegenbalg and Plütschau.

The lives of these, our first Missionaries, have been so often described that I shall presume them to be known to my readers. I will, therefore, in glancing over the history of the Tranquebar Mission allude only to a few salient points.

The two German youths arrived in Copenhagen, and were kindly received by Dr. Lütkens and by the King. They were then ordained by Bishop Bornemann and appointed as Royal Missionaries, otherwise, however, they did not meet with much encouragement in Denmark, and on all sides they were told "to dwell in the land and maintain themselves honestly." The good Danes did not consider that if the first Apostles and subsequent messengers of the Gospel had remained in their country, they themselves might have remained the poor fishermen and wild robbers they originally were. The two young men, however, did not suffer themselves to be led astray, but went forth in the name of God and at the command of the King towards the distant and unknown heathen.

The King had meant well, but had not considered that though Tranquebar was a royal possession, the government of it was in the hands of a hard-hearted trading Company, in whose pay and under whose orders were the Commandant and Council of the town. These did not wish any of their privileges to be interfered with, and did not care to have independent lookers-on and tale-bearers among them. Missionary work, therefore, met with difficulties at the very outset, which had scarcely been expected. When the Missionaries landed, nobody troubled their heads about them, and they had to remain almost the whole day in the open air, for hotels had as yet not been invented in India. This was a bad beginning, and if the Lord had not been with them, they might well have thought of turning back. But they remained and full of faith commenced their work of love.

This, however, was no easy matter, and if they applied for help to the Council or the Commandant, they met with nothing but cold faces, and secret and open opposition. The Commandant had received orders from the Company, his immediate superiors to suffer the Missionaries, but by no means to further their work, and when the Missionaries, ignorant of these secret orders, appealed to the letter "of our most gracious King Fredericus Quartus" they only poured oil upon the fire. The Commandant and Council, in reply advised them "to be more cautious in making use of the exalted name of His Majesty, and to conduct themselves with courtesy towards those in authority, lest it might be necessary to have recourse to other means; which, perhaps, they would not like." Nor were there "other means" wanting, for Ziegenbalg was imprisoned in the fort for several months.

From the commencement the Kingdom of God has always followed the royal road, that is to say, the road of its King. But this King went about in the guise of a servant, and spiritual eyes were required to recognize him as a King. But as sensual men have not the Spirit (Jude 19) they also have no spiritual eyes. Therefore they despised the King, mocked and persecuted Him, robbed Him of His clothes, and crowned Him with thorns, nailed Him to a cross and gave Him vinegar to drink. His Kingdom is, therefore, like himself despised, mocked and persecuted by the sensual children of this World even to this day, and this must continue so; or else how could the King's subjects be made to imitate Him? The Lutheran Mission, commenced to carry its cross from the very first days when the first two Missionaries landed at Tranquebar.

After eight years faithful work in Tranquebar, Ziegenbalg travelled back to Denmark and Germany, for he had at length discovered that the secret and open opposition to his work originated not with the Commandant at Tranquebar, but with the hard-hearted trading Company in Denmark, and so he went there in order to cut the evil at the root. In 1709, the Missionary Gründler, had been sent to his assistance. Plütschau had already been sent to Denmark, but at the time he was not properly aware of the root of the evil, and with all his love and faith, Plütschau had not the power or the talents of Ziegenbalg. In Europe, Ziegenbalg was everywhere received with the greatest joy. Money was collected in Germany for the Church that was wanted and for the spread of his work, and was sent to Denmark for transmission, and in Denmark itself all obstacles seemed to disappear. The King appointed him Dean, and sent him out afresh and everything seemed to be in the best order. Arrived again in Tranquebar, Ziegenbalg commenced with renewed vigour. He built the large Church, called New Jerusalem, which is still our Mission Church in Tranquebar. It is in the form of a Greek Cross and is large and roomy. Above the Altar, there is a large tablet upon which are inscribed suitable Bible texts in the Portuguese, Tamil and German languages, on both sides of this tablet are ornamental copper plates with Latin inscriptions. The plates and inscriptions were placed here by the Rev. Ben. Schulze in memory of Ziegenbalg and Gründler who lie buried beneath them. Before Ziegenbalg set out for Europe, he had already built a small Church not far from the Sea shore, which he had called Jerusalem, hence the name New Jerusalem for the large one. For some time native Christians were buried round this Church, and here also lies our first native preacher Aaron. But Church and Grave-yard have long since been devoured by the sea which, as at the Seven Pagodas is also constantly encroaching at Tranquebar. Eighteen years ago I saw the ruins of the Church-yard wall washed by the waves, but these have now entirely disappeared. But the sea too will restore its dead, when the Lord comes.

For about a year longer, Ziegenbalg worked with his old power and zeal, but then this man otherwise so fiery and seeking to overcome all obstacles, became suddenly quiet and reserved, for his spirit was broken. How this happened is a story of wheels within wheels, and is as follows:

In 1709, a certain Böringh was sent to Tranquebar together with Missionary Gründler. This man was, however, of quite a different school and of quite different views. He had been sent out to teach, and, therefore, thought that he had nothing more to learn. He had sharp eyes for all evils and abuses in the Mission, was not afraid to mention them openly, and ascribed to himself the power and gifts of a Reformer. In short, he had all the virtues and faults of many a young Missionary of the present day.

This love of reforming, before a Missionary has done anything, or before even he is able to preach an intelligible Sermon, has been the cause of many an evil, and in almost every Protestant Mission. And so common is this evil that the Church Missionary Society, the most respectable of all English Mission Societies, again and again impresses upon their new Missionaries the necessity of paying their elder colleagues every respect and conforming with their decisions, until after some years of faithful and diligent work, and after a thorough knowledge, not only of the language, but also of their peculiar customs of the people, they may be fitted to form opinions of their own. For the language is nothing more than a key to the understanding of the people, and it is possible to understand the language, and yet to be as strange to the people as the man in the moon. Bövingh was, as it were, a forerunner of the harvest to follow: he would learn nothing, but be master of all things. And so it did not last long before he himself found out that he was fitted for anything but for a Missionary. Two years afterwards he left the Mission, and in order to justify himself made a great clamour against it. Whilst Ziegenbalg was in Denmark, this evil spirit was never able to show itself above ground, but after he got back to Tranquebar it stalked abroad, so that the gentlemen in Denmark quite lost their senses. For they not only almost ceased to support the Mission in Tranquebar, but they also kept back the money which Ziegenbalg had collected in Germany. Not content with this, they sent out many long letters in which they upset the hitherto-practice of the Mission, and showed to the Missionaries a new method, which one cannot help wishing, they had themselves adopted, even were it only for one week.

There are two ways to carry on a Mission: the one is the Paulinian, and the other the Ottonian. The Paulinian is, of course, the one to be preferred. It begins with praying and fasting (Acts XIII, 3.) 'They prayed and fasted and laid their hands upon them and sent them away.' There is nothing of box and baggage packing in this method. But little money too is needed, though still something, as is written (Philip. IV, 16.) "For even in Thessalonica ye sent once and again unto my necessity." Money is as much a gift of God, as the bread which it buys. The one as well as the other is gained by human toil and human skill, neither the one nor the other springs ready-made out of the ground. Not many preliminaries, therefore, are required for this Paulinian or Apostolical Mission. But two things are absolutely necessary, *viz.*, Apostles and Apostolical conditions. Where one has no Apostles to send, and where the conditions and circumstances are quite different, we can, it is true, learn of the Apostolical Mission, but must relinquish the attempt to re-produce it. There is no good in one lame man calling out to another, "Don't limp!" It is better that dwarfs should do what work they can, than that they should tear out their hair, because they cannot do Giant's work, and in the meantime do nothing at all.

The other method is the Ottonian: Otto was a pious Bishop of Bamberg, where his staff, &c., are shown to this day. When the heathen Pommeranians drove out of their country the poor Monks who had come to preach to them, and called after them: "Yours must be a poor god that can send no better messengers than you are," Otto started forth in person. No doubt, he prayed and, perhaps, fasted also; but the most remarkable part of the commencement of his Mission is the packing of boxes and baggage. The noise of nailing them down could be heard at a distance. From a far people could see how they were packed, and nine (9) waggons were filled with them. Otto wanted to prove to the savage Pommeranians that the God of the Christians had other messengers than poor Monks. So Otto started on his road with many waggons full of boxes packed with gifts for the poor. At the same time he took with him to their nobles a letter of reconciliation from their liege Lord, the Duke of Poland, and added to this, his heart was full of love and his lips overflowing with the grace of God through Christ towards everybody. In this way what was impossible to the poor Monks without any Apostolical power, became possible to Otto. He baptized 7,000 heathens at Kamin, and induced the proud Stettiners to change their heathen temples into Christian Churches.

Ziegenbalg had his choice between these two methods, for the royal instruction only forbad him to take anything from the heathen, but did not forbid him to give them anything. For an Apostolical Mission, a country, circumstances, and last, but not least, the power, were all wanting. For an Ottonian Mission, on the other hand, everything was peculiarly adapted; for there were quantities of poor starving heathens. And, not unnaturally, his love displayed itself more readily towards these than towards the rich and the well-fed. He protected the poor, taught them with great patience and diligence, fed and clothed them during their time of instruction, and when they were baptized, endeavoured to help them to a respectable livelihood. Their children he received entirely into his house, taught and maintained them, and so tried to make them useful men and pious Christians. For all this, of course, he required money, his own he did not spare, and besides, found pious Christians who were glad to give him a share of theirs. In this way, he built Schools and Churches, erected a Printing Press—which had been sent to him from England—and even built a Paper-mill, partly in order to get cheaper paper, but partly also to provide his poor Christians with labor and an honest employment. And no one who saw his restless unselfish activity could help being surprised. Many a widow and orphan did more, they blessed him and praised God who had sent him. But what did the Danish Mission Directors do? With contemptuous letters they robbed him of all courage. Want of courage, however, is in India a fatal disease, and there are many who have fallen victims to it, and amongst these must be reckoned Ziegenbalg and Gründler.

Five weeks before his death, Ziegenbalg gave over charge of the Mission to Gründler, and then wrote to Denmark: "The cause of my sickness is mental; for during the last year and a half, my post has caused my heart many a struggle, sorrow and pain, and has given me many a restless night. These have been always increased by the many events which occur during such work. Some letters also which we received in 1717 and 1718 from Europe, have aided not a little to break down my spirit to such a degree, that I can no longer transact the duties of my post with my former pleasure. And as at the same time I have remarked, that since my return from Denmark, the work has been much less supported than before, this has caused me much grief, for I had hoped for far better results from my wearisome voyage there and back, than I have as yet seen. These mental trials and sorrows have had such a strong influence on the *motus vitales* and on all portions of the body that for eighteen months I have had severe bodily suffering. I accept such trials with submission, and have a trust in God that He will in some way give help, so that I may again be in a condition to be useful to the work. May His holy will be done!" This holy will of God was done, and on the 23rd February God released him from all trouble. Amid many tears, Gründler prepared his bed in the quiet vault in front of the altar, and 13 months afterwards laid himself by his side.

Ziegenbalg had landed in Tranquebar in July 1706. He went home in October 1714; returned in August 1716, and died in February 1719, so that altogether he only spent 10¾ years in this country. But it is wonderful how much he had done during that time. It is not, however, the number of converts that is so remarkable, for at his death, there appear in the Tamil Church Registers only 226 names, and in the Portuguese books about an equal number. But Ziegenbalg exercised a remarkable influence over heathens living in distant parts, which he maintained by friendly correspondence; learning from them of their religion and customs, and telling them in return of Him who alone is the Way, the Truth and the Life. Ziegenbalg dived deeper into a knowledge of the religion of the Tamulians, and ventured further into their jungles of divinities than most Missionaries up to the present day. His little book on the Malabar gods, though published for the first time, 150 years after his death, has been judged worthy of a translation into English and has been printed in Madras.

Ziegenbalg did his work thoroughly, zealously and by the employment of all his powers. May the Lord send many a successor in his work among the Tamulians whose life may equal his, and whose end may be as his was!

Gründler was now left alone, and all the burden of the work, and the responsibility fell upon his shoulders. Added to this, there arrived the worst of all the Copenhagan despatches, so that Gründler broke down, and for two months lay ill. The Danish Directors had allowed themselves to be led by their Secretary, the Candidate Wendt, into quite a new groove. They had conceived the idea of an Apostolical Mission, and had embraced it with pietistic one-sidedness. The instructions which our Lord gave to His disciples (Matt. 10) were now applied without limitation to the Missionaries in the Tamil country. Messieurs, the Directors, however, did not seem to remember that with these instructions our Lord sent His disciples to their own countrymen in Judea, and actually forbad them to go to the heathens or even to the neighbouring Samarians. So, they despatched one of the cruelest letters that probably any Missionary Society of any country has ever penned. I will only quote a few sentences as an example, and also to show the tenor of the former letters which had so crushed Ziegenbalg:

"The Lord sent forth His disciples empty handed; He even forbad them to carry in their girdles, gold, silver or precious stones; He told them to carry no scrip, nor shoes, nor staff, nor to have two coats. Test yourselves by this model. Think for a moment of what little weight the trifles of this world must be in comparison with one soul, and reflect what, at the day of revelation, the judgment of a righteous God will be between them. Bearing in mind this day, and having regard to the souls of the heathen, we had far rather that your bodily state were like the description given by Paul to the Corinthians I, IV, 11-13; miserable and shameful, poor and insignificant—Yes, we have a faith in the tender love of our God and our Saviour Jesus, that He will some day make it so (that is to say, that the Missionaries in Tranquebar should suffer hunger and thirst, should be naked and beaten, should be reviled, persecuted and defamed, that they should be made as the filth of the world and the offscouring of all things! I scarcely think that the Mission Directors at Antioch who despatched Paul wished him to suffer all this!) "Yes, we wish," continues this letter, "rather that no single Thaler had ever been sent to India, than that the entrance to the Kingdom of Heaven should have been closed by earthly things. It is worthy of remark (and is no doubt of great convenience to you) that you already have houses where you can regularly meet. But should this or that building hinder you from going among the heathens, or deprive you of time or opportunity of preaching the Gospel, we would wish that not one stone remained upon the other, but rather that living stones should be hewn for a spiritual edifice, until at last, each flock should establish such conveniences or learn to do without them. We would wish that even in Tranquebar you should hold no Sunday or Feast-day preachings, and no morning or evening Services, provided only that the heathens could hear the sound of the Gospel" "(so that, supposing the Christians might wish to hear the sound of the Gospel they would have to run to the heathen, to hear it there !)" "Amongst the bodily, outward and wordly conditions of the Mission must also be reckoned the Schools and the Seminary. You may say, that without these, the whole Mission at which for twelve years we have worked with so much diligence would fall away; but we would answer and repeat, Let perish, fall away and be destroyed everything that detracts from the principal work of going among the heathen and preaching the Gospel by mouth; for such institutions as these are only of good if they promote and help these objects." So far the Fathers in Denmark, and it is only to be regretted that they did not conceive the idea of sending out the author of this epistle, the Candidate Wendt, without gold, silver or precious stones in his girdle, without shoes or staff, and the wish that his state might be soon miserable and contemptible might soon have been realized.

Gründler read this letter amid many tears and showed it to his friends. The Commandant, a Herr von Nissen, was so indignant at it, that he exclaimed: "then Missionaries should be like soldiers who carry everything upon their backs! But before the gentlemen of the Mission Directory demand this from you they should first of all set you a good example, for they live in big houses, well furnished from top to bottom."

The first answer which the Directors in Denmars' received to their cruel letter was the news of Ziegenbalg's death. Such an answer they had scarcely expected, and they mourned sincerely for him. But soon afterwards came other fruit of their writing: Gründler's death. First of all, however, Gründler went through their last letter point by point, and answered it with such patience, and in so noble-minded a manner that we cannot restrain our admiration. From this letter I will quote a few sentences:

"The gentlemen of the direction of the Mission quote to

us the two Missions, Matthew 10 and Luke 10, in order that by them we may carefully examine ourselves. Now I will point out some differences in our position. Our Mission goes to the heathen, who as yet know nothing of the Messiah but only of many idols; not to brethren of the same race, but to an entirely strange people. The former could enter the houses of their own people, but we, among the heathen, may not enter a Malabar house, but must find out rest-houses of our own, where, however, we must ourselves provide everything. Apostles and Jews ate together and, therefore, Christ says: "When ye enter into a house say first, peace be to this house! and in the same house remain, eating and drinking such things as they give." The Malabars, however, will not suffer us to eat with them or even to touch their food and cooking-utensils. Therefore, when we Missionaries go forth with our Catechists, we must ourselves carry our brass pot, our rice, and our brass pan in which we cook a few vegetables. The Apostles were not allowed to take with them gold or silver or precious stones, no scrip, nor two coats, nor shoes, nor any staves. The reason is placed by Saint Matthew in Christ's mouth, "For the workman is worthy of his meat," and by St Luke, "For the workman is worthy of his hire."

We Missionaries, however, when we go into these countries must necessarily take for our subsistence, gold and silver and brass, or I will say: Pagodas, fanams and cash, for these heathens do not as yet understand the saying, "The labourer is worthy of his hire." Besides, we must get our Catechist, who accompanies us, to appoint a Philip, as a dispenser, who must buy for us in the villages, and prepare for us some rice and some fishes or instead of the fishes some vegetables. Purses here are not wanted to carry the money, but a piece of linen in which to tie it. Scrip and bags are not necessary, for we carry no refreshments with us; in this warm land we find one coat to be quite sufficient and, therefore, do not require two. Shoes and staves are, however, necessary; shoes at one time on account of the burning sand and at another on account of the hard soil. Staves are required partly to enable us to get over the swamps and the water, and partly on account of the snakes which abound here. I only mention such differences, in order that it may be known in what respects we can be exact imitators of the Apostles when we go out among the heathens, and in what respects we cannot on account of the country and the people. For I maintain that both of those Missions which were intended especially for the Jews, and to which the distinct injunction was given : " go not into the way of the Gentiles, and into any city of the Samaritans enter ye not," " cannot in all respects be held to apply to all Missions."

" If, however high, well born Sirs, you think that a heathen obtains more worldly benefits with the Mission than in his own household, and might, therefore, be induced to embrace our religion ; your opinion is not a correct one. When in our congregations the mothers bring forth children, most of them have not enough to cover their child with a piece of white cloth and bring it to be christened. For which reason the Mission-chest gives them two ells of cloth in which to wrap their child. When members of our congregation die, the most of them have not sufficient wherewith to buy a cloth to carry them to the grave. I have now been here for 10 years, and during these ten years, I do not know of more than six persons who have been buried in coffins, and among those six was the late Senior of the Mission and his little son. The others are all buried in linen cloths. Yes, out of twenty who may die there will scarcely be one who has enough to buy a piece of linen to be buried in. So much for their worldly benefits! The Apostolical congregations had houses and fields which they could sell, and then laid the money at the Apostles' feet, with which they were able to make such good provisions for the Missions, that seven almsgivers alone had to be placed in charge of them. In our congregations, however, there is very great poverty."

" From this it may be seen to how great an extent those who join our Mission are benefited in their worldly affairs. As far as I myself am individually concerned, I could live in Europe with better health and at far less cost. But I know that I am not in the world for things earthly and temporal ; and I care not whether in it I am prosperous or miserable. Heavenly things are my aim ; for these I strive and press forward. As long as the Mission is God's work, God will provide for this poor Mission. In this respect our faith induces us to cast all our care upon the Lord ; He will make all things well."

" To keep closer, however, to the matter of Mission expenses, the example of the King of Spain, Philip II, may, perhaps, be remembered. When his ministers advised him not to incur any more expense in a Missionary work, on the Phillipian Islands, which had already cost him several millions, and had not been of much good, the King asked if his Missionaries had been totally unsuccessful in preaching to the heathens, and whether they were not able to win over to Christianity at least one soul during the year. The Ministers were obliged to answer, yes! The King, thereupon, replied: "then all this money has been well spent."

"The writer of this letter wishes that we should be like the description of Paul, I Cor., IV, 11—13. At that time no Christian heart would have wished Paul to undergo such sufferings, but, on the contrary, they showed the greatest compassion; lovingly they gave food and drink to the hungry and thirsty Apostles; they clothed the naked and bound up the wounds of those who had been beaten. For, these sufferings were to a certain extent an obstacle to their going amongst the heathens, rather than as-far as bodily matters were concerned, their movements were facilitated by them. For, if they were beaten, they had to remain in quiet until their wounds were healed. That such sufferings are among the unmistakeable marks of Christ, which true Missionaries must also bear, is true enough, and they form a portion of the imitation of Christ. The Missionaries in Tranquebar, however, have not been without their share of such marks. But as you have the faith in the gracious love of our Lord and Saviour Jesus Christ that He will make, us Missionaries, poor and miserable, may the gracious God in Christ Jesu in return pour over you and us His spiritual as well as temporal blessings in an abundant stream—*Amen.*"

In this quiet and dignified manner was Gründler able to answer the whole of the long letter, and he then set about selling the Mission property. He began with a little house and garden in Poreiar, which had formerly been his own favorite residence, and he also sold by auction a small house in the town. But a consolatory letter from Aug. Herm. Franke, the strong in faith, again gave him a little courage and pleasure, so that he stopped any further sales; and when in September, three new Missionaries arrived in Tranquebar: Schultze, Dal and Kistenmacher, Gründler again revived. He gave himself great pains to teach the new Missionaries the language and the customs of the country and felt himself especially drawn towards Benjamin Schultze, in whom he correctly discerned real power. Franke had sent out the three new Missionaries unordained, and not *vià* Denmark, and so Gründler first ordained Schultze, that he might represent him in everything. Gründler himself proposed to make a journey to Copenhagen, as Ziegenbalg had done before, in order to talk about things personally and set matters right. First, however, he wished to spend some time in Madras, in order to preach to the heathens there. He, therefore, wrote to the Governor of Madras and requested permission to rent a house in the so-called Black Town, in order from thence to preach to the heathens, and requested him also to afford such help as might be required.

But this revival of Gründler was only the last flicker of his dying life-flame. His strength, devoured by a violent fever, soon decreased. Nevertheless, he caused himself to be put on board ship, in order to travel by sea to Cuddalore, where he had already been, and he trusted the sea-voyage would give him some relief. But his state grew so much worse that he was obliged to turn back, and arrived in Tranquebar quite exhausted. In spite of this, on his last Sunday on earth, he put on his robes yet once again and tottered to the Church. Schultze, who was conducting the Service, was terrified when he saw him enter the vestry, "But, you cannot stand!" he exclaimed, "I must," was Gründler's curt reply, and he endeavoured with copious draughts of water to still his inward fire. He then stepped in front of the Altar, and stretching out his hands, blessed his poor congregation. This was his farewell to his flock; and on the 19th March 1720, "he fell softly and peacefully asleep in his Saviour." On the following day, Schultze laid him to rest by the side of his friend Ziegenbalg. His widow wrote to Prof. Franke: "As far as my dear husband is concerned, the true cause of his death was the sorrow and grief which the cruel letter of the Mission Directors caused him. I can assure your Reverence, that from that time, my deceased husband was unhappy, and had no longer any pleasure in his work, as formerly. In this way his strength was consumed from day to day, until at last the Lord freed him from all his sufferings.

In this way both of the first Lutheran Missionaries of Tranquebar had been laid to rest. They are both buried in the Church which they built, in front of the Altar, from which they so often administered the consolation of eternal life, and in view of the pulpit from which they so often proclaimed Him, who is the Resurrection and the Life. Gründler was a humble, faithful and 'thorough' servant of his Master; may God grant us many such good and faithful workmen, and an end like his end!—*Amen.*

The flock in Tranquebar was severely tried. For some years they had seen their Missionaries no longer working with their former pleasure, and then they had to bury their beloved pastor. Gründler did what he could; but he soon fell sick, so that he could no more; and when at length he recovered, the letter of the Danish Directors lay upon him like a night-mare, and prevented every free movement. At last he began to tear down his own work by selling the Mission property, and then at last he too succumbed, before the new Missionaries had been six months in Tranquebar, or had mastered the language. It can scarcely be imagined how severe was this trial to the young inexperienced congregation, only just won from idolatry and living in the midst of heathens.

In the same way we can scarcely comprehend the difficulty of Benjamin Schultze's task. He was the only ordained Minister, and had now to bear upon his shoulders, not only the Tamulian, but also the Portuguese flock, without being master of either of the languages. His colleagues were even still less so. Missionary Kistenmacher was always sickly, was not able to adapt himself to the circumstances, and at last died. Dal, a Dane, took time. He troubled himself very little about Tamil, and after years had not mastered Portuguese. On the other hand he was strong in heartless criticisms, and had a bitter pen—and he passed these unkind and severe criticisms not only on his overworked colleague Schultze, but also on Ziegenbalg, whom he had not known, and on Gründler, of whose humble and manly piety he himself had been a witness. A youth such as this, who knew nothing of the country or the people, and who understood nothing of the Mission work, for he had not yet even learnt the language, was able in cool blood to call such precious servants of God "cheated cheats." Dal lived long enough to see the thorough falsehood and sinfulness of his judgment, but I can nowhere find that he ever retracted it.

So much the more commendable appears Schultze's action at this juncture. Returned from Gründler's burial, he called his colleagues, spoke to them words of encouragement, and made them promise him to labor faithfully at the work. He then fell with them upon his knees and prayed God to grant them strength and His blessing for this purpose. After this he called the congregation, and through an interpreter, for he was not yet able to speak to them himself, he consoled and encouraged them. They in their turn felt the consolation offered and begged him to administer the holy Communion. This he did as well as he could and begged the people to pardon his mistakes in Tamil. They then reassured him, said that they had understood everything, and were rejoiced to see that the Lord had so far helped him. This pleased him and four weeks afterwards he began to preach in Tamil, and he preached so willingly and so zealously that when suffering from swollen feet, the effects of a violent fever, he caused himself to be carried into the Church and preached to them sitting.

He soon saw that it was absolutely necessary to learn Portuguese, and this he naturally found much easier than Tamil. He then made a practice of preaching every Sunday morning in both Tamil and Portuguese, and in the afternoon to catechize in Tamil: and when after the burden and the heat of the day he retired to his lonely room, he gave himself fresh heart, and strengthened himself in the Lord with a good German hymn. One Sunday evening after he had sung, "Love, that art to me a model," &c., and had felt strengthened by it, he thought to himself—"Yes! you can sing that, but what can the poor Tamil School children do? If only somebody could translate it for them!" And so he at once set about translating the hymn. The words came easily into his mouth; first one verse was finished and then another, and by two hours after midnight he had got the whole hymn finished. This gave Schultze courage and pleasure, and during the next week he went on and translated "And now we beg the Holy Ghost," "Alone to God on High be praise," "Now thank we all our God," and afterwards some others. These he taught to the School boys and sang them over together with them, until they had got the tunes by heart. It is true that these translations were by no means perfect, but they supplied a want and were gladly sung.

Whilst Schultze was thus doing his duty amongst his flock with great diligence and self-sacrifice, he did not forget the heathens. Every week he had a day set apart for them, and when he went out he took his school children with him to the number of about 40. Arrived at a village he stopped in the street and struck up a hymn. A German tune sung by 40 throats soon collected a number of people, and when the sound of the last verse had died away, Schultze uncovered his head and prayed to God for these heathens and then only he addressed them. After the address, a conversation shorter or longer according to circumstances, ensued between the heathens and himself and assistants, and then the troup of Evangelists went away to another village. For six years Schultze thus travelled over the Tranquebar territory with its 30,000 inhabitants, so that scarcely one remained who had had no opportunity of hearing his voice. His Missionary results were also quite equal to the previous standard. During 14 years, Ziegenbalg and Gründler had baptized and received 452 Tamulians and Portuguese or about 33 in a year. During the six years that Schultze passed in Tranquebar, he had baptized and received 174 Tamulians and Portuguese, or about 29 per annum. At the same time he was as good as alone, for Dal, not knowing the language was unable to help him. Schultze also worked diligently on the translation of the Bible which Ziegenbalg had commenced, and in which, after completing the New Testament, he had got as far as the Book of Ruth. Schultze finished all the remaining books of the Old Testament.

Schultze had, like Ziegenbalg before him, often longed to preach the Gospel to the distant heathens living beyond the little Danish territory. But he was not able to leave Tranquebar; besides the Tranquebar territory was surrounded by the country of the King of Tanjore, where travelling was unsafe, let alone preaching. In the Mogul's territory which was not far distant to the north, it was certainly much safer and much more open; but he could not travel thither, because he was not able to leave Tranquebar for so long a time. In June 1725, however, there came to Tranquebar three new Missionaries Bosse, Pressier and Walther. The two last were able men and commenced the work of the Lord vigorously. But they were ignorant of the language, and so Schultze had to remain in order to instruct them in this as well as in the Mission affairs generally. He, therefore, remained until the spring of 1726, and then left Tranquebar on the Monday after Sexagesima. Like Gründler did shortly before his death, he sailed in a little boat from Tranquebar to Cuddalore and journeyed from thence to Madras and even still further on foot. On the road the words of the Gospel of the day from which he had preached in Tranquebar on his last Sunday, were continually sounding in his ears, "There went forth a sower to sow," and so Schultze went forth sowing his seed, until at last he settled down in Madras where we shall find him again.

In Tranquebar there were now three Missionaries in Schultze's place besides Dal, who, to be sure, was there also. But five more years lasted before Dal was ordained, so that he had to go through a probationary time in Tranquebar for eleven years. The management of the Mission never came into Dal's hands. It was undertaken for the present by Walther and Pressier. About this time the Gospel began to spread in Tanjore, though the Missionaries were not yet able to travel there. Christians from thence came to the festivals in Tranquebar and also to the Communion, and were ministered to in other matters by native assistants until the Missionaries were at last able to come themselves.

Many faithful servants of the Lord labored in Tranquebar in succession or together, and served each the Lord according to the talents with which he had been endowed, and the circumstances that surrounded him, until in 1837, the last of them, A. F. Cämmerer, fell asleep. From this time the two Danish congregations in Danish territory, (for the other congregations in British territory had gradually passed into English hands) were ministered to though inefficiently, by the Danish Chaplains. Germany had by degrees become as poor as Denmark had been in the commencement and had no longer any Missionaries for the Tamulians. For without faith there can be no messengers of faith. And Germany had through "philosophy and vain deceit after the tradition of men and the rudiments of the world" lost ever more and more of her faith. But when God fetched a scourge from Corsica, and chastised Germany with it in a manner she well deserved, she got no help from her philosophy. But the Lord helped her, when she again turned towards him, and soon afterwards there were again messengers of faith. In 1840, only three years after Cämmerer's death, another German Missionary, Cordes, landed in Tranquebar. The whole town was in a state of excitement when the news came that a German Missionary to the Tamulians had arrived in Madras and was on his way to Tranquebar. Europeans as well as natives were equally well pleased, for our fathers had left a good reputation behind them. Even to this day there still live in Tranquebar, two sisters, children of the Missionary Doctor Martini, who were both born in the last century, and who still like to tell of the quiet and friendly habits of the Missionaries of that time.

But if the beginning of everything is difficult, it is often even more difficult to rebuild what has tumbled down. In Madras already Missionary Cordes received all kinds of well-meant advice against wasting his energies in the out-of-the-way Tranquebar, &c. He was told that Tranquebar was not even worth the experiment of re-building. But his Lutheran conscience led Cordes to Tranquebar, for here only was to found a Lutheran congregation with all the forms of Lutheran worship, though it is true that it may be said to have been in its last gasp. Besides, his instructions were to go first to Tranquebar, and it is always right and proper to allow one's self to be guided and to be led as it were by the hand into the path which God wishes one to follow. One's own paths may be more interesting, but are never the best.

Arrived in Tranquebar, Cordes was received with open arms, and although everything was not exactly as it ought to have been, by degrees matter got into order. The Danish Chaplain, who had been in temporary charge of the Mission, soon allowed him to help in the work, and when he went home, handed over everything into his charge. The Tamil congregation also soon met him with entire confidence, and even the local Government, though but little inclined to let the old German work again get into German hands, approved of Cordes' work, and when the Chaplain left, entrusted to him the care of all the congregations.

When Tranquebar was sold to England, the Governor, however, once more came forward with his wishes; he was of opinion that the Missionary power of Germany had departed, and that it would be better to hand over the Mission to the Gospel Propagation Society ("a rich English Company," as he styled it,) which had already taken over the Mission station established in English territory. And those who had formerly spoken against doing anything for Tranquebar, were now only too willing to do too much for her. Even Spencer, the Bishop of Madras, thought it worth his while to stretch out his hand for it; for he wrote to Cordes and expressed his anxiety lest Tranquebar should be now left orphaned and forsaken, and his willingness to protect her. Cordes answered that so far was the idea of forsaking the congregation removed from his thoughts, that he intended to continue the Tranquebar Mission as a Lutheran one! It should, however, be remembered to the praise of the Danish Missionary College that it distinctly announced to the local Government at Tranquebar that the Mission must remain Lutheran. On this account, said the Governor, he handed it over to Cordes.

As far as the Tamil congregation is concerned it should also be remembered to their honour, that they neither allowed themselves to be led away by the wealth of the so-called Company, nor blinded by the pomp and influence of the Bishop. It remained not only true to its German Missionary, but also addressed to the King of Denmark the prayer that they might be given over into the hands, not of the English, but of the Lutheran Society, "lest they should also lose in spiritual matters, what, owing to the sale of Tranquebar, they must necessarily lose in temporal matters." Their prayer was heard. In 1847, the royal Mission College at Copenhagen formally gave over to the Lutheran Mission all their lands and buildings together with some 1,500 Christians, 14 Schools, 5 Catechists, 16 teachers, &c. From that time peace with the S. P G. Missionaries could naturally not be very great, especially as it soon became apparent that the Lutheran Mission in Tranquebar had really again come to life. As in the commencement, the work of the Lord began again to spread from Tranquebar and to extend far into the land of the Tamulians.

Missionary work is a work of fighting and struggling, for the heathens do not allow themselves to be won to the Kingdom of God without a struggle. They defend what they have, which they have received from their forefathers, and the more so as it is so closely bound up with their country and their mode of life. As Missionaries, therefore, are obliged to be continually fighting, it is no wonder that they sometimes quarrel among themselves. It was thus with the very first Missionaries who went to preach to the heathens. They quarrelled, and as it now seems to us, about some very trifling matter, and so bitter was the quarrel that they parted. And yet these were the most self-denying Missionaries that ever lived. Their names are known as Barnabas and Saul. But their quarrel and separation tended only to the furtherance of their work, and this alone might teach us to have patience with the disputants. In the Lutheran Mission there has also been no want of quarrels from Ziegenbalg's time to the present day. And there will be such as long as ever there will be a Lutheran Mission, and should there be no longer such a Mission, there will be quarrels as long as ever there are Christians living in the world.

> " All envy now and hatred quell,
> Let peace and love among us dwell,"

is a beautiful and proper prayer, and is being heard continually, but it will be fully and completely answered only when we reach home and are no longer in a foreign land.

As in the old, so in the young Mission all the Missionaries who came to Tranquebar did not remain in the Tamil country. Many returned home, and now and then some one or the other raised an evil clamour. Bövingh had made a beginning in Ziegenbalg's time and he found many imitators. But the work of the Lord must continue to spread " through good repute and evil repute, and the evil repute may, perhaps, be as necessary and as useful as the good. Like its King the Kingdom of the Lord must wear for the natural man, " neither form nor comeliness," nor has it had any from the days of the Apostles. How could it otherwise be *His* Kingdom ? But it will receive both when the King will put on His form and His comeliness. Until then we walk in faith and not by sight.

Tranquebar is again as it was in the beginning the centre of the Lutheran Mission in the Tamil country. The " Senior" of the Mission resides there who, in the Mission Council, regulates the whole Mission. The experience of many years that the admission of newly arrived Missionaries to an equal vote and rank is the cause of much trouble and much confusion has never led to any good. Newly arrived Missionaries must, therefore, study the language, the people and their relations for two years and then pass an examination in Tamil consisting of a sermon (*ex tempore*, not read from manuscripts) and fluent conversation before they are allowed an independent charge and an equal vote. But because the Missionaries are no longer in Tranquebar, or even within easy reach of each other, but for the most part are scattered over almost the whole extent of the Tamil country, so that a frequent meeting would be attended with great expense and loss of time, a regular Mission Council has been constituted from out of the Missionaries resident in or near Tranquebar, which is presided over by the Senior and consults over and directs the various circumstances of the Mission. Once a year, generally in February, all the Missionaries assemble in Tranquebar for a Synod, in which the Senior presides and to which he renders an account of his management during the year. When the business-part of the meeting is over, two addresses are generally given, one learned and the other more practical which are afterwards discussed by all the Missionaries in debate. As, however, several native preachers work together with the German Missionaries, on their account a rule is made to speak Tamil only on the first day, on which also practical matters are generally discussed. During latter years, a Mission feast has been added, at which the different Missionaries give a short address regarding their work and the spread of the Gospel. A German Service closes, as it had commenced—the proceedings, and a participation in the Holy Communion forms a fresh bond of connection, whilst at the same time it invigorates the Missionaries to renewed work and to renewed struggles in their, for the most part, solitary posts. The Synod, therefore, is to the Missionaries generally and to the Senior especially a week of hard work though at the same time a welcome opportunity of strengthening in the Lord and renewal of brotherly love. The Seminary where the teachers, catechists and preachers are educated is also in Tranquebar, as also the Central School to which every Missionary can send the pupils to have them educated in further training. In addition there is still at Tranquebar a Printing Press as there was during the time of Ziegenbalg in which all Church, School and house books are printed, the editorial labor of which, together with that of a Tamil monthly paper, is entrusted to an especially appointed member of the Mission—Mr. Blomstrand.

The Portuguese community which lasted from Ziegenbalg's days to ours has ceased to exist as such; that is, a Portuguese Service is no longer held; a few members, however, of the old congregation still live and they attend either the Tamil or the English Service which is still held in Ziegenbalg's Church alternately with a German Service. This little European congregation numbers some 60 souls, whilst the Tamil one consists of about 700; to these must be added the two suburbs of Tranquebar, Tiroomenyam under the charge of the Central School, Mr. Scheffer, with 117, and Manikraman under the control of Missionary Blomstrand with 300 souls. Poryar, once inhabited by Gründler and given up by him, has again been worked, and since 1842 a Missionary has resided there, at present Missionary Schanz. His flock consists of 900 souls living in or near Poryar. In and around Tranquebar there are, therefore, more than 2,000 adherents of the Lutheran confession; some 350 Christian children are also educated there, and about 100 heathen children also take part in the instruction given in the Christian Schools. From 1706 to 1869 there were, on the average, 100 converts christened or received every year, for the number in the Tranquebar Church books is at present 17,440.

In spite of all this, Tranquebar is still essentially a heathen town, and the little territory, formerly Danish, is essentially a heathen country in which the old idolatry with its rites is still practised. After the faithful work of 160 years, and after so many prayers, can it then be that the old territory with its 30,000 inhabitants is not yet converted? It is not! and if it would not shock the reader, I would add that there is not much prospect of its being so converted. And even though every year more or less heathens may be instructed and baptized, still even by these means there is no speedy prospect of converting the whole. And why not? I shall be prepared to answer this question fully and satisfactorily as soon as I get an answer to the much older question: How was it that Moses, with all his signs and wonders and with a whole race of Priests and Levites, was not able to convert his own people although he had them under his sole direction for 40 years? or the other question: Why it was that the twelve Apostles, with the fullness of the Holy Ghost, with 500 brethren to help them and with many signs, wonders and powers, were not able to convert the town of Jerusalem not to speak of the little country of Judea and Samaria? The Apostle Paul has already given the answer, only many a Missionary friend would seem to have forgotten it. It is written in 2 Thess., III, 2, and runs: "*For all men have not faith.*"

The different Mission-stations of our day are in many respects like the cloisters of the middle ages in heathen Germany. By them there was established in the midst of heathendom and idolatry a service of God of whom the heathen had no conception. Cloister-schools were established in connection with the cloisters, and in the same way there are one or more schools in every Mission-station. In this way the saving truth is brought home to old and young and there are continually some to be found who have a yearning towards it. In these solitary Mission-stations a light is kindled in the midst of heathen darkness, and if the light of the knowledge of Jesus Christ does not spread so rapidly as the light of the sun travels through space, the reason of it is that the heathen devilish atmosphere is so thick. When, however, everything is ready, there will no doubt arise a Bonifacius, who will not only collect and rule, but who will also hew down the idolaters' oaks with a sharp axe. Even in the Roman Empire, heathendom, long since rotten and crumbling, did not fall, in spite of the three centuries of preaching of the Apostles and their disciples, until the converted Roman Emperors overturned it by force and forbad its practise on pain of death. And what is a European oak compared with an Indian banian tree? Will the 200 millions of India at once form themselves into a Christian community merely because it is the wish of a handful of poor powerless strangers? No deeply rooted tree can fall unless assailed by a mighty storm. Will the deeply rooted, thousand-trunked banian of Indian religious life suddenly fall down under a serene sky?

A stream does not forsake its customary bed without mighty earthquakes. Will the deep and mighty stream of Hindoo religion forsake the bed in which it has flowed for thousands of years whilst bright sunshine is all around? It is possible that these storms and earthquakes are not far removed from India, but if they are to prove beneficial to the people, it is necessary now to preach of Him, who has said: "Call upon me in the hour of need and I will deliver thee," for how can they call upon Him of whom they have not heard. Need, however, teaches prayer and supplication. The hope even for these millions may, therefore, remain undisturbed. In the meantime, let every Christian rejoice with the angels of God over each heathen who throws aside his idols and calls Christ his Lord!

---

2. *Madras.*

Madras is situated some 170 miles north of Tranquebar, and in the good old times a journey thither in a bullock coach always lasted nine days, and often even more. But in the last ten years the roads have been improved and bridges have been built so that the distance can now be done in about seven days. There are also now railways in the Tamil country and by these, though none touches at Tranquebar, it is possible, by wide detours, to reach Madras in two days. So altered are the times.

The first Mission-station from Tranquebar was founded in Madras—other stations followed, either from Madras, as Cuddalore, or from Tranquebar as Trichinopoly and Tanjore. Madras is now the largest town in the Tamil country, and built like Nineveh with many gardens between, so that the different parts of the town seem to have little connection. In the middle of this large town is Fort Saint George, in which are most of the Government offices. If an official lives at the Adyar, a river in one of the southern suburbs of Madras, he has a drive to his office of some six miles, and the distances from the west and the north are not much less. Half a million men inhabit this scattered town, and every family lives in a separate house. The palace-like buildings of the higher English officials lie far apart from each other, each one in its separate 'compound' so that often one house is scarcely visible from the other. Shady trees fill the compounds, and flowers surround the houses. The poor who pass by may well think each to be a little Paradise. Snakes, however, of many a form are not wanting in these Paradises, and the Indian sun is one of them. Near the Fort is the so-called "Black Town" the town proper of the natives. It is built mostly of one-storied houses and is inhabited by a dark brown race for the most part with naked bodies and voluble tongues. Here and there the leisurely Tamulian is sometimes seen in a hurry and the 'mild Hindoo' with his face marked with passions. If only the hideous idol marks did not so disfigure the foreheads of the men! The old women too manage to give themselves a regular demoniac appearance by smearing their foreheads with Siva's ashes. But we will gladly leave the narrow crowded, heated and noisy streets, for their smell is intolerable.

Here in this Black Town, but in that portion which is near the sea, where the air is purer, and it is more possible for a European to live, Schultze founded the first Mission-station in Madras. We saw him leave Tranquebar on the Monday after Sexagesima in 1726. As far as Cuddalore he travelled by sea, in order to avoid the extortions of the Tanjore kingdom. For it was their custom to squeeze from each traveller, even from strange natives, tolls in payment of the protection they enjoyed—supposing they were fortunate to get through without being robbed. But the extortions practised were so oppressive that a rich native, who had himself suffered from them, offered the Mogul a considerable sum on condition that these tolls should no longer be demanded from travellers. The Prince consented, and two years before Schultze's arrival all the tolls were abolished. Schultze, therefore, as soon as he was outside the kingdom of Tanjore, was able, thanks to the unknown Tamulian, to travel free and unhindered. He first went from Cuddalore to the great pagoda town, Chellumbram and back again, and then commenced his journey to Madras after having preached to the heathens in Cuddalore and visited their schools. For the present he did not stop long in Madras, but went towards the north as far as Pulicat, the northern boundary of Tamil land. From thence he left the sea and struck inland towards the west everywhere preaching the Gospel to the heathens.

Benjamin Schultze appears to have been of strong constitution, and at that time of good health; for he did all his travelling on foot, with only one native companion who carried the most necessary articles and a mat of rushes. His food was rice and curry as it is prepared by natives, plentifully supplied with red pepper, and not always free of sand which grates between the teeth. His table and his crockery consisted of a leaf-plate, as made by the Tamulians from the nearest tree, a number of leaves stitched together with thorn-like needles, so that a round surface is presented. On this leaf-plate the curry and rice is piled as much as is required, and this was the way that Schultze fared. He had brought, however, with him, from Tranquebar, one article of luxury—a spoon. This he pulled out ot his pocket, sat down on the mat, and so enjoyed his Indian meal. At night he spread his mat in or near a hut and slept in peace. It was the hottest time of the year. He had often, during the heat of the day, to take shelter under a tree and to suffer from headache. No wonder, though it is a wonder that he escaped sunstroke and death. In this way he travelled about for months, visiting the heathen schools and preaching in a hundred different villages, until in July he arrived in Madras, bare foot, limping and sick. But in fourteen days his giant-like nature had recovered and he was ready to commence his labor of love.

He first of all only asked for the permission of the Governor of Madras to live there and establish a school. The Governor, however, not only gave him this permission, but also promised him assistance and protection. Schultze then returned to Tranquebar to consult with his colleagues, and so to found the Mission in Madras with their approval. The brethren were unwilling to lose him and Dal, especially, would not hear of Schultze's departure, although he did not hesitate to criticize many of his actions and to report them to Europe. But as there were already four Missionaries in Tranquebar, there was not the slightest reason to keep him there as the fifth, especially as they did not willingly allow themselves to be led by him. He, therefore, again turned to Madras, and, though unwillingly, was allowed by his colleagues to go in peace.

Schultze hired himself a house in Black Town, in the midst of the natives and published, by a notice affixed to his door, that he would instruct all children that might be sent to him. In a short time he had not only a school of children, but also so many grown up visitors that he had to assign a special time at which he was to be spoken to by all. Every morning he taught for an hour in the school, and then from 9 to 10 he remained under the verandah of his house to speak to all who might choose to come. In this way the Gospel was soon made known to many.

But again and again there came to him men who spoke only Telugu and whom Schultze could, therefore, neither understand, nor could he preach to them of Christ. He, therefore, began to study this language. Telugu is a sister language of Tamil, the most melodious of the Dravidian languages, and so, especially as he had no ordinary talent for languages, Schultze soon mastered it. In a short time he wrote a Grammar of the language and translated into it the Catechism and, subsequently, he translated the New Testament and indeed the whole Bible.

There is, however, a language spoken on the Ganges and the Cauvery, and understood on the Indus as well as the Palar. In the south of India it is generally spoken by the Mahomedans and is called the Mahomedan language, (Tulukku pashei). But in the north of India it is spoken by the Hindoos, and in the Presidencies of Calcutta and Bombay even Europeans are obliged to learn it. Hindoos who come from the north to the south frequently can speak nothing but this so-called Hindustanee. It is written in both Arabic and Sanscrit characters. It has, however, nothing in common with Arabic, but has with Persian to which it is nearly related; as, however, many Hindoos from the north who could only speak this language came to Schultze for instruction, he commenced to study this language in order to be able to assist them. It is not a difficult language and a knowledge of it is even now useful to the Missionary in the Tamil country who wishes to work among this people. Schultze wrote also a Hindustanee Grammar and made several translations into the language. In this way he spent the hot hours of the day (when he must needs be under a safe roof) in useful labors in which he was unwearied.

With the catechumens Schultze was at first very cautious. For all over India, and especially in the larger towns there are vagabonds who do not object to being instructed, if during the same period they can get food, as indeed is only fair when the persons are really poor. And these men often allow themselves to be baptized solely on account of the Baptismal cloth, just as the old Saxons and Pommeranians did. The younger Missionaries are often hoodwinked by such persons, who indeed are like the wind; they come, no one knows whence, and go, no one knows whither. Schultze, therefore, required that every one who wished to be considered and instructed as a catechumen should first tell his place of residence and his means of living. Even in the present time this rule is a good one and especially so in new Mission-stations where the Missionary has no congregation by his side to warn him against such people. In this way Schultze spent two years in Madras teaching and preaching. From 1728 to 1730, he collected a congregation of 200 souls, in spite of the exertions of the Jesuits who tried to make the people suspicious of him. In 1730, Missionary Sartorius came to help Schultze. Sartorius was a good, pious man and lived in peace. But in 1832, there came one Geister, who proved a great plague to himself and to others. Amongst the rest he gave Schultze much trouble; and as Schultze was then sick, for he suffered much in the chest, he withdrew himself almost entirely and kept to his literary labors. But when in 1737 Sartorius and Geister went to Cuddalore, and Schultze was again unfettered, he baptized in a short time over 100 heathens. Schultze lasted until 1742 and spent, therefore, 16 years in the Black Town of Madras. Then, however, he broke down entirely, so that he had to return to Germany where he lived, in the 'Waisenhas' at Halle until 1760, ever ready and eager for work, until at last he entered upon his rest over seventy years of age.

Benjamin Schultze was one of our most gifted and laborious Missionaries of the greatest abstemiousness and unselfishness. He baptized of heathens, or received from the Roman Catholics, some 700 souls, and many heathen heard in many places and in many languages the tidings of the Gospel from his lips. It is true he had his peculiar manner, but when we call to mind those teachers who have preached the Lord's word, and through whose labors so many have been brought to believe, we should imitate the faith in which they served the Lord here, in which they died, and in which they are now before Him in eternity. As to their faults they died with their bodies, and we should suffer them to be dead and buried with them. For that is the most honorable and the most fitting thing for us to do.

Schultze handed over charge of his station to John Phil. Fabricius who had arrived two years previously from Tranquebar. Fabricius received his salary as Schultze had before him, and as the subsequent Missionaries did, no longer from Tranquebar, but from the Christian Knowledge Society in London. Fabricius was a pious, humble man with a sincere love for peace, of which, however, as far as worldly matters are concerned, he enjoyed but little. He ruled the Mission in Madras for 46 years; for 33 of these from 1749-1782, he was assisted by his friend J. C. Breithaupt, and these years were the richest with blessing for the Mission as well as for the lonely Fabricius. His times were times of war. Already in 1746, whilst Fabricius was yet alone with his flock, the French took first the Black Town and afterwards Fort Saint George. The Mission lost its property and Fabricius, with his flock, took refuge in the Dutch possession of Pulicat, a day's journey from Madras. There he remained with his people, or at least with the greater number of them for three years, in peace and quiet, though in many a need, until at last he was able to return to Madras.

In Madras he found but one portion of the Mission property remaining: the churchyard. The three following years were years of much distress. Then, however, help came. The Romish Priests, as usual, had mixed in political intrigues, and during the French occupation their conduct had been such that the English Government found it necessary to punish them. A fine large Church in Black Town was completely demolished, and another in the suburb of Vepery was confiscated. The Church in Vepery was made over to Fabricius together with 500 Pagodas (= 1,750 Rupees) as compensation of the losses he had suffered. At last, therefore, the Mission in Madras had a roomy Church and space enough to extend itself still further. The year 1752 closed for them in peace and joy, and for six more years the congregation, faithfully ministered to by their pastors, was allowed to develop in peace.

But in the year 1758 the French were there again. Again the congregation took refuge in Pulicat, but the two Missionaries wished to remain at their posts and the French General not only promised them every protection, but also gave them a military guard. This, however, did not prevent all their possessions being robbed, and when there was nothing more to be stolen they were ill-treated. So there was nothing left for them but to escape also to Pulicat. This time, however, their flight lasted only for a few months and then were again able to return and continue their peaceful labors.

In spite of all this distress, perhaps, in consequence of it, there came ever more souls that enquired after the way of salvation, and not only heathen but Papists also. In the same proportion the enmity of the Romish Priests increased and spent itself in evil slanderings. This moved Fabricius to take up the pen against them and he brought out a pamphlet in which he demonstrated the errors of Popedom as they had been proclaimed and denounced by the Apostles beforehand. He also published a little book for the better instruction of catechumens which is used to the present day. His greatest literary work, however, was the revision of the translation of the Bible by which he also established the Tamil Church language. Perhaps no language in India has so masterly and so popular a translation of the whole Bible as Fabricius has produced in Tamil. In the same way he finished the translations of the German hymns which Ziegenbalg and Schultze had commenced, and in this he displayed a singular talent for many of his translations are even better than the originals. Nothing since then that had been attempted in Tamil can compare with Fabricius' "Hymnologia Germano Tamulica" in idiom, knowledge of the language or depth of feeling.

During 46 years Fabricius and Breithaupt collected from the heathens and the Papists some 1,600 souls. This is no large number for so long a time, and for two such faithful and able workmen and comes far behind in comparison with the results of Schultze's labors. The times, however, were unquiet and both Fabricius and Breithaupt were quiet retired men. In 1782, Breithaupt fell asleep and the brethren in Tranquebar sent to the assistance of Fabricius who was over 70 years of age, the able and already experienced Gericke. But Fabricius would not accept him and Gericke had to return. For Fabricius, too, was peculiar, just as his predecessor Schultze had been before him only each in his own fashion. For six more years Fabricius remained at the head of his flock and performed all the ordinary duties, but as far as governing was concerned his day was past. He had still always the same friendly smile for all, and distributed his alms at the same window to worthy and unworthy, needy and unneedy alike, but the careful examination of each case and the punishment of misdoing was a thing of the past. On the other hand, indeed, he allowed himself to be misled by deceitful persons into ways which he had not intended and situations which were not beseeming. It was only in 1788, when he was 77 years old, that he allowed Gericke to return and take over charge of the Mission. Even then he always liked to be in his place in the Church, and amidst all sufferings which his peculiarities brought upon himself and others, his friendly smile never forsook him until at last death closed his eyes. His faults are buried with him, but his memory lives and will live as long as his heartfelt hymns are sung, and they are sung, not by Lutheran congregations only, but as far as the Tamil tongue extends.

Gericke was already 46 years old and had labored for 21 years amidst the Tamulians, especially in Cuddalore and Negapatam, when he took over charge of the Mission in Madras. He remained the head of it, until his death, for fifteen years. He was a faithful and industrious workman and beloved by all. In Madras as in Tranquebar there was a Portuguese as well as a Tamil congregation to both of which Gericke preached, and as the English also wished to hear him he preached to them also in the evenings. Naturally with this distribution of energies the Tamil congregation suffered and did not increase; the Portuguese community, however, did. During the first 21 years of his Missionary life, Gericke had to travel about a great deal and had been continually troubled by the horrors of war, and so it remained till his death. It is true that at this time there was no war and his head-quarters remained at Madras, but still he had to undertake long journeys. In this way he visited Negapatam, which though only 18 miles from Tranquebar is some 200 miles from Madras. He even went as far as Tinnevelly and during one journey baptized there over 1,000 heathens and thus greatly strengthened what the late Reverend Schwartz had begun at the now-so-prosperous Tinnevelly Mission. He also frequently travelled to Vellore some 80 miles from Madras, for Vellore was a garrison in which there were British troops. But in spite of these long journeys he did good work in Madras and earned there much love. His chief work seems to have been amongst the Europeans and Portuguese, *i. e.*, half castes. From his last journey to Vellore he never returned. His palanquin was ready for a start at night but he did not feel well. Then he said to his servant—*Nân pogirèn*—I am going. 'But you are too weak' replied the servant. *Shumá iru; nân pogirèn.*—Be quiet, I am going! and so he went into the joy of his Lord. The grief at his death was universal and, though the distance was so great, his body was brought to Madras and buried there with many honors. About four thousand persons of all classes followed his coffin both heathens and Christians, and many wept. His private fortune he bequeathed to the Mission, and during the troubled days that ensued, this was its chief support.

When the brethren in Tranquebar heard that Gericke had gone home, they sent Missionary Rottler to Madras and soon afterwards Missionary Paezold who had previously worked with Gericke in Madras for a short time returned from Calcutta. Dr. Rottler was preferred by the English and received the appointments held by the deceased Gericke. Paezold took charge of the Tamil congregation in Vepery. Neither, however, possessed the ability of the former Missionaries and became more and more dependent upon the English society. Indeed, what could they do? There was no prospect of any more German Missionaries; and Tranquebar itself was nearly dying out. Dr. Rottler also allowed himself to be used as a means of drawing over the congregations; but when the stern churchman Bishop Middleton was not ashamed to offer the 70 years old Dr. Rottler re-ordination, then Rottler perceived that he had gone too far; but it was then too late. In 1816 the Bishop issued instructions direct to Missionary Paezold, who had no longer the energy to oppose this unauthorized interference. In the following year Paezold died and now Lutheran Catechism and Liturgy began to be continually edged out as, indeed, was only to be expected. A committee over which the Bishop presided was formed, which, in the name of the English Society which had hitherto paid the salaries of the German Missionaries in Madras, without, however, defraying the station expenses—took possession of the Mission property and the control of the congregations passed over into its hands.

From this time Missionaries of the Gospel Propagation Society, the inheritors of the Christian Knowledge Society were sent out to the congregation; Missionaries who displayed plenty of honest zeal, but only little knowledge of the peculiar circumstances of the people. Besides this many an evil had crept in which could not be borne. The only way to abolish them, however, was by evangelical and not by arbitrary measures. For many years there was much heartburning and many disputes, and the end was that the most influential of the community separated themselves entirely from the Mission, and appointed their own Catechist, who held service for them and buried their dead in a newly purchased ground. These people were, of course, denounced as baptized heathens, with whom no Missionary would have anything to do; but this they contradicted every Sunday by their Christian worship at which manuscript sermons of the late Fabricius were read, and from day to day their conduct proved, that they had not degenerated into heathenism, but remained Christians, though feeble and weak. When, however, the Mission in Tranquebar again revived, this congregation at once turned to the quarter from whence the Gospel had first of all come to them, and from which Missionaries had been sent who had faithfully ministered to them for 100 years.

The brethren in Tranquebar would not have been Lutheran Missionaries if they could have left the prayer of these poor people unheard. They set, however, cautiously to work, and first of all sent a Missionary to enquire into all the circumstances and to report to them. This, of course, excited the indignation of the abovenamed Society led on by the Bishop, and they gave vent to it in the public papers. One amongst them, at least, was a sensible man and had pity upon them. This was the late Rev. Brotherton, who, only three years ago in Tinnevelly, fell asleep in the Lord. He made no disguise of his wish that the congregation in Madras should be given to the charge of the Tranquebar Missionaries, so that it might not be entirely neglected and perhaps forced to fall away altogether.

In 1848, the connection with Tranquebar and the reception into the Lutheran Church was at last effected, but under conditions which necessitated considerable discussion. The hardest of these conditions was that the congregation should provide for its own wants. Hitherto the Tamil Christians had believed in nothing so firmly as that the first duty of a Missionary was to provide not only for Church and school requirements, but also to maintain and protect the poor. Under the Danish Royal instructions the Missionaries were prohibited from taking anything from the converted heathen, which rule, as in the commencement most of them were very poor, not unnaturally extended also to the requirements of the congregation. The Missionaries, therefore, were compelled to bear all the costs themselves. The out-stations being only copies of the principal one at Tranquebar, it became a rule everywhere that the Gospel should be preached free to the heathens. No wonder then that the congregation at Vepery were taken aback when it was made a condition that they should provide for their own requirements; as, however, they already had been for two years separated from the English Mission, and had during that time borne all such costs, and as their position could not remain a permanent one, they at last consented and agreed to accept the conditions.

There were still some 400 souls who had held out so long, and to these the Reverend Kremmer was sent as pastor. Great was the joy that they at last had another German Missionary among them who was ready with German love and humility to serve and care for the least among them. At the first celebration of the Lord's Supper there were 90 communicants which was a larger number than that often communicated in Gericke's time. Their numbers also increased by new additions, and everything seemed to go according to their best wishes. As in the olden time the congregation again had a German Missionary to minister to them with the Word and the Sacraments and to regulate their ordinary conditions.

But the Kingdom of God is not to be built up without fighting and quarrelling. Many of the people thought that it was sufficient if the Missionary preached to them, administered the Sacraments and looked after and managed the schools, and that he had no business to trouble himself with their domestic life. But because he did so trouble himself and where he discovered sins which called for repentance, anger and passion was excited which led at last to a separation. Some 60 souls formed themselves into a kind of rival congregation andalsoheld a service. As, however, they could not be received back again unless they repented and confessed their error, and as this was just what they were not willing to do, they turned to the Bishop and to the same society from which they had been so long separated. And the Bishop? He received them at once and it was proclaimed in the papers how great a victory had been gained. This victory was not, however, of much importance for most of the people returned penitent, and the Vepery congregation which now resided and held its services in the adjacent Pursewaulkum, continued to increase and to prosper.

For a long time the congregation had to meet for worship

very hot especially for the Missionary. After eight years, however, on 6th December 1856, a new Church, for which the people had longed, was consecrated. The building was done by one of the elders of the congregation, and thus an edifice arose which certainly would not satisfy the lover of strict Church architecture. In the interior, however, it is roomy enough, it is light and is easy to preach in. The congregation, therefore, is no longer in want of a room wherein to assemble, nor of the Word of God when they have assembled. The simple elementary school has also been raised, so that English instruction is given in addition to Tamil, and several teachers have their time fully employed.

The congregation in Madras has grown from the 400 souls which it numbered in 1848 to 1,200 and so is of about the same size as it was in the time of Fabricius. As, however, they no longer live in one place but are scattered some as far as St. Thomas' Mount (where the Apostle Thomas is said to have found a Martyr's death—situated some ten miles from the Church in Pursewaulkum) the Rev. Kremmer has ample to do. One of the younger Missioneries is generally appointed to assist him, who especially looks after the school and the distant stations, for joined to the Madras station is that of Sadras a 12 hours' journey distant from Madras.

The congregation continues to provide for its own wants, and Mr. Kremmer does not neglect to keep them up to their duty. Most of the new converts from the heathens are, however, either unable to assist or are themselves in want of assistance and the task, therefore, does not grow lighter but heavier with time, and the Mission hitherto has had to assist: and unless some rich converts come over who are prepared to spend their fortunes in endowing the Church, it is probable that the Mission will have to assist still further, for the property which the German Missionaries collected and bequeathed remains, of course, together with the Churches and buildings in the hands of the English Society. Were it still in our hands it would be ample to cover all the expenses of Church and school. As it is, help from home is always required for Madras, but surely no money from home could be better spent than in spreading the Gospel among the heathens and in the upkeep of the in a native house, which was not only too small, but also means of grace amongst these poor Christians. May the Lord bless the congregation at Madras with all needful gifts so that it may fulfil its calling as a congregation of the Lord!

Cuddalore.

About 120 miles south of Madras two rivers flow into the sea at but little distance from each other. The one is called Gadalam and is said to be derived from Garuda-nadi or the Garuda river. Garuda is the name of the bird sacred to Vishnoo upon which he sometimes is represented as riding. One day in his travels, Vishnoo came to Tiroovandipuram, a holy Brahmin's Settlement, 5 miles from Cuddalore, by the side of Mount Capper. The god was very thirsty; in his extremity he applied to the snake that was dedicated to him, but the poor worm did not know how to help his godship. He then applied to his faithful Garuda who opened his mouth from which a stream of water poured forth, which continues flowing to this day and is, therefore, called the Garuda-nadi. The other river rises in the uplands of Mysore 220 miles from Cuddalore; it is called the Pennar and is even more holy than the Gadalam. Every day Brahmins are to be seen, men and women, who wade through the Gadalam, walk a mile further and then perform their ablutions in the Pennar and carry from it their drinking water in brightly burnished copper vessels. The idols, too, are carried to be bathed in the Pennar. They say that the water of the Pennar is more wholesome, but the probable reason is that the Sivaites—of which sect there are the most Brahmins here, will have nothing to do with Vishnoo's river. Over both rivers there are large anicuts built of stone to damm up the floods which during the monsoon rush down in large volumes, and from which the water is led off by thousands of channels far away into the interior, in order to irrigate the rice fields. There is besides near Cuddalore a tank many miles in circumference, which holds water the whole year round and distributes it to the rice fields far away. In this way the neighbourhood of Cuddalore is very fertile and yields two and sometimes three crops in the year. The rice fields form level plains divided into fields of large squares each about a quarter of an acre in size, in order each to be able to retain the water; and the eye never wearies at gazing on the wonderful green of the young crop, and at the waving golden colored ears of the ripening fields. The monotony of such a view is varied by groves of waving palm trees. These cocoanut palms, the most beautiful and the most useful trees of India, encircle the rice fields as a frame does a picture, and present to the eye of the wondering stranger an ever changing view varying in form and in extent, but always lovely. There are, I doubt, few other places in India which are so well calculated to remind one of the Fairy Island, Ceylon. In fact the whole district or collectorate of Cuddalore, or, as it is termed South Arcot, is a very interesting one. The country is watered not only by rivers, but also by large tanks. One of these is so large that it contains 12 square miles and pours forth its water from 18 sluices, so that it irrigates 22,000 acres of land and produces for the Government a yearly revenue of Rupees 1,15,000. After the district of Tanjore, that of South Arcot is the richest, *i. e.*, the most fertile in the Tamil country. There are also in the district many objects of interest. Mighty ruins of former impregnable fortresses and large pagodas with columns tumbled down or still standing excite wonder. Large beds of fossils invite study, and a petrified forest in which by mere chance I found and measured trunks 50 feet in length, still offers an insoluble riddle since no one has been able to find out the name of the trees which here lie turned into stone. Besides thousands of small and moderately sized temples, there are two which are among the five holiest of the Tamulians and the largest in the world, viz., those of Chellundram and Tiroovanamalei. But the most important of all I have not yet named and that is a dark colored mass of human beings above one and a quarter millions who inhabit the district of Cuddalore. And this mass wanders from temple to temple in order to worship dumb idols.

In the middle of the 17th century the Mahrattas were masters of this district and had a Governor at Gingee (pronounce Ginjee). Gingee was so important a fortress that once when an English army marched against it, it marched back again to Madras at the mere sight of it (1752). To this day the ruins of the fort and the shatterred temples are wondered at, but human dwellings are sought for in vain in the once so powerful town. Wild jungle grows over all, and monkeys and other wild animals are the sole representatives of the former citizens of the fortress.

In 1684 the English East India Company received permission from the Mahratta Governor of Gingee to settle down at Cuddalore and build a fort. They built the fort on the left bank of the mouth of the Gadalam opposite the town of Cuddalore which lies on the south or southern side. To the north-west of the fort lies Manjacoopam and Poodoopollium with the suburb Samandalam as their boundary. Of the former Fort St. David there are now only a few just noticeable ruins. The French whose capital was at Pondicherry only 13 miles distant often besieged and sometimes took it. In one of these attacks the French retired so suddenly that they left their dead behind. General Wangenheim, a Hanoverian, was at the time Commandant of Cuddalore. After the attack had been repulsed he rode over the battle field and noticed among the dead a young French officer in whom he discerned signs of life. He had him carried to his house and carefully tended, so that he recovered and was subsequently exchanged. Many years afterwards when the French under Bernadotte entered Hanover, Bernadotte enquired after General Wangenheim who was presented to him. 'Do you remember,' he enquired of the General, 'that in the battle at Cuddalore you had a young French officer carried from the field and carefully nursed in your house?' 'Perfectly,' answered Wangenheim, "I have often since thought of the young man and wondered what had become of him." "The 'young man' stands before you, exclaimed Bernadotte, and thanks you for his life!" and the enemies embraced. But besides warriors, messengers of peace also came to Cuddalore. Even Ziegenbalg preached the Gospel in Cuddalore and under the large banians at Samandalam where our Church now stands. In 1717 Gründler also visited Cuddalore and started a Tamil and a Portuguese school, which in 1718 Ziegenbalg again visited. These schools, however, did not last very long. In 1726 Benjamin Schultze landed at Cuddalore on his way to Madras, and was received by the Governor and other officials in a friendly manner. He visited all the heathen schools of the town and preached in and around Cuddalore in many places. Amongst others he visited five native schools in 'Devipatnam' "situated to the north of Fort St. David;" which Schultze mentions as a populous place. Now not a single house remains standing though the name Devipatnam still exists. During the many sieges of the Fort St. David the town seems to have been burnt and destroyed. Two European houses now stand upon the site, but the rest is brought under the plough.

In 1737 Sartorius and Geister were sent from Madras to Cuddalore in order to found a station there. They, too, were kindly received by the English, and commenced their work. But in the next year the able Sartorius died and Geister was left alone until in 1740 Kiernander came to assist him. In the war troubles of 1746 Geister left the town which was besieged by the French, he went to Batavia and from there intended to go home, but on the way was called to his eternal home. Kiernander had remained quietly at his post awaiting better times, on his journey out he had distinguished himself by his quiet, reserved manner, and storms never deprived him of his composure, and this stood him in good stead at Cuddalore. For, when in 1745 he had baptized a youth of good family, and had sent him for further instruction to Tranquebar, the elder brother, Rungan, openly accused him to the Governor of having secretly enticed and kidnapped him. Not content with this he raised a regular tumult and came with several hundreds of his followers in front of Kiernander's door, where, amidst loud cries, he demanded that his brother should be restored and the baptism removed. Kiernander went out quietly to the mob, and said: 'I am very glad to see so many of you together, for I shall be the better able to preach the Gospel to all of you, and I trust you will prove attentive hearers.' 'No! No!' they shouted, 'we have not come to hear, but to get back Tirupully (the baptized youth) and we want this and that, and the other.' Kiernander then quietly explained to them that one brother was not necessarily the slave of the other, and had a perfect right to leave his brother and go elsewhere; that Tirupully, who was now called Isaac, had voluntarily gone to Tranquebar and that he valued his baptism too highly to suffer it to be again taken away from him. Upon this some were pacified and went away; others, however, remained and continued to make an uproar until at last they again went to the Governor. There, however, they got nothing until at last they tired even of shouting. Isaac eventually became an able Catechist, and served the Mission faithfully for many years.

In 1750 Hüttemann came to help Kiernander, but the

times were by no means quiet ones. The French besieged Cuddalore, and in 1758 took it. The Missionaries were allowed to retire with their property and many Christians followed them. Kiernander did not wish to remain idle and carried out the long-mooted plan of establishing a Mission in Bengal. For in Bengal through gratitude of the Great Mogul Shah Jehan, and after the Portuguese had been driven out, the English had obtained a firm footing. Both, however, the banishment of the Portuguese and the settlement of the English are events too important to be passed by without some mention. Shah Jehan's wife, the Empress Montaz Mahal, the same to whose memory her husband afterwards built the Taj Mahal, the greatest and the most costly Mausoleum in the world, was greatly displeased with the image-worship of the Portuguese, who even to this day carry it on as bad as the heathens; for the Empress was a strict observer of the Koran, and otherwise, in her fashion, pious and good. When the Governor of Bengal reported to the Emperor and complained that the Portuguese stole children and sent them to other places as slaves, the Emperor, under the advice of the Empress, sent him the curt answer, "Drive these idolaters out of my Empire!" Accordingly the Mahomedan Governor marched against the Portuguese, besieged them, and after 3½ months captured their fort on the Hooghly. The Portuguese had some 60 ships there, almost all of which were burnt. On the largest of these the Portuguese had laden their treasure, and in it some 2,000 people took refuge. The Captain of the ship, however, was like the others hard pressed, and when he saw that escape was impossible, he blew the ship into the air, with all its treasures, its living freight and himself also. Thus in 1633 ended the power of the Portuguese in the Hooghly. After some years it happened that the subsequently celebrated daughter of the Great Mogul, Jehanara approached too closely to a light and her clothes caught fire. She was saved, but was so badly burnt that the anxious father summoned all the most skilful physicians in his Empire, and promised to the one who should cure her the most splendid rewards. At this time the English had a Settlement in Surat, and as their physician enjoyed a good reputation for skill, he also was sent for. The Governor of Surat at once despatched Dr. Gabriel Broughton and he succeeded in curing the Princess. "Choose your reward!" exclaimed the thankful father to the Doctor, when he saw that his daughter was cured. Dr. Broughton, however, asked for nothing for himself, but all the more for a permission of free trade and a settlement for his company. The Emperor at once granted this request, and so in 1640, the English commenced to build on the Hooghly seven years after the Portuguese had been driven out though not through their agency. This was the origin of Calcutta. Thither Kiernander went and soon collected a numerous congregation consisting principally of the many European half castes. Under peculiar circumstances he also gained a considerable fortune which, however, he faithfully employed to the advantage of the Mission. At his own cost he built a Church which is said to have cost him 100,000 Rupees, and he also built a Mission house, &c. His attention was, however, for a time too much engaged in earthly matters. At last he lost all his fortune and died at the age of eighty-nine (1799) in poverty, but thanking God that he was freed from all the trammels of this world. His Church stands to this day, and is still called Kiernander's Church. The late Chaplain, Mr. L. whom I lately met, informed me that he, together with the Trustees, had made over the Church to the Church Missionary Society, in order to remove it from the innovations of the Ritualistic Bishop Milman of Calcutta, and to preserve for it a simple Evangelical worship. He also told me that Kiernander has descendants in Calcutta who are in good circumstances.

After two years Hüttemann returned to Cuddalore; in 1767 he received an able and faithful assistant in Gericke, and there followed some years of quiet work. But the life among the Europeans was a very godless one as may be gathered from some letters of Hüttemann's written to the authorities of Cuddalore a year before his death. These letters are preserved amongst the records at Cuddalore where I was furnished with copies of them. I will quote only a few passages. In October 1870, Hüttemann writes to Secretary Tallowfield:

"When I had the pleasure of seeing you last night, you were pleased to tell me that the Commandant and Council of this place desire me to officiate at the funerals of the soldiers. I took the liberty to tell you, that if I received no addition to my small pay of 5 Pagodas, I would consider it beneath the dignity of my clerical office to have more burden put on me—and this the more as it is well known that the physician of the Hospital or the Commanding Officer receives the pay thereto appointed, and it would be a crying injustice to require of any man the service and allow another one to put the pay for it into his pocket. And besides this, the Burial Service is specially adapted for the use of the living, but at the funerals of the soldiers there is no one present, and the Clergyman must appear in the ridiculous sight of a papistical sorcerer, who blasphemically pretends to help by his acts the defunct into heaven. But if a man has lived in sin, if he has by an ungodly life made himself unworthy of happiness, then no prayers after death will avail him anything. His case is sealed for all eternity, even if the whole world could be given for the redemption of his soul. As a Missionary I am not obliged to read the English Liturgy and to preach. And if I were to bury soldiers, how am I to get there? (the distance was about three miles); shall a man of my age walk a foot and expose his life and his health to the tropical sun without any reason whatever? And besides this to inhale the pestilential effluvias of the dead bodies, which are mostly covered by veneric ulcers and are carried about without a coffin,—in spite of the regulation that requires it—only covered by a miserable piece of cloth, a dreadful sight for a European. After the Government has obtained such large territorial possessions, it appears but their duty to support a proper number of Chaplains, to teach the people the principles of the Protestant religion and of morality, without which no Government can exist, but must at once sink down into a hateful band of assassins and rogues, a band in which the most crying injustices are committed; a band, which must be considered as an open conspiracy against the God of heaven and the Father of all men, to put down his reasonable creatures into slavery and to the level of brute cattle and hurtful pavians, &c., &c."

Of course, Hüttemann received no redress from such letters as the foregoing, but nevertheless, he expressed himself willing to conduct the burials. But the eagles of war soon collected to devour these carcases. The French as well as Hyder Ali marched down from Mysore, devastated the country and besieged Cuddalore. Famine and disease soon made their appearance, and in the midst of these pressures Hüttemann died. Soon afterwards Cuddalore fell into the hands of the French. Gericke writes thus: "An English prisoner of war is about to be sent to France, and I seize the opportunity to inform you in haste that since the 3rd of April Cuddalore has been in the hands of the French. Since then it has pleased God to make us still less than we were before. Only two of the native school children remain, the rest are all dead. An epidemic fever carried off one-third of our congregation whilst I was lying, as I thought, on my death-bed, suffering from the same disease. As soon as the town was captured, our Church was converted into a Powder Magazine; we now hold our Tamil Service in the school and the Portuguese one in my house, where I also continue to hold English Service. Besides my own family there are many English prisoners of war here who attend Service. The houses in which the late Mr. Hüttemann lived have been occupied by the French, otherwise the officers have been very friendly towards me. General Dulchemin received me most kindly when I went to visit him in his camp before the town was captured. Hyder Ali wished to get the town as much as the Frenchmen did, and they say that it is due to my intercession that we did not fall into the hands of that tyrant. The French have always received my requests for others favorably, especially in behalf of English captives, and have helped where it was possible to do so. Admiral Suffrein sent me a very kind answer to my letter, and the Governor in Cuddalore seems to be always glad when he can meet my wishes. At the same time we are in a very disagreeable position. Prices are rising, and the whole country has been turned into a wilderness, at least three-fourths of the inhabitants have fallen by sword, hunger, and disease! I have heard nothing of my brethren and friends in Madras and very little from Tranquebar. The distress is so great everywhere that it seems best to continue my work here; God has guarded us wonderfully hitherto and will do so in the time to come. The time is one of suffering."

Gericke, however, was not able to remain in Cuddalore, but went from place to place for some time. He remained chiefly in Negapatam and at last came to Madras in 1788 in order to relieve Fabricius. Cuddalore was looked after by a native Catechist and occasionally visited by Gericke, until at the commencement of this century, Missionary Holzberg was sent there, who remained in Cuddalore until his death in 1824. Missionary Rosen succeeded him until 1829, and after him Cuddalore was supplied with English Missionaries.

The old Mission at Cuddalore did not prosper better in English than in German hands, and had not the German Missionaries bequeathed to the Mission a property of rice fields, palm trees and buildings, it would have been long ago given up. As it is, however, the various sources of income of the Mission are amply sufficient to meet the expenses of the small station with its 160 souls, especially as it is only presided over by an ordained native.

As in most of the other Missionary Settlements of our forefathers, the Mission in Cuddalore was again revived in our time. The older of the native Christians remembered the German Missionaries and loved the quiet and familiar way in which they held intercourse with the people.

In the years 1853-54 several of the old Christians who had come originally from Tranquebar turned to us, and were received by the Rev. Kremmer on a journey from Madras to Tranquebar; and in the village of Tuknambakam several heathens received instruction and baptism from the same Missionary. At the commencement of 1856 Cuddalore was formed into an independant station and named Sadras—Cuddalore. In Sadras a number of Christians had been collected from among the heathens and the Papists, and in 1854, the Rev. E. R. Baierlein had taken up his residence in that dreary place. Whilst he was studying the language, he also built a little Church, since the Christians whose number was increasing could only assemble in the verandah of his house for Divine Worship. The Church was built out of the old bricks of the house of the former Dutch Governor, and the site was given to the Missionary by an English official personally unknown to him. In July 1855, the Church was consecrated, and Mr. Baierlein preached his first Tamil sermon in the Church he had built.

The new Church had not cost much money, but it had cost the Missionary his health, for he had worked at the language and the building harder than a tropical climate permits. The seed of disease had been sown, and on a journey through a hot jungle he was attacked with sunstroke, so that he barely escaped with life. Instead of being able to take charge of his new station, Cuddalore at the beginning of the year, he was obliged, accompanied by another Missionary, to travel to the Neilgherries and was not able to return to his post before the end of the year, nor to take up his residence in Cuddalore before March 1857.

'The beginning of all things is difficult,' says a German proverb, and this was the case in Cuddalore. The reception by the Collector, the Regent of the district was stiff and formal; for he did not care to have Missionaries in his District, much less in his vicinity. The English Chaplain, however, said candidly to the Missionary, "I don't know whether I can extend to you the right hand of fellowship; for you have probably come to overturn our (English) Mission." What answer could be given? Mr. Baierlein expressed his pleasure at this candour and said, "allow me to give you the same answer, as under similar circumstances, I was in the habit of giving to the wild Indians of North America." "Which was?" he asked—"It was this: wait and see!" This answer rather took the old gentleman aback, but he was obliged to take the advice, and subsequently became a good friend of the Missionary.

In order even to avoid the appearance of angling after the small remnant of the old, now English, Mission, the Missionary rented a house in the new town, three English miles distant from the old town, and went quietly to work. The times, however, were by no means quiet ones; for one evening the Magistrate sent him a sword, a pistol, and a rifle with bayonet and cartouche box full of ammunition. These were strange weapons for a Missionary. But it was in the year 1857, when the rebels of North India were taking town after town, and were cruelly murdering European communities one after another; men, women and children, for they aimed at exterminating all Europeans in India. The rebellion, however, did not extend so far south and the weapons were not used.

The Magistrate was also desirous that the Missionary should not make use of his other weapons; his spiritual ones, for as he saw that the Missionary was frequently preaching here and there, he let him know in a friendly manner that in these unquiet times he should be especially careful not to give the people a cause for uneasiness. Nor did the Missionary act contrary to his wishes; but when the country again became quiet, he travelled from one end of the large district to the other and preached everywhere the name of the Lord Jesus; especially he was fond of preaching in front of the temples, and often to large crowds, of the living God who cannot be shut in temples nor can be served by oiling of idolatrous stones.

By the grace of God the flock soon increased, and with it the school, so that it became necessary to obtain a piece of ground. Though it was possible to provide for the school there was still no suitable place for worship, nor was there a spot where the dead could be buried. The Catechist buried them secretly, before dawn, in an old Military Churchyard. This, however, could not go on in this way. The Missionary tried on all sides to find a piece of suitable ground, but heathens and Papists were against him, and would not allow him to purchase a small piece even at a large price, supposing he had had it to give them; and the English though not opposed were not anxious to help him. Wherever he looked it was in vain. At last weary of seeking, and despairing of finding, he came one day to Samandalam a suburb of Cuddalore, which is mentioned by Ziegenbalg in his reports, and there found a piece of jungle, full of thorns and thick bushes. For this piece of ground he applied to the authorities and obtained it. He at once commenced to fell the wood and to build some mud walls for a dwelling. A thatched roof was soon put on and during Easter of 1859 he occupied his new house, and at Christmas of the same year he was able to consecrate his stone built Church, built beneath the old banian trees where Ziegenbalg had preached. For a change had come over the scene. The English at first mistrustful had become friendly, and when for six months they had no Chaplain, they requested the Missionary to hold service for them on Sunday evenings. This was done, and in gratitude for this service they helped him to build his Church. Two years before, it was with the greatest difficulty that he had been able to hire a house, and even when a house stood empty it was refused to him. To the living no shelter was allowed, and to the dead no resting place. So narrow is this wide world sometimes. But now within two years he had a house and Church and space enough to spread further. Thus the Lord helped, and in the course of time he helped still further; the mud hut grew into a substantial firm dwelling, and the Church received a steeple with a bell and a harmonium.

The living stones also were not wanting, and together with the heathens, Papists also came and allowed themselves to be taught and received in our Church. The latter have to be instructed exactly the same as heathens, and it is often impossible to avoid accepting them as they live in the midst of our Christians, and if we did not, nobody else would trouble himself about them. They are in the habit of going to their distant Church only once in the year, and many of them had not gone for many years. Their instruction and reception is, therefore, a sort of kindness. It, however, seldom meets with a reward and Catechumens from the heathens afford generally more pleasure than those from Roman Catholicism. Their ignorance is just as great and their superstition finds plenty of nourishment in the outward pomp and show of the Popish Church. But still the truth of the Gospel, which they often hear with great joy and receive with apparent willingness, will not be entirely lost on them.

Outside Cuddalore and in a region where it had been least of all expected, the Lord opened a door. From the district round the large pagoda town of Chellumbram the heathens came singly and in groups of 40 and 50 to be instructed and baptized. This work was a joyful one, for as they were willing hearers of the Word, it often fell upon good ground and took root. In course of time they came from thirty villages. Mission work, however, is a work of fighting and struggling, when the Catechumens returned to their villages as Christians they had many things to suffer. The heathens mocked and hated and oppressed them, and they had many wants which they had not before. Especially they wanted a burial ground, for our Christians attach much importance to a decent burial, and it is a commendable feeling which should not be suppressed. Then they also wanted ground on which to build a school and here and there a mud church, for buildings cannot be erected in the air. The heathens, however, were resolved not to let us get a firm footing anywhere. In one village they boasted loudly, that even if seven Collectors should come there, they would not let us have a hand's breadth of land, and they had some reason for this, for the whole of the country consisted of rice fields and there was but little dry land suitable for building available and it was also extremely unlikely that a Collector would ever come into this remote region. The Missionary, however, had promised his Christians a visit, and as there was nowhere any shelter for him, they erected a hut of leaves. The Munsif was a very proud man, being descended from a high but impoverished family; indeed the Christians begged the Missionary not to go there as they feared that the proud heathens would send him away mocked and laughed at. Thus warned, he prayed for help from above and his prayer was answered. The village is some 36 miles or more distant from Cuddalore. During the night he travelled 26 miles in his bullock coach, as far as Chellumbram, spoke to his Christians there and then started before dawn with a Christian as guide; he rode 10 miles before sunrise, and when it arose had reached the village. Arrived there he sent a message to the haughty Munsif that he would be glad to speak to him. He allowed himself to be waited for, and then sent the village writer and the village Curnam in front of him. At last he himself arrived walking as slowly and majestically as a North American Indian chief. The Missionary commenced an earnest but friendly conversation and remained in the village 4 hours, and by the time the sun had got hot, and the Missionary had to start to ride 6 miles to the nearest shelter, the old gentleman had become so friendly that he accompanied him for more than a mile, caused him to be carried by his people through a deep channel, whilst he waded through by his side and at last only returned after repeated solicitations. He is reported to have said to the villagers that he would not move another finger against the Missionary, and he kept his word. The Missionary received two pieces of ground instead of one and built his Church of mud in peace. In this manner the Lord gave us many a conquest in that district. In 1866 Chellumbram and the neighbourhood with 500 Christians was converted into an independent station and entrusted to the Rev. Wolff who now resides there. Sadras had also been previously detached from Cuddalore, and again added to Madras, since from thence it can be reached by Canal in a night whereas it is a 4 days' journey from Cuddalore.

Cuddalore, therefore, again became a small station with only about 200 Christians. Since then fresh doors have been opened 40 miles to the north and 17 miles to the south, so that the number of Christians who belong to Cuddalore has again risen to 400. The Church Register opened by the Missionary in 1857 showed, until the end of 1870, 988 of whom 700 were baptized from the heathens, about 200 Papists, who came for instruction and were admitted, the remainder being baptisms of Christian children. The care and the trouble spent in the erection of this new station has not, therefore, been spent in vain, for in less than 13 years nine hundred heathens and Papists have been collected together. Though, in proportion to our wishes, this is only a small number, still it is large when compared with the general results of these last sorrowful times. Mission work is a work for eternity. It is true that godliness has the promise of this life and of that hereafter; it is true that the outward temporal life of the Christians is very different to that of those who live without God; it is true that joy in the Lord is the strengthening of life here, and the consolation of everlasting life does not suffer even the most bitter sorrow of earth to penetrate to the inmost depth of the soul; true it also is that a man who has seen Naples may yet in spite of Goethe's dictum, be unhappy. But a Christian who has known the Lord and has Him in his heart never can be. Still the joy in the Lord *here*, and bliss in Him is something small and insignificant; *there*, in the light of the eternal sun, of the Lord himself, *there* only will it be clear and visible, how much, how inexpressibly much has been won by the salvation of one single soul. And if the angels in heaven, who live in eternal joy, are yet able to rejoice over *one* sinner that repenteth, how much more shall we be able to rejoice over the hundreds who have turned from darkness to light, from their dead idols to the living God! May the blessing of the Lord rest upon, and His saving love preserve our station of Cuddalore now and in the future, and whoever loves Him let him answer—*Amen*.

Trichinopoly.

Trichinopoly is situated in a dry region though not far distant from the Cauvery. It receives on the average 10 inches less rain during the year than Madras, and during the hot months the heat is on the average 4 degrees (Fahrenheit) greater. In the cooler seasons, however, the nights are much colder than at Madras or indeed anywhere on the coast. In the middle of the town is a rock rising some 330 feet above it, from which there is an extensive view over the whole country. Of course, as it is in the land of the Tamulians, a pagoda is built on the top of the rock, another larger one is situated half-way up, and at the foot of the rock there is a fine large tank provided on all sides with granite steps. The whole has a very pleasant appearance, and the houses of East Indians form the façade of the square. These houses, however, are uncomfortably hot, for the rock warmed by the rays of the sun reflects considerable heat. Some years ago so great a crowd of worshippers attended the feast of Ganésa, whose temple is on the top of the rock, that a serious accident occurred. Thousands of persons were thronging up the steep granite steps, when for some unaccountable reason a panic occurred amongst those who were on the top. They rushed back, and in their turn forced back others, and before those at the bottom of the rock could learn what had occurred, 500 persons had been trampled to death, and since then the Police keep the crowds in order. Trichinopoly has a central situation and in it meet all the roads from north, south, east and west; the trade carried on is, therefore, considerable. It is no wonder then that in the struggles between the French and the English for the sovereignty of Southern India, Trichinopoly soon became a central point. At first it belonged to the King of Tanjore, but it was wrested from him during the first half of the 15th century by Visavanada Naick, the King of Madura and converted into a fortress, which subsequently caused the destruction of the kingdom of Tanjore. The Madura Kings, however, did not hold it long but soon lost it to the Mahomedans, and the cause, strange to say, seems to have been a slipper. As an emblem of his authority the Mahomedan Governor of Arcot was in the habit periodically of sending round to the tributary States a slipper, supposed to belong to the Padishah, or great Mogul, and to which, carried in State upon an elephant, every tributary Prince was expected to do homage, to meet the slipper on the borders of his territory; and to conduct it in State to his capital. This slipper was sent to the Rajah at Trichinopoly, Ranga Kistna Naicker. He seems, however, to have been too proud to perform the required homage and not strong enough to resist it, and, therefore, like an Indian he had recourse to stratagem. By excuse of illness, he failed to meet the slipper on the borders of his kingdom, and by continued excuses and promises eventually got the ambassadors and the slipper into his Palace. Arrived there the Padishah's envoys expected that their slipper would be worshipped, but the courageous Tamil King requested them to place it on the floor. They, unaccustomed to such usage, declined. "What! said the King, bring sticks and tell them to place the slipper on the floor, and then we will see." Frightened, the ambassadors obeyed, upon which the King put his foot into the slipper and then exclaimed: what does your King mean by sending only one slipper; does he think that we have only one leg? Go back to your country and fetch the other slipper! whereupon the ambassadors were beaten and sent away in disgrace. The King who thus dared to set the Mahomedans at defiance died in 1707. The sovereignty of the Padishah, as the manuscript terms him, had probably been imposed before and the incident thus related probably refers to the shaking off of the hated yoke by a Prince more powerful than his predecessors. After the death of this King the Mahomedans again invested Trichinopoly for which they would seem to have had a great affection, since a large number of them settled down in it and have imparted to the town more of a Mussulman than a Hindoo appearance. But even whilst the town and neighbourhood belonged to and was occupied by a Nabob, there was an English garrison there, where it has continued to the present day.

In the year 1760 a movement took place in Trichinopoly originated by a native soldier named Setianaden, who had been converted by the writings of the Tranquebar Missionaries. In consequence of this movement, in the following year, first Missionary Dame travelled there from Tranquebar, visiting on the way the small congregation which had been collected at Tanjore by the German Captain Berg and ministering to them with Word and Sacrament. In the same way, in May 1762, Chr. Fr. Schwatz went to Trichinopoly accompanied by Missionary Klein, and as they found more work than they had expected, Schwatz remained there, Klein returning to Tranquebar alone. Schwatz had already served for eleven years in Tranquebar where he had become the favorite of every one. His quiet, cheerful disposition and his gift of always speaking the truth in love, proved of good service to him in Trichinopoly, and he soon had not only a small Tamil and Portuguese community, but had also to preach to the English garrison. The brethren in Tranquebar had given their consent to Schwartz remaining in Trichinopoly, for there were then five other Missionaries in Tranquebar. Even the Danish Mission College subsequently gave their consent, and continued to pay to Schwartz his salary, although he also received a stipend from the English Society for his services in Trichinopoly. And as the English never like to be served for nothing, he also received a third stipend as garrison preacher. But the more he received, the less he spent upon himself, for he was and remained unmarried and was contented with little. The Danish Mission College not only loved him, but also praised him highly almost because for some time he had sent no reports.

Schwartz, therefore, was Missionary at Trichinopoly and soon built a Church towards which the English residents contributed about 7,000 Rupees. Here he preached on Sundays from 8 to 10 in Tamil, from 10 to 12 in English and in the afternoon in Portuguese. In addition he also made frequent journeys to Tanjore and wherever his calling summoned him. In 1777, Schwartz handed over the station of Trichinopoly with 400 Christians to Missionary Pohle, who like Schwartz had come with the consent of the Missionaries from Tranquebar to Trichinopoly. But what had been praised in Schwartz was strongly censured in Pohle, and he was ordered at once to leave Trichinopoly and return to Tranquebar, or else to return the cost of his outfit and passage. At that time there were six Missionaries, so that there was probably rather a want of work than of workmen. In addition Schwartz had already left Trichinopoly and had settled down in Tanjore. What then was the humble and pious Pohle with the 400 Christians he had received from Schwartz to do? Rather than forsake them, he resolved to return his outfit and passage money, and so he remained at his post for 40 years until the Lord called him not to Tranquebar, but to his eternal home.

After Pohle's death in 1818 the flock in Trichinopoly was but meagrely attended until in 1826 it came into Schreyvogel's hands. Schreyvogel had come to Tranquebar as Catechist in 1804 and after nine years' service had been ordained. After his ordination he continued to labor there for 13 years until he came to Trichinopoly. Then, however, the English Bishop and the newly arising English Missionary movement so influenced him that he accepted an Episcopal re-ordination, and went over entirely to the English Church. Of course he took his congregation with him. After his death in 1840 the congregation passed entirely over to the English, in whose hands, the longer it has remained, the less at home it has felt.

Ten years afterwards when our Mission in Tranquebar began to revive, many of these Christians began to long for their mother Church. It devolved upon our present Missionary J. M. N. Schwartz, the namesake of Chr. Fr. Schwartz to bring back into their Church many of these erring sheep. Of course at this there was a great outcry in the enemy's camp. Their mode of proceeding was, however, a peculiar one. To take over congregations and considerable Church property, collected by our German Missionaries after infinite labor and time, was to them right and proper enough; but that some few of these Christians should wish to return to their mother Church was unintelligible; it excited their displeasure, and so violent did they become that they made themselves heard in other quarters of the globe. Of course they made no mention of the Church property which they retained. It seems almost to be considered a crime to return to the Lutheran Church, or even to remain faithful to her to the end; but nevertheless what Pastor L. of the United Church in Silesia told me 25 years ago is true: "This is certain: the man who is logical in his Christianity must become a Lutheran!"

Trichinopoly has, therefore, again become a Lutheran Mission station though the town has not much to do with us, and contains but few of our Christians. On the other hand in the two districts into which the station is divided there live in 35 villages about 1,000 Christians of the Lutheran confession. Missionary Handmann was, until a short time ago, the Missionary at Trichinopoly. As assistants he had a native Pastor, twelve Catechists, ten Teachers and four other Mission servants. It may, therefore, be expected that the seed is plentifully sown among the heathens of the district, and may the Lord pour His rich blessing upon it! As there are Christians in so many places and as in each there are many congregated together, they have themselves the best opportunity of becoming to their heathen neighbours a light and the salt of the earth. It is, however, often very difficult to convince Tamil Christians that they themselves are under the greatest responsibility to the heathens around them, with whom they come in daily contact, and to whom they have so many opportunities of showing Christ by word and by deed. The Hindoos are in a perpetual state of stagnation, and though by means of Christianity individuals may be brought to life and action, yet they are apt to fall into a kind of Christianity according to custom; and at all events it is not less necessary with them than with others, to be continually urging them on to prayer and to their religious duties lest they should fall into slumber. Elsewhere it is perhaps not much better, but the heat of the tropics makes the universal evil of laziness still worse. The heathens of the Trichinopoly district seem besides to be as hard as the greater part of their soil is. May the merciful God pour out a rain upon this and other hardened heart soils! Missionary Handmann has commenced to build a Church aided by some of the officials and Officers who are not opposed to our Mission. May his successor (Missionary Kahl) soon succeed in finishing it and in filling it with honest citizens of Trichinopoly, citizens who, though their skins may be brown, have had their garments washed and made pure in the blood of the Lamb.

Since the above was written Missionary Kahl, one of our most promising young Missionaries, has received higher promotion than the mere independent charge of a Missionary station. He has been promoted to a better country where he has entered into the joy of his Lord, and has joined in His presence the faithful band of Missionaries who are singing the praises of the Lamb whose servants they were on earth.

Tanjore.

The kingdom of Tanjore is the heart and the noblest part of the whole of the land of the Tamulians. It embraces the Delta of the Cauvery: *i. e.*, the district where the Cauvery divides into many streams and overflows the country. In this well-watered region the streams of people from the north soon found it pleasant to dwell. Even before the Christian era this seems to have been a well regulated country, and though the people of Southern India are very different from those of the north they do not, even in those days, seem to have been far behind them in civilization. The kingdom of Tanjore has probably always only been a small kingdom although it extended some considerable distance to the north; but in the earliest times it recognized the advantages of its situation and knew how to profit by them. The question was how to raise the mighty mass of water from the bed of the river into channels on a higher level, and so distribute the water to the level fields on all sides. This has been done in days to which no date can be fixed, by a giant-work, by a dam built across the Cauvery out of hewn stone brought from a long distance.

This dam is over 1,000 feet long and 60 feet broad, is furnished with many sluices, and no one knows its age. The English have repaired and greatly strengthened it, they have also built a bridge over it and otherwise improved it. By means of this dam which for centuries has been able to bear up against the enormous floods which in the rainy season, come down the river, the water is raised so high that it can be carried to the most distant fields. This giant-work is assisted here and there by many smaller dams so that the water is always again and again dammed up. In this way a regular net work of channels is formed, and more than 2,000 bridges are necessary to keep the communication open. By these means above 670,000 acres of land are irrigated, and the amount of water required to keep up the necessary supply, especially at the commencement of the season, before the seed has grown so as to afford shade, and when the hot sun draws up in evaporation large quantities of the water spread over the fields, is about 2,200,000 cubic yards in every hour! Afterwards when the rice has grown to some height and casts a shade over the ground, less is required, and shortly before the harvest, none at all. On an average 26 million cubic yards of water are required every day for these fields, and from the time of sowing to the time of harvest, not less than 6,500 millions. There is, however, not merely one crop raised in the year, but on many fields two and sometimes three, each of which requires the same amount of water. What enormous structures, and what an amount of science is required to conduct these almost incredible masses of water so that each of the hundred thousands of fields has a sufficient supply; and not too much! For the seed dies from an over supply of water, equally as it does from a deficiency. Arrangements are, therefore, made not only to lead the water to the fields, but also to lead it off again in other low lying channels when there is too much. From this water, or rather from the fields which are covered with this water and produce rice, the Government receive a revenue of Rs. 3,920,032. In addition to this the Government receive from salt, spirits and other sources of revenue more than another million. The entire population of Tanjore is not quite two millions.

At the same time the kingdom, or as it is now termed the district of Tanjore, is much more lightly taxed than it was before. The Government lose annually in ground-rent about 700,000 Rupees which properly belong to it. The people, however, do not benefit by this, but a kind of middle men named Mirassidars. These are a species of landed proprietors who do not cultivate the land themselves, but rent it to the farmers. Into their pockets goes the surplus amount and they are the only persons who benefit by the light assessment. The farmers themselves have to pay very high taxes indeed to these go-betweens. As the latter have no other employment, and as idleness is the commencement of all vice, they are rich not only in money but also in crimes, and litigiousness is carried to such an excess among them that two District Courts of Sessions are required in Tanjore, whereas all other districts have only one.

It is considered 'good tone' amongst these people to have several law suits at once which have lasted, perhaps, for years. They secure English lawyers from Madras to whom they generally have to pay 2—3,000 Rupees only to get them to come. Travelling expenses and each day of detention forms an additional charge. Sometimes such a lawyer does not speak more than 100 words for his 2—3,000 Rupees, but it is a point of honor with these natives to get an English Lawyer. The Judges, in spite of their high pay Rupees 28,000 annually, are greatly plagued individuals for not only are the witnesses whom they have to hear, and whose depositions they have to write down in their own handwriting, generally purchased on either side, and perjured; but also the documents brought forward to support the perjured witness are in a great many cases forgeries. As long as this refers only to property and estate it can, perhaps, be borne, but when, as is often the case in every month the matter is one of life and body, and when upon such doubtful evidence a man may have to be sent to prison for many years, may have to be sentenced to penal servitude on the Andaman Islands for life, or may have to be doomed to the gallows; then the matter becomes a difficult one. Many of the Judges spend a sleepless night after having passed a sentence of death. In no country is it an easy thing to sentence two, three, and sometimes four or five or more persons to death, and so cut off their opportunities for repentance; but in India where some men become so nervous that they do not like to kill a mosquito that has stung them till the blood comes, the task is even a more difficult one. I know strong and healthy men, who, when passing sentence of death turn pale, and when it has been passed tremble in every limb.

Tanjore (literally Tandjávoor) is a regularly built and cleanly kept town, and contrasts favorably with the majority of Tamil towns. The suburbs are not so good in proportion. The town was once very strongly fortified, and deep moats and high walls are still to be seen, though in a state of decay. The royal palace is a very large building with many large open Courts and with so many passages, that, without a guide one might well be lost. Some of the wives of the last King still live in it but otherwise it is uninhabited, and creates a wierd and melancholy impression although it has been lately repaired. In one of the halls the Judge who was my companion ordered the gold embroidered cloths and the jewel-set-arms of the last King to be shown to me. The greater part of the Crown jewels have, of course, been taken possession of by the Government, but the Judge showed me several large chests filled with jewels worth many hundred thousand Rupees, which are the private property of the still living Royal wives. It is their private property but the keys of the boxes are in other hands! and this alas! cannot be otherwise. A whole suite of rooms were walled up, and I enquired if they were in a ruinous condition. Oh, no! answered the Judge, but no one has entered them since the last century. And why? I asked. When the town was captured the last time, the King did not wish that his wives should fall into the hands of his enemies, and those are the rooms in which he caused them all to be put to death. I asked no more questions.

The celebrated Pagoda situated by the side of the town, was also fortified. Near this Pagoda Schwartz built his first Church for English and Tamulians, and was not frightened of the noise or the hatred of the heathens. And he does not appear to have suffered from it, perhaps because it did not frighten him. This Church still stands and contains the celebrated monument (sculptured by Flaxman) which the father of the last King of Tanjore caused to be erected to the memory of Schwartz. Above the Altar is a large wooden tablet on which the Ten Commandments, the Creed and the Lord's Prayer are inscribed. The Church, however, is but seldom used now; for the congregation lives not in the town, but in the suburb, where Schwartz had already built a small Church for them, and near which he himself lived and died.

Chr. Fr. Schwartz is the founder of the Mission at Tanjore, as well as at Trichinopoly. In the year 1778 he came to Tanjore from Trichinopoly and remained there until his death. He lived and labored in Tanjore for nearly 20 years, although before he took up his residence here, he had already spent 28 years in India. There were, however, a good many Christians in Tanjore before Schwartz settled there, and he often visited them from Trichinopoly. Even before he had come to Trichinopoly there had been Christians in Tanjore, who for the most part had been collected by other Lutheran Christians from among the heathens and the Papists, for the Missionaries of Tranquebar were for a long time not permitted to come to Tanjore.

It seems to be God's peculiar pleasure to make use of insignificant instruments and to commence the extension of His Kingdom in a quiet and unobtrusive manner. The outward signs of power and influence in this world, not only do not further the still-working of the Spirit of God, but only too often stand in its way. In this way it was by means of a despised pariah, a subordinate officer in the army of the King of Tanjore that God chose to commence and to enlarge his work. This man was called Rajanaicken, and was by birth a Roman Catholic. He was very fond of reading and read all the palm leaves (for books were but rarities in those days) which the Catechists could give him. These palm leaves, however, contained for the most part legends of the Saints and of the miracles of Mary, all of which left Rajanaicken unmoved. But when he read of the Lord Jesus Christ and how he suffered and died for us, his young heart was fired, and he longed to read more. His craving remained long unsatisfied until at last a Roman begging Friar brought a little book without a title which contained the four Gospels and the Acts of the Apostles. This book had been given to the Friar by Benjamin Schultze at Tranquebar, and he had torn out the title page so that he should not be punished by his priests. Rajanaicken begged the Friar to give him this book, which he did, but with the caution that he should not show it to the priest. Rajanaicken read the little book with such delight, that he soon began to copy it, for fear it should be taken away from him. In this way he copied two of the Gospels on palm leaves until he became certain that the book would not be taken from him. What he read, as he himself said, poured oil upon his lamp of faith, so that the flame burnt high. From time to time he received other little books from Tranquebar, and at last joined the Missionaries altogether. He did not, however, come alone but brought with him two soldiers to receive fuller instruction and to be baptized. When Rajanaicken had reached from a knowledge of the Saints to a knowledge of the Saviour, he could not rest but felt himself compelled to publish to all the world where only the source of salvation and life, of peace and of joy was to be found. For this prophet's labor he, of course, received a prophet's reward, he was bitterly hated and persecuted, and especially by his former comrades in religion, who in spite of the many proofs of the good influence of his teaching, continued to prefer the Romish twilight to the bright light of the Gospel, and the heathen ceremonial service to the worship of God in spirit and in truth. Rajanaicken, however, rested content with the grace of God, he forsook the service of the King of Tanjore, and entered the service of the King of Heaven, whom he served as a Catechist with singular fidelity for upwards of 40 years, although in his last years subject to many weaknesses. In the year 1771 he fell asleep with the words of Stephen, "Lord Jesus receive my spirit," and entered into the joy of his Lord.

There was a Prince in Tanjore named Telungarajah who was favorably inclined towards Christianity, and with whom Missionary Schultze had already entered into correspondence. When Schultze was no longer in Tranquebar, this Prince invited Missionary Presier to visit him in Tanjore, and sent a carriage to bring him. Thus the first Lutheran Missionary came to Tanjore and preached the Gospel. The time of Tanjore, however, had not yet come, and the enmity of the heathens and mahomedans was too great.

In Schwartz's days things had changed. The King sent for him, and conversed with him for a long time. He put several questions to him regarding Christianity and permitted him to explain to him the whole plan of God's salvation for man. "How is it," asked the King, "that some Europeans will not worship images, whilst others, like the French and Portuguese do worship them?" "The worship of images is distinctly forbidden in the Bible," answered Schwartz, "but because the word of God is kept back from the people they fall into error and into idolatry." "How can they arrive at a knowledge of God," asked the King, and Schwartz answered: "God in His great mercy has revealed himself to men in a two-fold manner. First, through the works of the creation; the heavens, the earth, sun, moon, &c., by which He displays His great power, wisdom and goodness so that all these works are for our instruction. God reveals Himself daily to us in His care; everything that we eat and drink warns us to recognize Him and to worship Him in gratitude. The second means, that He has given us, by which to arrive at a knowledge of Him is His word. From this we are enabled to see with certainty what is necessary for our salvation, which we could not understand from a mere contemplation of the creation." Schwartz then asked for permission to explain the most important doctrines of the word of God, and on this being received he continued: "The chief doctrine is with reference to God and His honor. The word of God teaches that God is a spirit of infinite wisdom but without a corporeal form or material body, such as we have. It is, therefore, derogatory to His honor when men attempt to represent Him by an image. The word of God teaches us further that God is omniscient, holy, just, merciful and omnipresent. Judge for yourself whether it is possible to make an image to resemble Him! Is a figure of wood and stone which has neither holiness nor the power of doing anything a fitting representation of the all-powerful, holy and omniscient God? Is not the true God dishonored by such, and a knowledge of Him rendered difficult." After dwelling further upon this head Schwartz began to speak of the second point, of man's evil nature. He said, "a soul which fears God above all things, loves Him and trusts in Him, whose thoughts, wishes and cravings are all directed towards God, towards His honor and His praise," such a soul is pure and holy. But let us look within ourselves and we find that our inclinations and our cravings are all set upon earthly and carnal things. And from this we may be certain that our souls are not in a fit and proper state, that they do not please God and that they are wicked; and God's word further teaches us with reference to ourselves, what we ourselves feel to be the case. The third point, continued Schwartz, "is how we are saved from our misery of sin by our Saviour," and he then requested the King to be allowed to narrate to him a beautiful parable, contained in the word of God and which illustrates this doctrine. "Let me hear it" said the King, and thereupon Schwartz related the parable of the Prodigal son and explained it. He showed how we have fallen away from God and have become lost in mind, in will, in body and soul; that husks are the best reward to be expected from the service of sin and the devil; that we should allow ourselves not only on account of our own misery, but also on account of the rich mercy of God, to be induced to return to Him; and lastly, how always ready He is in His inexpressible mercy to receive those who turn to Him in heartfelt repentance. It was thus that Schwartz spoke to the King and to a number of his noblemen. After some refreshment had been brought to him, he continued: "We Christians are in the habit of thanking God for His mercies and of requesting Him to give us grace to employ the powers which we have gained by the enjoyment of the gifts He has bestowed on us in His service." The King then requested that Schwartz should pray. Accordingly in the midst of these heathens Schwartz prayed, and when the King added: "I have also heard that you are in the habit of singing," Schwartz sang to him the three first verses of the hymn in Tamil:

"My God I bring my heart to Thee,"

and then read out the remainder of the hymn to the end. The King was much satisfied and said that he had never heard such things from a European, of course because the majority of Europeans are in the habit of only showing their Christianity in Church or, perhaps, a little in their own households, but of keeping it carefully concealed from every body else. Schwartz was very graciously dismissed, and soon afterwards started back for Trichinopoly for he had only come to Tanjore for a visit. The King, however, said to Captain Berg, "it is my decided wish that that Schwartz should live more with me, so that I may have the advantage of his good advice." The Brahmins, however, knew how to counteract the King's wishes, and succeeded so well in their counsels to the King that they managed to get him confined in prison by the Trichinopoly Nabob for two years, from whence he was only unwillingly released at the intercession of the English.

When Schwartz had taken up his residence altogether at Tanjore, he often saw the King and conversed with him, but it never came to a conversion for the intrigues of the Brahmins and the King's own flesh were too strong for that. In 1787 he (Tolossi Rajah) died; when on his death-bed delivered over his adopted son to the care of Mr. Schwartz, saying, "this is not my son but yours." Schwartz, however, thought this responsibility too much for him. Had he undertaken it, and had he brought up the lad, of about ten years old, as a Christian, the future of the kingdom of Tanjore would very likely have been a different one. But Schwartz declined the responsibility, and upon his advice the boy was given in charge to the King's brother Rama Sami, who acted as Regent during the Prince's minority. As Regent he was at first friendly towards Schwartz and presented him with a village of an annual revenue of Rupees 1,000 for the maintenance of his schools. But he himself rather wanted to become King, and besides this he was urged on by corrupt Brahmins. His supporters, therefore, alleged that the old King when he died had not been in his right senses, the adoption was not valid, and his brother, who now called himself Ameer Singh was the rightful heir to the throne. The Governor of Madras sent an Official to investigate the whole matter. This gentleman went very cautiously to work; he selected twelve learned Brahmins, caused them to be separated from each other and then proposed to them the several questions—Schwartz also was present and translated the answers. Like a miracle it happened that the answers of all the twelve Sages were exactly alike and each was in favor of Ameer Singh's claims. The Regent, therefore, became King and the lad Serfojee was put aside. The fact, however, was that this conclave of Brahmins had been treated no better than the conclaves of Cardinals assembled to elect a Pope have been generally treated. The Brahmins had all been bribed and succeeded not only in throwing dust into the eyes of the Madras Government through their Official, but also into the eyes of Schwartz the guardian of the young

Prince. But though the deception was publicly known Ameer Singh still remained for many years on the throne, which, however, was no peaceful seat. Willingly he would have been entirely rid of the young Prince Serfojee, but Schwartz protected the boy that had been entrusted to him, and when he found that Tanjore was no longer a safe place for him, he took him with a military escort to Madras. Schwartz remained in Madras for a year and Ameer Singh would have liked nothing better than that he should have never returned. He did return, however, quite safe and sound, and brought the young Missionary Paetzold with him who was learning the language under his tuition. Paetzold has described the pleasure with which the King saw the return of the aged Schwartz. "Whilst Mr. Schwartz was in Madras the superstitious King collected a lot of prophets and magicians and asked them to state whether he would return safe from his journey to Tanjore again, or whether he would die on the way. The prophets employed all their art and then told the King 'that the old Padre would not return alive but would be drowned in a river.' Upon this the King caused considerable presents to be given to them. But it was not long before our dear old Padre returned safe and sound. But when Herod saw that he had been cheated by his wise men he got very angry. If the mad, wild, cruel and ignorant man, called the King of Tanjore could or dared (as for his life he would like,) he would kill Mr. Schwartz to-day rather than to-morrow. He is Mr. Schwartz's determined enemy. If any body would only get rid of him, this tiger would make the murderer the richest of men or perhaps his Prime Minister. Mr. Schwartz has, therefore, a military guard in his garden." This blind hatred did not improve the King's situation, and even before Schwartz's death he was deposed and Serfojee was raised to the throne.

As Mr. Schwartz had in Trichinopoly to minister to the English so he had also to do in Tanjore, and had much to do with political matters. The story of his embassy to Hyder Ali is well known. Mr. Higginbotham in his valuable book, 'Men whom India has Known,' says that Hyder wrote to the English Government: "Do not send to me any of your agents, for I do not trust their words or their treaties; but if you wish me to listen to your proposals, send to me the Missionary of whose character I hear so much from every one; him I will receive and trust." Schwartz only accepted the appointment after hesitation. Hyder received Schwartz with great cordiality, and apparently arrived at an understanding with him though what that understanding was remains a mystery. The treaty, however, whatever may have been its form, was not effected. A bag of Rs. 300 which was placed in Schwartz's palankin as he was leaving, this honest ambassador of God and man would not at first accept, and only eventually did so when Hyder's officers informed him that it was as much as their heads were worth to take it back to their master again. Schwartz took it but only to give it to the Government of Madras on his return, and when they in their turn refused to accept it, he requested to be allowed to invest it as an endowment to his school. This was in 1780 or only two years after his settlement in Tanjore, so that his integrity and piety had already made him famous before the guardianship of the young King of Tanjore attracted to him still more attention. In 1783 Schwartz was again sent on an embassy to Tippoo, Hyder's son, but this obstinate and foolish Prince refused to see the man his father had chosen to honor.

Schwartz lived and labored in Tanjore nearly 20 years. During this time he collected a flock of nearly 3,000 souls, who were, however, not all in Tanjore, but as is often the case in the Tamil Mission, scattered amongst many villages. Schwartz lived and held his Service in the suburb of Tanjore, and his Christians lived around him. His Church in which he preached in Tamil was but small and was afterwards considerably enlarged. Considering the high respect in which Schwartz was held by the people, by the Kings of the land and the English Government, now growing daily more powerful, one might have expected that hundreds of thousands of Tamulians would have been won by him. For in him were combined so many things to prove advantageous. A thorough knowledge of the people and their customs, a winning manner which made him the favorite of every one, a great influence with the mighty ones of the country, no family ties to trammel him, an experience gained after nearly half a century's work, and the very considerable sums of money which were at his command. But here again things did not fall out according to worldly calculations. As through the acts of the mightiest Apostles only so many believed "as were ordained to eternal life," so it was here. And though the dead should rise from their graves and the angels in heaven should become Missionaries, the world would still remain the world, and the way to life would remain a narrow one until the day of judgment. Schwartz has well said: "Let no Missionary waste his time in vain complaints. We should be witnesses of our Lord, not only converters of souls. It is true we wish that as Peter's sermon converted 3,000, so we might be able to see a rich and visible blessing rest upon our labors. But, there is a time to sow, and a time to reap, and then, perhaps, if we received such blessings we might not, perhaps, preserve our humility of heart. The best thing we can do is to *work diligently,* and then *to pray that God will bless our work.*"

As the end of this faithful servant drew near, many of the brethren came from afar to see him once more. Janicke and Kohloff were with him. Gericke came from Madras and brought the young Holzberg with him. Pohle came from Trichinopoly and Cämmerer from Tranquebar. To Cämmerer who had only been seven years in India and had been Schwartz's pupil in Tamil he praised the goodness of God who had found him worthy to be a Missionary with which no other service in the world could compare. True, he said, there comes many a cross, "but my brethren! they are good for us. By means of them our hearts are more drawn towards God and we are kept in humility which the proud and obstinate heart so willingly loses sight of—and we always receive more of the good than we do of the evil. Ah! when I think how like a father God has hitherto led me, out of what troubles he has saved me, and in spite of my many sins truth has so patiently dealt with me I must exclaim, Blessed be His name! Believe me the joy is inexpressible to have forgiveness of sin through Christ. Ah! what has not my Saviour done for me a poor sinner!" A few hours before going Home he sang with a loud voice the hymn:

'In Christ I have my life and dying is my gain,'

and then fell asleep, whilst those around him were singing the last verse of "O bleeding Head so wounded." This was on 13th February 1798. Schwartz was over 71 years of age and had served the Mission for 48 years. Next day he was laid to rest in the Church he had built, but instead of singing there was nothing heard but weeping, and when Gericke tried to preach his funeral sermon he found he could only read the burial liturgy. On the following day only was his funeral sermon preached.

Probably no Missionary has been so much loved during his lifetime and so greatly honored at his death as Ch. Fr. Schwartz. The English Government erected a monument to his memory in the Cathedral at Madras with a long inscription full of his praise. And even Serfojee the heathen King of Tanjore, whose tears had fallen upon Schwartz's body, placed a monument to his memory (sculptured in Europe by Flaxmann) in the Church which Schwartz had built near the large pagoda, and the King composed the following inscription :—

"Firm wast thou, humble and wise,
Honest, pure, free from disguise,
Father of orphans, the widows' support,
Comfort in sorrow of every sort.
To the benighted dispenser of light
Doing and pointing to that which is right,
Blessing to Princes to people, to me ;
May I, my father, be worthy of thee
Wisheth and prayeth thy Serfojee."

His native Christians also erected a monument to him, but not in stone or in metal; they erected it in their hearts "*The memory of the just is blessed.*" Eleven years before his death Schwartz had prepared the son of the old Missionary Kohloff so far that he was able to ordain him. The younger Kohloff, whose service in the Mission, added to that of his father's amount to more than a century, was during the last eleven years Schwartz's Assistant, and then his successor, with him there labored for shorter or longer periods Janicke, Horst and Hanbroe, who all went to their rest before him. Kohloff lived until 1844 and, therefore, saw the commencement of the revival of the Tranquebar Mission. After his death the changes in the congregation were numerous, and anglocizing could go on without obstacle. Eight years after Kohloff's death, after the German arrangements had all been shoved on one side, many of the flock turned again to their mother Church. When Missionary J. M. N. Schwartz received them again into the Lutheran Church, they begged that the services might be conducted exactly in the same way as they were in the time of Chr. Fr. Schwartz. They had, therefore, by no means forgotten the faithful shepherd who had left them 50 years before.

Tanjore is, therefore, again one of our Mission-stations, and

Missionary Ouchterlony has been the resident for many years. Our flock there now numbers nearly 900 souls, of whom one-half live in or near Tanjore and the remainder are scattered in 30 villages. It is true that the property left by Schwartz, together with the Churches and houses, has remained in the hands of the English Missionary Society who received it when Germany forgot to remember the land of the Tamulians. Before the close of the last century the Rev. Paetzold of Madras thus writes regarding this matter: "According to right the Gospel Propagation Society has no Mission, *i.e.*, no proprietory claim upon any East Indian Mission. The Vepery Mission, Church and buildings comes from the Catholic Armenians, who, because they intrigued with the French, had to give up both, whereupon the Government handed over both of these to the German Missionaries at their request. Fabricius and Breithaupt their predecessors and successors kept everything in proper order at their own cost. In Cuddalore Huttemann built and repaired, and now Gericke keeps in order the half-deserted station, with no Missionaries appointed to it, out of his private pocket. Tanjore, Trichinopoly, Palamcotta, Combaconum, Ramnad, &c., were all founded and put in working order bySchwartz, the Churches were founded, built and repaired by him, as best he could at his own expense, and are in the strictest sense of the word Schwartz's own private property. But Schwartz says, No, they are the property of all honest, faithful German brethren who may succeed me, for as long as they may remain in India. When there are no longer any, those may take it who like. That the G. P. Society has contributed nothing, not even one penny, towards the building of all the Churches and Missionary buildings; nay, further that they have not even taken any notice of such, is an indisputable fact." So far Mr. Paetzold—But it has happened as Schwartz prophesied. When there were no longer any German Missionaries 'those took it who liked' and it only remains for us to be glad that it has fallen into the hands of those who, though they oppose us whenever they can, employ not only this money, but also many and large sums in addition in the interest of the Tamil Mission. They have inherited the externals, the essentiality, the pure Word and Sacrament has remained with us. And besides the good and faithful God has again helped us in the erection of the most necessary Station-buildings, and to a fine roomy Church at Tanjore. We, therefore, look forward to the future with confidence and believe that He who has hitherto helped will do so in days to come. He will help us if we remain faithful to Him until death. And to this faithfulness unto death may He in His mercy help us all!—*Amen.*

Combaconum.

Combaconum is situated in a very fruitful and populous portion of the old kingdom of Tanjore, and possessed a royal palace. Village succeeds village and the whole region is like a garden of God. Where, however, there are rich districts and King's palaces, there also will be no want of Brahmins. But where the Brahmins are numerous, miracles are also necessary, that the people may be attracted and subsistence provided for the Brahmins. Besides numberless miracles said to have happened once, the Brahmins have also established a miracle which continues to happen, and that regularly every twelve years. The Ganges, though 1,000 miles distant, fills once in 12 years the big tank at Combaconum with its water. As to bathe in the Ganges is a work of great merit, and as owing to its distance the performance of this work is difficult; hundreds and thousands flock to this tank and in it wash away their sins so effectually that they have no need of any further purification. As elsewhere the Brahmins and their followers are here also much opposed to the Gospel. If in any place Brahmins represent the Pharisees, and anywhere deserve to be called whitened sepulchres, it is here, for I know of no other place in Southern India where Brahmins hold secret meetings at which they eat meat, the object of a Brahmin's abhorrence, and drink brandy, and yet according to outward appearances are strict Brahmins. People like this who are not even honest, as regards their own religion are, of course, the least likely to be affected by the Gospel. "Have we not rice to eat, and clothes to wear as well as you? why should we become Christians? and as we are so much better off than you, it is clear that the blessing of God rests upon us and not upon you!" This is what they say, and one cannot even answer them with the illustration of the beast fattened for the slaughter-house, which gets as much food as it can eat whilst we regulate the diet of our own children and deny them many things—because they do not fatten their cattle. The parable of the Prodigal son is equally lost upon them, because they are far removed from the husks, and fatten upon the marrow of the land. To certain men and classes of men the Gospel remains a folly until their death and to them nothing applies except what applied to the Pharisees—" Woe unto you !"

When during the middle of the last century Christianity spread further and further from Tranquebar, some Christians were found at Combaconum, who were ministered to by Chr. Fr. Schwartz from Tanjore, as Combaconum is much nearer Tanjore than Tranquebar. Schwartz kept a Catechist there and built a little Church. But this has shared the same fate as everything else that our Missionaries built and collected. In our days some Christians, however, still remained, so that in 1856 Combaconum was again made into a station, together with Cuddalore. Missionary Meischel looked after the station from Mayaveram as there was as yet no building for a Missionary. But the flock increased even under these circumstances. Since 1860 we have had a Mission building near the town constructed for a Missionary's residence,and for holding Divine Service. Originally it was lightly built but has since been thoroughly repaired. The Rev. Wansky who, since 1867, is stationed here, has seen his congregation slowly but steadily increase.

At the present time Combaconum has about 400 Christians who live scattered in 23 villages. May the All-powerful God soon change the righteous Pharisees into poor sinners, fitted for the Kingdom of God; but in the meantime continue to collect the poor and the miserable and those who lie under the hedges so that His Kingdom may be full. For there is yet room there!

Mayaveram.

Between Combaconum and Tranquebar lies Mayaveram, distant from Tranquebar a night's journey or about 18 miles. The neighbourhood is very fertile and the land is irrigated by water from many channels. As far as the eye can reach there is nothing to be seen but rice-fields, the monotony of the view, however, is here and there broken by small groves. And wherever is a group of trees, there one may be sure is also a little village, even though there is nothing to be seen of it. The houses are all very low, consisting chiefly of mud walls and palm leaf thatch, so that the trees tower high above them. In this fine fertile neighbourhood it is pleasant living, especially for the Hindoo, whose scull is like an earthen vessel and is burnt all the harder by the heat of the sun without causing him any suffering. The brain of a European, however, is in danger of melting, and his lungs pant for air in this region where there is at times scarcely a breath to be felt. Mayaveram is the principal place in the neighbourhood, and is a pretty little country town with broad streets, and a large much-frequented pagoda, together with many smaller ones. During the last century Christianity seems to have taken no root here, for the people wanted nothing. And where there is nothing wanting the Physician of the soul can give no help, for the full man requires no food, nor the healthy man a doctor. After 1813, when by order of Parliament, India was thrown open to the Mission there came several Missionaries to the Tamil country, some English and some German sent by English Societies. Especially active was the then youthful Church Missionary Society. Her elder sister the Gospel Propagation Society had already taken possession of the inheritance of our fathers, to which after our fathers had died out, they had a certain right.

The Church Missionary Society, however, had to begin anew. It is true they attempted a Mission at Tranquebar in opposition to ours, but the Danish Government wisely declared that they could not suffer a second Mission in the small field of Tranquebar. So they were obliged to leave Tranquebar, they did not, however, go far but settled down at Mayaveram where they built two Mission houses and a larger building for a school. This was in 1823.

These intentions upon Tranquebar by no means prospered. During 18 years there died, got sick, and left Mayaveram, not less than six Missionaries, of whom the first three were Germans in English employ, and the last three Englishmen. The seventh Missionary, an Englishman, was even too much of a Churchman for the Church Missionary Society, and so he was dismissed. This station with 38 Christians stood then empty, and was in danger of falling into the hands of the heathens. This excited the pity of the pious Collector, H. Stokes, in Guntoor, so that together with other friends he purchased the station and presented it to our Mission, with the condition that we should always keep a Missionary there. This was a noble act of a noble and pious man, in whose house I have seen Officers of high rank, a General at their head, kneeling down with him to pray to God that He would extend His Kingdom in India. In the year 1845 Mayaveram became a Lutheran station.

In spite of many struggles with the heathen land proprietors, the Lord's work gradually spread until out of the 38 Christians there came at last several hundreds, so that a large Church had to be built. During the last years under the ministration of the Rev. J. M. N. Schwartz the work has so greatly prospered that the hundreds have grown into thousands, and the large Church has been quite filled. Frequently on a Sunday there have been no less than 400 communicants and indeed so many as frequently to be a severe strain (in this climate) upon the physical powers of the Missionaries. Mayaveram has, therefore, become our largest station and reckons nearly 1,800 souls in 120 villages. The Rev. Mayr assisted by a native pastor, with a candidate for Orders, and 15 Catechists, now presides over Mayaveram, since the Rev. Schwartz has undertaken the duties of Senior at Tranquebar. May the faithful and merciful God continue to increase the poor and the miserable, so that the eighteen hundred may grow into as many thousands and be a light to shine throughout the whole of this populous country. We have a great God and it is fitting to ask of Him great things!

Nagapatam.

Nagapatam, or as it is generally called Negapatam, signifies the snake-town, and this name has, as those of many other Indian towns, its origin in Indian mythology. It is situated on the mouth of one of the branches of the Cauvery, in a fertile but unpicturesque neighbourhood of the old kingdom of Tanjore. The Portuguese settled here and were driven out by the Dutch. The Dutch built, as they did in each of their Indian Settlements, a fort. It is proverbial and perfectly true that the traces of the Portuguese are Churches—of the Dutch, forts—and of the English, roads. The Dutch carried on considerable trade between Negapatam and Ceylon and their distant possessions in the Sunda Islands. In English hands Negapatam, as well as Tranquebar, Sadras, Pulicat, &c., fell into decay and commerce all centred in Madras. When the railway, however, was finished from Trichinopoly and Tanjore as far as Negapatam, the trade at Negapatam began to revive, so that the town was rescued from thorough ruin. Our old Missionaries already labored in Negapatam and especially Gericke, who lived here for several years until in 1788 he became Fabricius' successor in Madras. But in Madras he did not forget Negapatam but visited it from time to time until he died. Even in his Will he did not forget Negapatam but inserted a clause by which he provided that a portion of his property should be devoted to the maintenance of Negapatam. To this day the English congregation accordingly receive annually Rupees 630, whilst the remainder, and by far the larger, part of the property goes to the benefit of the congregation at Madras. We look with pleasure on the traces of the labors of our old Missionaries, although the fruit of them has passed into the possession of others.

As Negapatam began to revive by means of the railway, and as Tranquebar still continued to decline, many families emigrated from Tranquebar and Poreyar to Negapatam, where some of them obtained appointments in the railway, and others engaged in trade. This was the commencement of our congregation in 1862; and in 1864 it was converted into a station. The congregation at present consists of over 230 souls, and is one of the wealthiest and most respectable of our Mission. It has, however, unfortunately had to suffer many changes in its Missionaries, having had since 1864 almost as many pastors as there have been years. These changes have not had very evil effects, since the congregation consists of old Christians, descended from Christian ancestors, but the good effects of a permanent supervision have been wanting. The Rev. Mayr who looked after the station from July 1866 to March 1870 took the first steps towards building the necessary Church, and was even subsequently active with regard to it, until on 3rd April 1872 the Church was consecrated. It is especially pleasant to record that the congregation bore a large share of the expenses of this building. May this congregation fulfil its high calling and let its light shine not only to the heathens but also to the Papists! May the grace of our Lord be the sun and shield of the congregation and station of Negapatam.

Pudoocotta.

Pudoocotta means Newcastle, and is also a piece of the

old Tanjore kingdom. It is a wooded hilly bit of country of about 1,300 square miles and some 300,000 inhabitants. A number of tanks collect the rain water and irrigate the rice-fields. The cultivators, however, spend most of their labor in the production of pulses, which do not require irrigation. The inhabitants are for the most part Kaller, *i. e.*, rogues. The golden age for their caste is, however, past and gone, they have changed their calling, and have become tillers of the field in which employ they are as honest as their neighbours. The town of Pudoocotta is regularly built with straight and pretty broad streets. In the middle of the town is the palace of the King, for his Brahmin flatterers call him the Maha Raja, *i. e.*, the great King. The Brahmins hold him tightly in moral—or immoral—bondage, and the English Government is compelled to hold him in pecuniary bondage. Of course, the English Government only adopted such measures when his proclivities for running into debt were found to exceed all bounds. For instance, at the annual feast of Durga, thousands of Brahmins who came flocking from a distance were fed for 10 days and then presented with gifts, so that one of these feasts cost above Rs. 30,000, beyond the personal expenses the King incurred. The father of the present Prince was a simple, but rich, clever and influential Zemindar. In their last struggles he continued firm to the English although all his neighbours were against them. Out of gratitude he was converted into a Prince of Pudoocotta. He built the palace and did much to improve his little territory. His son, however, the present Prince gives the reins to the Brahmins and does nothing but enjoy himself. He will probably be the last Prince of Pudoocotta as his father was the first. The time of Indian Princes is everywhere past.

In Pudoocotta the American Missionaries of Madura had collected a few Christians and had opened some schools for the heathens. As they wished to centralize their powers, the station with its tumble-down mud house was offered to and accepted by us. The Christians numbered some 90 souls. This was already in the year 1849, and if a Missionary had been able to go there at once the number would have increased. But not only had we no Missionary but no dwelling for him or means wherewith to build one. And so one year passed after another and it is only to be wondered that the Christians were not altogether scattered. This they did not do but increased to 117 souls. At last in 1869 Pudoocotta received its own Missionary in the Rev. Kahl, and he has already succeeded in building a house. Unfortunately soon after he had to be transferred. The Rev. Zorn has been his successor in Pudoocotta.

In a smaller degree our Missionary in Pudoocotta stands in the same relation as Schwartz once did in Tanjore. There is a small heathen royal Court, ruined by Brahmins, with a good humoured but weak King; a number of Christians in many villages, but as yet no Church. May he equal Schwartz in activity and may he like him win many souls to the Lord! and let this be the prayer of all those who wait for the coming of our Lord Jesus Christ and by whom His appearance is looked and longed for!

Coimbatore.

The district of Coimbatore was formerly a portion of the Great Pandion kingdom of Madura. Under Hyder Ali it was annexed to Mysore where it remained until taken possession of by the English. It is the most mountainous and the best wooded district of the Tamil country, for here are the Neilgherries or blue hills, the highest point of which is above 8,000 feet in height, and which form an invigorating place of retreat for the sickly Europeans from the plains. There is a regular alpine air, though with an Indian sun, and no snow or ice. A residence there is strengthening to wearied men but not sufficient to bring about the recovery of those really ill. Recoveries are something like the red cheeks which the children from the plains so easily get on the hills, and again lose immediately they return to the plains. A large town, Ootacamund, is situated some 7,000 feet high, and offers everything which a European in a foreign land can desire. Churches, schools, libraries and public gardens and many a quiet forest where the wearied limbs can again get accustomed to walking. In the winter months it is very cold and the thin air is very piercing, but it never comes so far as to freeze. The sun perpendicularly above the head is, however, very treacherous. Two thousand feet lower there is a smaller town Coonoor, which is preferred by those who are too weak for the cold winds and the heavy rains of Ootacamund. There is plenty of room for many other towns, without, however, much prospect of any being built, for although the cool oasis amidst the glowing heat of Southern

India, is such a blessing, it can only be enjoyed by the wealthy.

The slopes of these hills are planted with coffee and tea, for which the plains are too hot, and many plantations produce excellent crops of both. Otherwise, however, they are covered by dense forests and the valuable teak tree is here at home. More important, however, are the teak forests in the south of the district, in the Aneimalei hills, (=the elephant hills. These hills are as high as the Neilgherries, but almost entirely uninhabited. Here the Government has taken the teak forests under their special protection. The trees are felled under the supervision of Government Officials, dragged to the edge of the precipices, down which they are rolled, then taken in carts for several days' journey, thrown into the Ponany river, and floated in rafts down to the sea on the Western Coast. Here they are placed in ships, and go by sea to Bombay where they are used for Government purposes. The timber destined for Madras is taken by yet longer detours to the Cauvery, floated to the sea and then taken by ships to Madras. In this way teak-wood becomes expensive, but as it is almost the only wood in India which will stand the climate, and is not touched by the white ants, it is almost indispensable for building purposes.

The Aneimaleis being uninhabited by men are a favorite residence of elephants, tigers, leopards, bears, bisons and whatever else crawls upon earth. In addition it is for the greater part of the year—the rainless months—the abode of fever, and a short residence only is sufficient to bring a man under its sway. This fever king, who has his emissaries in the jungles of the plains is the true Procrustes of India, who uses the same measure for every one who comes within his influence without caring whether he be big or small, high or low, and presses him into the same cot. Whoever escapes his clutches never forgets his terrible hospitality.

Many of the wild elephants are caught and used for dragging down the felled teak timber. A reward used to be offered for their destruction, or rather for the production of their teeth, for each pair of which the Government gave Rs. 70, so that in four years 700 elephants were killed; a reward, however, is now no longer given and the destruction of elephants is forbidden. A price is also placed upon tigers and leopards, or rather upon their skins; these are killed in much larger numbers, but without being exterminated. They frequently pay a visit to the Neilgherries, and even to Ootacamund, where they have killed and eaten many a grass-cutter. English Officers are generally on their track, but these animals are very cunning and are no respecters of persons. I have met several Officers who can show dreadful scars, the results of their cruel embraces.

The district of Coimbatore has over a million inhabitants, and three-fourths of these gain a subsistence from cultivation. Besides rice and various pulses, tobacco and several kinds of cotton are grown. The cotton is not much exported, for 14,000 looms already wait for it and work it into the requirements of the district. As no machinery is employed, either for cleaning or spinning, the cotton is manufactured to-day just as it was in Menu's day, 2,800 years ago, and employs a large number of laborers.

In other respects also this district is rich enough. It contains 16,000 Brahmins, of whom 500 are priests, who serve the idols in more than 100 large pagodas, and 2,000 dancing girls who have to dance in front of the stone-gods with drums and pipes without number. In this district, and especially in and near the principal town Coimbatore, which is not otherwise remarkable for any thing, there resided a number of old Christian families, of whom in 1856 a number joined us. Some heathens also came, and this was the origin of the station of Coimbatore. The congregation is amongst the most prosperous of the Mission, many of its members are Government Officials, and they willingly contribute to the wants of the station. Five years ago a dwelling-house was built for the Missionary, which being erected by a professional man, especially appointed for the purpose, is said to be one of the finest in the Mission. A large school-house was at the same time rebuilt and is also used as a Church. Missionary Herre has labored here for many years, and his congregation now numbers 427 souls in 19 villages. It is a large and interesting field of labor, and we pray that the Lord will increase the number of His followers to as many thousands and give to each individual the grace to be a light and a salt of the earth to his heathen neighbours, so that the Missionary may labor with ever less grief and more joy of heart, until the Lord Himself shall come, Who is our life and our light as well at home as abroad.

Chellumbram.

Though not a large town Chellumbram is regularly built with broad streets, and an enormous pagoda in the middle. The country around is very fertile and is the richest portion of the Cuddalore District. When the young rice crops begin to shoot above the water, the whole country looks as if covered with green satin. For miles and miles as far as one can see this lovely green refreshes the eye now and then relieved by a cluster of cocoa-nut palms. A few months later the golden ears not unlike wheat, wave to and fro in the wind, and involuntarily tune the heart to offer up thanks to God for these His rich blessings.

But the richest blessing of this rich country are the believing souls who live scattered in more than 30 villages. By degrees some 500 persons came to Cuddalore to be instructed and baptized, and of the majority I can say with confidence that they received instruction with actual longing, and soon learnt by-heart the five chief points of the Catechism. In the same way they quickly comprehended the further explanations, so that it was a real pleasure to teach them. And when they returned to their villages, they were not idle, but proclaimed the good tidings to their relations and neighbours who also came. The Christians themselves are the best spreaders of Christianity, each in his own village and in the most natural manner.

In this way the work of the Lord grew in and around Chellumbram until it became too great to be properly attended to from the 30 miles distant Cuddalore. As just at this time the Rev. Wolff returned from Germany, Chellumbram was separated from Cuddalore and made over to him in 1866. The change was to have taken place gradually but actually occurred more suddenly than had been intended. At the same time the young Christians lost their native preacher, who had labored among them for some time and had won their confidence. The results soon became apparent. By the grace of God those already collected remained faithful to their new pastor and his assistant. A sudden change, however, of a Missionary establishment has always an injurious influence upon a newly collected congregation, and although there may be no one to blame. The hope, therefore, which Mr. Wolff expressed when he took charge of Chellumbram, that in the same year he would be able to double the number of Christians (490) was unfortunately not fulfilled. In latter years, however, the work has again begun to increase.

As Chellumbram was made into a separate station, it was, of course, necessary to build the requisite station buildings, and Mr. Wolff has succeeded in erecting a good Mission-house and out-buildings. In the first of these there is not only ample room for his own family, but also for the accommodation of guests and brethren passing through. As such visits are rare in Chellumbram the pleasure of the kindly hosts is all the greater that they have a guest, and that of the guest also that he can find shelter in a Christian household, in a region where but lately there were no Christians to be found. A small school is near the house from which from time to time the sound of our German hymns in the Tamil tongue are heard as far as the dwelling-house. It is to be regretted that the station was not built in the middle of the town of Chellumbram, although it is situated only a few minutes distance from it. Inside the town the heathens would have seen more of our Christian services and even the Christians from the villages, prefer, as is also the case in our smaller towns of Germany, to go to a Church in the town.

At present Chellumbram reckons 673 Christians in 48 villages. May the merciful God and Lord of the harvest soon see fit to carry into effect the hope of Mr. Wolff and soon double the number of his converts, and may the hundreds be changed into thousands all filled with life and light from above! Chellumbram is one of the few stations in our Mission where there is no rival. Even the Papists, although they have a few Christians scattered here and there have neither a priest nor a station in Chellumbram. Our Missionary at Pudoocotta is the only one who enjoys similar good fortune, but Chellumbram has the advantage over Pudoocotta that the Christians live for the most part within easy distance and the country is a pleasant one and well populated. May God soon raise up faithful native assistants in and around Chellumbram, and make this station as spiritually a rich and fruitful field, as it is naturally. Oh! Lord, send faithful workmen into Thy harvest. That is, a prayer which is needed for each station in the land of the Tamulians and also for Chellumbram. Therefore let all those who love the Lord Jesus Christ pray for this!

Conclusion.

We have now visited each of our Mission-stations in succession and have seen how they originated and how much progress each has made. If we look back upon the whole, we are bound to admit that the work of our Missions spreads each year more, and that there has been an improvement everywhere and in each station. It is true that as regards interior arrangements our Mission cannot compare with the English and Romish Missions. We are in great need of more places of worship and of School-buildings, and here and there of Mission-houses and station-buildings. It has been well said that tents and not houses is the proper expression for our condition of life among the heathens. To whom could the words, "We have no abiding place here but look for the one to come," better apply than to the Missionary amongst the heathens. In a strange land which can never become his home, amongst a people whose inward feelings as diametrically opposed to his own as their color is to his; amidst the strangest dialects, where the tones of his mother-tongue are but a rare sound, who than a Missionary could more truly sing:

"I am a stranger here on earth."

Yes, tents is the proper expression for our condition of life, but the country will not suffer us to live in tents, or without houses. The people too have seen so many and such different 'travelling saints' that they will not trust them, and the question "whence is he?" is a stereotyped one in the mouth of a Tamulian. In such a country and with such a people it is, therefore, necessary for the Missionary to have a safer roof than a tent offers, and a dwelling, so that he may give an answer to the question—"From whence?" and that his people may know where to find him when they wish to come to him for help. However, often as he may go to them and visit them in their villages, he must still have a house; not only does the climate render this necessary but also the Missionary's calling.

Although we are much behind in our internal structures, in the rounding off and arrangements of our congregations, in protection of their rights and in accustoming them to their duties; as regards our direct task that of collecting heathens for the Kingdom of God, God in His mercy has by no means allowed us to be behind our neighbours. In the last 10 years from 1862—1872 we have baptized 4,600 heathens, besides nearly 3,000 children born in the Mission of Christian parents. This is a much larger number than any equal number of Missionaries* have baptized in the same time anywhere in the land of the Tamulians. Tinnevelly excepted; not excepted, however, the Papists in spite of their large number of Bishops, Priests, and Nuns, buildings and means. To God be given the honor, for it is not we who have done this, but He who has brought them to us and given them to us, that we should instruct them and baptize them in His name and rear them up to Him.

If, however, anybody should ask: are all these thousands really and truly converted and faithful Christians? I would answer without hesitation; by no means. They are, however, all withdrawn from the degrading and indecent idolatrous worship and have been brought under the healthy influence of the Gospel. Their faces have been turned away from dead idols and directed towards the living God, turned from the darkness towards the light. This alone is a great gain. The light shines into their lives and clears up many a dusty corner. Many things which as heathens were natural to them they now leave off and are ashamed of; besides it is the Lord Who knows His own and not we. But when we see our Christians die with a full sense of their sin and guilt, and in a firm faith on Jesus Christ their Redeemer, we are bound to say, may my end be like theirs! and when we see blind old men, led by their grand-children, and leaning on a staff walk 40 miles to partake of the Holy Communion; when we see our Christians bring their children as far to be baptized, the parents having, perhaps, been only baptized two years before; when they allow themselves to be persecuted and beaten, because instead of working on Sunday they insist upon going to Church, and when we see them every Sunday walk 17 miles to Divine Service, the mothers carrying their children, we cannot do else but say: The

* Of Missionaries there were 12 in 1862 and 16 in 1872.

Lord's work is going on in their hearts, the Father is drawing them to the Son, the Holy Ghost illuminates, quickens and sanctifies their hearts. And this is what has been done under mine own eyes; how much more might not be gathered from the testimony of the rest of the brethren!

Our work is not, therefore, entirely in vain although the days are small, and we still smaller instruments. Therefore, wherever in our distant home there are Christian hearts which lift themselves to God in simple and child-like faith, may then our work be remembered before the Lord. The work—our task is enormously great; our strength is insignificantly small. Let, therefore, a sigh now and then arise to God for our work as also for ourselves.

CHAPTER IV.

THE ENGLISH EPISCOPAL MISSION.

Until the commencement of this century the Government of India would not permit any English Missionaries to come to the country. This Government had its Head Quarters in London, and was called "The Honorable East India Company." Although the Government consisted of Englishmen only it would not give its sanction to any English Missionaries. When at last some English Missionaries: Carey, Marshman and Ward ventured to come to India, (Calcutta) they were not permitted to labor as such, but were obliged to settle in the small Danish territory of Serampore, even there they were hard pressed by the English Government, and some were actually sent out of the country. But whilst India was so shut against English Missionaries, the Germans who came to Tranquebar, were not only allowed to travel all over the country, and to build stations where they liked, but the Governor of Madras was friendly towards them and sometimes aided them. Even in Calcutta, the Tranquebar Missionary Kiernander was allowed to build a station without being in the slightest degree prevented by the Government. It seemed as if God had intended the country for the English but the Mission for the Germans. Whilst, however, the English were always more diligent in taking possession of the length and breadth of the land, the Germans became always more neglectful of the Mission. They relinquished one station after another, and at last did not even know how to keep their last post, Tranquebar. Under these circumstances, the Mission also had to become English.

In the year 1813, the Charter of the East India Company had to be renewed by the Crown, and at this opportunity the friends of the Mission in England tried to move the Government to insert a clause in the Charter, in which, for the future, Missionaries should be permitted to go to India and labor there. But they appealed to deaf ears, to the Government as well as to the East India Company. There was, therefore, nothing left to them but to appeal to the country and to see how much Christian consciousness was left in the people. This step was not a fruitless one. Lord Castlereagh, the ministerial leader of the House of Commons, and the real governing power of England, had given to a petitioner this answer: "The country in general seems to be indifferent regarding the Mission to India; all interest appears to be centred upon one or two Societies." "If that is your Lordship's opinion," returned Mr. Fuller, the petitioner, "you shall soon have an opportunity of judging to what extent public opinion is on our side." When the country came to hear of these cold words of the cold Lord Castlereagh, there arose a movement from one end to the other. Petitions poured in from every quarter of the kingdom, from large towns as from little villages; from individual congregations, as from corporate bodies. Every post brought more of them. For eight weeks they kept coming in, nine hundred in number, until the ministerial table was full of them. "That is enough Mr. Fuller," Lord Castlereagh is reported to have said, and he introduced the clause: "That it is the duty of this country to facilitate the introduction of useful knowledge and of religious and moral improvement into India, and conveniences should, therefore, be afforded to persons who are willing to go to India for this object." Hitherto no Missionary was allowed to go to India without the permission of the Government, which permission, however, the Government never gave. The word 'facilities' was meant as showing that this permission was no longer necessary. But even this clause which shows on the face of it, that it had been forced out of Government, excited in the Lower House a debate which lasted a week, and it is remarkable that it was chiefly opposed by those who had been a long time in India—and who had left their Christianity behind at the Cape of Good Hope. First of all rose Sir Henry Montgomery who had been for 20 years in Military employ in Madras, and in opposing the clause he said: "If we wish to convert the Hindoos, we should commence by converting our own people, who now present an example of lying, cursing, drunkenness and vice. The Mutiny of the native troops at Vellore (which like all other evils had been, of course, ascribed to the Missionaries) was not caused by the Missionaries, but if they were allowed perfect freedom of action, such scenes would be repeated. For my part I am more anxious to save the lives of my 30,000 countrymen than the souls of all the Hindoos at such a price. Besides, I know of no instance in which a Hindoo has been converted, with the exception of a single one through the instrumentality of that respectable individual Mr. Schwartz." Thereupon Wilberforce got up, and pointed out that 20 years before he had proposed that Missionaries should be allowed to go to India, and that promises had then been made which had never been fulfilled. He spoke strongly in favor of Carey, Marshman and Ward of Serampore in particular, and of Missionaries in general. He spoke for three hours and in such a manner that even his opponents heard him with pleasure. But then there got up one old Indian after another who praised the religion and the customs of the Hindoos and described them to their hearers as worthy of paradise. Even Sir Thomas Munro, who subsequently as Governor of Madras, has left behind him a good name, spoke against the clause and said amongst other things: "If civilization should ever become an article of commerce, England could only gain by the introduction of Indian civilization." The most bitter, however, was a former Madras lawyer, and Wilberforce had to rise once more to defend the Mission. But although Wilberforce was almost the only one who spoke in favor of the clause, still it was carried, for the unmistakable opinion of the country which had shown itself in the 900 petitions could not be despised. In this way the door of India was opened to English Missionaries, and from that time dates the commencement of the English Mission in the country of the Tamuliáns.

The Church Missionary Society at once made use of this open door, and already in the next year sent out their first

Missionaries Rhenius and Schnarre to Madras, and others soon followed them, Schafter, Schmid, Lechler, Barenbruck and others. These were all Germans, but Englishmen also soon came: Ridsdale, Tucker, Ragland, Moody, Royston, Pettitt, &c. The Society for the Propagation of the Gospel also commenced to send Missionaries to India. The Christian Knowledge Society which had supported our old Missionaries who worked in English territory, Schultze, Fabricius, Gericke, Rottler, Paetzold in Madras; Schwartz, Kohloff, Pohle and others in Tanjore and Trichinopoly, retired from Missions to the heathens, and handed over this portion of its labors to the newly formed S. P. G. This society, therefore, became the heir of the congregations, stations and property collected by our Missionaries. It had in this way a good start in India, and especially in Madras, Cuddalore, Tanjore and Tinnevelly.

This society divides its work in the Tamil country into three circles; that is Madras, Tanjore and Tinnevelly. We will follow this division and commence with the first circle *Madras*.

In this circle the society has three stations, two in Madras and one at St. Thomas' Mount near Madras. The most important of these stations is still the old one in Vepery, where our German Missionaries labored for so long a time. There the Society has over 800 Christians; altogether in these three stations there are over 1,500 Christians. The Missionaries are not Europeans, but four are natives and the fifth is an East Indian. According to the Report of 1870, there were baptized in the three stations 40 heathens. In addition the Society maintains a Theological Seminary, with 18 pupils and an English-Tamil school, which is attended by 380 children, of whom 40 are Christian children and the rest Brahmins, Mahomedans and other heathens.

The number of Christians in the other circle that of Tanjore, which now includes Trichinopoly, is much larger. Here in 11 stations there are 4,700 Christians and the congregations are well organized and contribute according to their circumstances towards their own support. A considerable portion of the energies of the Society, is here also expended on the schools. Besides an English-Tamil school in Ramnad with 160 pupils—heathens—it has a so-called High School in Tanjore with 460 pupils and another such in Trichinopoly with 400 pupils. They attempt by these means to approach closer to the higher classes, but as the principal attention is bestowed upon subjects required for the Government Examinations, and as the Government Inspector only looks after secular subjects of knowledge, conversions to Christianity from these schools seldom occur. Besides these schools, the Society has also Seminary at Vediarpuram with 125 pupils from which it take its Catechists and Teachers.

This the once-so-fruitful field of our old Missionaries Schwartz, Kohloff, &c., seems now to have become like firmly trodden down soil. In our Mission, also, the fewest conversions of heathens take place in this field. There has been no want of faithful work, and, as far as the S. P. G. is concerned there have been ample funds, but neither have made the soil fertile. The wind bloweth where it listeth, and thus it is with the Spirit of God. May it please Him to breathe upon this part of the country and to awaken the old Christians to life and the heathens to the question, " what shall we do to be saved ?"

By far the most fertile circle in the whole of India is the third, that of Tinnevelly. The conditions here are, however, very different from those in any other part of India, and in order rightly to understand the results of the Mission it will be necessary to treat of them in detail.

Tinnevelly is the most southern of the Collectorates and lies between the 8th and 10th degrees of northern latitude. There is but little rain here for the western ghauts which divide Tinnevelly from Travancore retain the south western monsoon and the north-east monsoon is kept back by the most northern portion of Ceylon which lies exactly opposite the coast. The consequence is that in Tinnevelly there are large unfertile tracts of land, as opposed to the neighbouring kingdom of Travancore, separated from it by the western ghauts. Standing upon the southern spurs of the ghauts, both countries can be seen at the same time, and the contrast is astonishing. Travancore appears clad in a marvellous green, with hills and valleys, lakes, rivers and forests. I have never seen so remarkable a fertility as in Travancore. The famed fertility of Egypt cannot compare with it, and the most fertile parts of the Tamil country do not equal it. Tinnevelly, however, appears like a large burnt up plain with a few fertile green oases widely separated from each other. But these barren unpicturesque fields are well suited to cotton, which is here so extensively cultivated that not only is sufficient produced for the clothing wants of the people, but also many thousand bales are exported to Europe.

In the sandy tracts is the home of the Palmyra; an ungraceful but useful tree. The trunk measures from 60 to 90 feet in length without a single branch, and then comes the crown formed of fan-like leaves. These leaves are used for thatching houses, and mats and baskets are also manufactured from them and even vessels for drawing water. The single leaves form the so-called *oleis,* which are used all over India for writing upon. The writing is carefully scratched with an iron point and whole books and valuable documents are thus compiled. Even in the schools the lower classes use these as books. The young roots of the trees as well as the ripe fruits are eatable and the unripe fruits yield a tasty and wholesome food.

The most important product of this tree is its sap, which it yields most abundantly during the hottest months of the year. This sap taken fresh from the tree serves as a breakfast for the Palmyra farmer and his family, and is not only nourishing, but also pleasant to those who are accustomed to it. The remainder of the juice is at once boiled into a sort of sugar cake, which is partly used by the family at the noon-day meal, and partly sold to purchase curry and rice for the evening meal, the chief meal of the day. If, however, the juice is allowed to remain standing unboiled, it soon becomes changed into an intoxicating drink called toddy.

In order to draw off the sap of the Palmyra, the cultivator has to climb up to the crown; as, however, the trunk has no branches, this is by no means an easy task. It can only be done by strong healthy men accustomed to it from their youth. They tie their feet together fast, put them against the tree, they then grasp the trunk with their arms and draw up their feet, and so on till they reach the top 50, 60 or even 70 feet in height. This can only be done by strong muscles. A proper day's work consists in climbing 50 trees twice; for in the morning the juice which has accumulated during the night is taken, and at evening what has been produced during the day. Each tree yields from two to three measures. It is remarkable that the sap flows most freely just at the hottest time of the year. The best time for the sap of this shadowless tree is during the months when the sun is in the north, including the time when it is going towards the north in April and returning from the north to the south in August. When every blade of grass is dried up and disappears without leaving a vestige behind, when instead of clouds of rain there are clouds of dust filling not only the rooms but the eyes, the mouth and the nose; when the streams are dry and the wells are exhausted, and the largest rivers in India contain instead of refreshing water a glowing bed of sand; then the Palmyra, growing in barren soil, unseals its fountains and pours forth its juice without ceasing. How is it that this shadowless palm has so much superfluous sap of life? Dr. Caldwell wished to answer the question and dug deep into the ground, deeper and always deeper, in order to discover the course of its roots. But, however, deep he dug he always found the thread-like roots of the Palmyra burrowing yet deeper, until 40 feet below the surface of the earth he came upon water. Here the roots, caring nothing for the sandy soil, drunk in refreshing water, and penetrated even further between rocks and stones, so that the Missionary could follow them no more. The riddle how the Palmyra obtains its juice in the hottest weather was, therefore, solved; and this is what the Tamil poet means when he sings:

> If thou do'st a good deed ask not again in the instant
> What good will it bring me, what fruit?
> For see how the palm tree gives back at its summit
> The water it drank at its foot!

This also is the meaning of our Tamil translation of Psalm xcii, 12, "The righteous shall flourish like a palm tree;" when all around is scorched up and dry, the fountain of the righteous is full of water and does not cease to yield him refreshment. It is, however, a fountain, hidden deep, deep under the surface, but rooted in and nourished by the love of God.

It was amongst this simple race of Palmyra farmers, the Shanars, some of whom also cultivate the land, that Christianity has celebrated her most important victories in India. Living at the southern extremity of India and possessing only a barren country, they were not much effected either by the Brahmin immigrations or by the Mahomedan sway. The Brahmins suffered them to drag their idol-cars, but did not permit them to enter the temples. In this way they retained their own gods and their own worship. Their gods were demons, with an influence for evil only, and who had, therefore, to be conciliated by a regular devils worship, (of which the drinking of blood formed a part,) so as to induce them not to do too much evil or to refrain from it altogether. It never occurred to the people to ask for or to expect benefits of their hands.

Nor did they experience many benefits from man. Their much more crafty neighbours and the large landowners knew how to get from them one piece of land after the other. Under these circumstances, the Gospel, which speaks of a merciful God, Who has a heart which feels for man and Who delights in doing him good, found an easy entrance. It was to them like a draught of refreshing water after a long journey in a barren desert. Simple Christians from Tanjore first brought to them the tidings. Ch. Fr. Schwartz baptized the first converts and left with them a native assistant. He also baptized a Brahmin widow who owned a little property and who built a small Church in Palamcottah the chief town of Tinnevelly.

In the year 1792, Missionary Jänicke visited Tinnevelly from Tanjore, and baptized those who had been prepared. He was the prophet of Tinnevelly for he closed his report with these words: "There is every reason for hoping that in the future Christianity in Tinnevelly will spread yet further." In 1797 he again visited the district, and reports that in addition to the first Catechist Satiyanadan who had been ordained by Schwartz there were then laboring among the Christians four more Catechists and some assistants.

In the year of the good Jänicke's death, Gericke visited Tinnevelly from Madras and baptized in different places some 1,300 souls. His journey was like a triumphal march from village to village, and he writes of it: "We arrived at Bethlehem, a new village which also has a new Church built by the catechumens, in order that they might be baptized in it. I preached to them on the healing of the man sick with the palsy and spoke of the blessings they might expect in Christ if they turned to Him with upright hearts. In the evening they all assembled again; after their heathen names had been registered and their new Christian names written opposite, I preached to them about the history of Cornelius and baptized 203 souls out of 48 families. Each family was called separately and after they had renounced the devil and had made a confession of the Christian faith, father, mother and children and all the members of the family knelt down and I baptized them in the order the Catechist read out their Christian names. In a few instances it happened that the head of the family addressed a few touching words of exhortation to this or the other member of the family. The service lasted from 6 o'clock in the evening until midnight. Satiyanadan and the Catechist said: "This is like a new life; never have such things been seen in this country." Next morning the flock were again assembled for prayer, after which I installed the four elders whom they themselves had chosen. After this we visited some of the leading heathens. They had not been able to make up their minds to turn Christians, but expressed themselves as satisfied with what they had seen and heard. We then went to Pageladi where we held a service similar to the one in the last village. Here there was no Church, but as the whole village had declared for Christianity they had cleaned out their heathen temple and prepared it for divine worship. They had all been previously instructed by Satiyanadan and the Catechists. I addressed them regarding the history of Lydia and baptized 220 souls out of 53 families, and then appointed the elders. It was eleven o'clock at night before we started for Kundali. Here again the whole village was expecting me and was waiting to hear the word of God and to be received into the Christian Church. They too had converted their heathen temple into a place of worship; I preached to them of the jailor at Philippi and baptized 248 out of 62 families. The service lasted from 8 o'clock A. M., until 2 P. M. From there we went to Karakovil where also the whole village was waiting for me. The Catechists had already taken down the names of the different families; and after I had spoken to them, I baptized 204 souls out of 46 families. The service lasted from 7 P. M. until midnight. It gave me great pleasure to see all the inhabitants of the village, young and old, hastening to the Church. The Catechist and the Christians who had followed us from other villages said: 'Never whilst this was a heathen temple did they come in such numbers. The Lord Himself draws the people to His Word and Baptism.'"

The number of Christians had thus increased to 2,700 and the Word was making an active progress. But now there came one trial after the other, and each more heavy than the last. First of all persecution from their heathen neighbours and from heathen officials. Then there came a dreadful pestilence which carried away many and caused many others to waver in their faith. The worst of all was that through all these troubles which extended over a long period they had no Missionary to guide or to console them. It was not till 20 years afterwards that they came under the guardianship of the Rev. Rhenius, whose hands were, however, otherwise full, and it was only after 29 years that they received a Missionary of their own.

It might be imagined that after 29 years of trials, only a vestige of them would have been left here and there. But when Rev. Rosen came to count his scattered sheep he found there were still 3,000 souls remaining. During these 29 years they had, therefore, not only kept together but had also increased in numbers, although not a few had fallen away. Two native pastors ordained by Schwartz, sent there and maintained by him, had continued the work as well as they could. The Christians who had been compelled to yield to persecution collected together and founded a new village, Mudaloor—signifying the *first* place to which, in the future those could flee who were persecuted by their heathen neighbours. There is some thing prophetic in the very name of Mudaloor, for after it several other villages were founded—Nazareth and others. In both of these villages there resided native ministers who looked after their different flocks. It is true that Dr. Caldwell doubts whether these native pastors have not done more harm than good, but the English Chaplain, Mr. Hough, of Palamcottah, who visited them in 1817 and travelled about with them, speaks well of them; he writes:—

"The native Pastor Visuvanada lives in a village which is called by the Christians Nazareth, some 20 miles south of Palamcottah; and Abraham, the other Pastor is in Mudaloor, some miles further. If I may judge from what I saw during my stay amongst the people of both villages, both they and the Christians of the neighbouring villages are greatly attached to their Pastors; and I am confident that it is only necessary for the native Pastors to be properly supported and guided, to render them of most efficient service to the congregations under their charge. Even my short visit caused to all of them an indescribable joy, and the good people came flocking from every village and hamlet. When I catechised those who were represented as the most leading men, I found them far better instructed in their religion than I had expected; and if the length of time is considered during which they have been without a Missionary, it is most satisfactory and encouraging to find that the gentle Spirit of the Gospel has always kept them in union. The two abovementioned villages consist entirely of Protestant Christians, and there is nowhere an idol or a temple to be seen. The quietness that reigned here, contrasted with the noise in heathen villages seemed to surround the spots with a kind of sanctity, which led me to forget that I was in the middle of a heathen country. One of the native Pastors led me to a place near the village where a number of women were sitting under the shade of some cocoanut trees. They were spinning cotton and at the same time were singing Lutheran hymns. After the service, a large portion of the congregation showed no inclination to separate, but sat down in front of the door and sang their hymns until late in the evening. In this group there were two old men who had been converted by Jänicke 20 years before, and these men sang me some hymns which Jänicke had taught them. What they sang and said, was not so intelligible to me as the language of the younger people, but you will believe me that they were amongst the most interesting of the members of the group. I mention this, perhaps, trivial incident in order to show that there seems to be more here than the mere name of Christianity, and that the opponents of Missionary work are in error when they say that there are no real Christians amongst the native Protestants; even if the labors and expenses of the Society had met with no other fruit they might still point in triumph to these two villages and prove that their work had not been in vain. Some heathens living in the neighbourhood of these villages said to me frankly that they were quiet and well conducted places." (*Rise and Progress of the Tinnevelly Missions, London*, 1845.)

Up to that time, however, the Society had borne none of the labor and expense in the Propagation of Christian Knowledge in Tinnevelly. Indeed it does not seem to have known anything of these Christians, until it was stirred up by this good man and induced to take an active part. The Christians up to that time had probably never even heard the name of the Society. It was up to that period a pure German work supported by German funds. This same clergyman, Mr. Hough, *introduced* the Common Prayer Book, for as he took the trouble of instructing the Catechists in it, it is clear that up to that time they had not used it.*

Not until 1829 did the Society send the first Missionary, Mr. Rosen, to Tinnevelly, and after that time sent many important men, such as the late Rev. Brotherton, who was indeed an Israelite without guile, Thomas Caldwell, &c. These men have done much and the Society has given them ample funds for disposal. Perhaps the institution which has met with the best results is the following: They have every where village schools, as our Mission also has, to which the Christian children are sent; but all children who, in the village schools, display any talent, and pleasure in study, both boys and girls, are collected in the chief stations in boarding-schools for boys as well as girls, and there further educated. The cleverest boys are collected in High Schools and trained for Teachers, Catechists and Preachers. The girls also are placed in an institute and educated as teachers. In this way the Mission brings up a generation of well educated people, and especially has done much to raise the status of women. They have gained the same experience as we have in our boarding-schools, that although all the children do not turn out well, it makes a very marked difference to have women in a congregation who have been properly trained in a boarding-school. Whilst the others sit quite silent, these take a share in the Liturgy, sing from full hearts, and at the Sermon exhibit an attention and capability of comprehension quite different to that of the rest. In domestic life also they are much cleaner and more regular than the others. The Missionaries remark in their Reports that as far as girls are concerned, day-schools do not answer all purposes. It is

* The Tinnevelly Mission, by the Rev. G. PETTITT, London, 1851, page 9.

true that they have everywhere day-schools for girls, but it is only those who have been brought up in the boarding-schools under the immediate eye of the Missionary and his wife, not merely educated, who form proper examples to the other women. These are generally married to the Teachers, Catechists and Pastors, and thus form Christian families very different from those taken from among the heathens, or left by the Mission in their primitive state. The boarding-schools, therefore, are not concentrated in one station, but there is one wherever there is a Missionary, and it is intended to establish more or else to enlarge the existing ones.

According to the Report of 1873, the Society has now over 14,000 Christians in Tinnevelly living in 280 villages, and 5,000 catechumens under instruction. Nineteen clergymen of whom the majority are natives labor in this field, and during the year reported on, baptized over 700 heathens. There are over 3,000 boys under instruction and over 1,000 girls. In many of the best stations quite a quarter of the whole community is being instructed. The expenses of the Society are, of course, very large. It has considerable endowments in India, and receives from Government a grant-in-aid for the schools. The Christians, also, contribute generously. On the whole, the expenses of the three circles during 1869 appear to have been quite 228,000 Rupees. Only 128,000 Rupees, however, of this sum was sent by the Society from England, the remainder was drawn from the abovementioned sources, to which also must be added the subscriptions collected in India.

Those who sow abundantly will also reap abundantly. In consequence several of the congregations in Tinnevelly have got so far that they bear the expenses of their own Pastor and of their own schools, and others are on the way to be able to do the same. The Society, therefore, sends almost every year less sums. Whilst in 1869 they sent Rupees 128,000, in 1871-72 they only sent Rs. 123,879. If the work goes on unhindered in this way, it is to be hoped that in the next generation these congregations may become entirely self-supporting. The European Missionaries and the friends of the Society will then be free and can be employed in collecting fresh congregations from among the heathens.

2. *The Church Missionary Society.*

The second Society of the Episcopal Mission is the Church Missionary Society. This Society at once seized the opportunity of the renewal of the Charter of the East India Company, and in 1814 landed her first Missionaries in Madras, Rhenius and Schnarre. They first went for a short time to Tranquebar and then settled down in the so-called Black Town of Madras. Rhenius, who was soon aided by Schmid, made himself in a short time remarkable. Even in my time there still lived in Madras many persons who well remembered his preaching in the streets. His work, however, soon spread far beyond Madras, but in consequence of some misunderstanding with the Society, and because Mr. Hough, the Chaplain of Palamcottah begged so earnestly for Missionaries, he was transferred in 1820 to Tinnevelly, whither was followed in the same year by Mr. Schmid.

In Tinnevelly the remarkable gifts; and the great zeal for work, which Rhenius possessed, found ample field. He founded on all sides schools, which were for the most part under the supervision of Schmid, who, however, also travelled about and preached to the heathens. Rhenius retained the principal post of preaching to the heathens and collecting congregations. His cheery, kindly and winning manner furnished him every where with an introduction, and before three years were over 136 families out of 17 villages situated to the east and west of Palamcottah had come to him for instruction. In the following year there came 293 families from 18 villages and in 1825, 293 families from 89 villages; so that after 5 years' work, 4,300 souls had renounced idolatry and had turned towards God.

The reasons that so many thousands were so suddenly converted were various; the chief one seems to have been their astonishment that an European should speak their language, and trouble himself about them, the Shanars, a race forsaken, oppressed, though not standing in the status of servitude nor addicted to drunkenness. Rhenius was not deceived. He said: the majority of these people are not impelled to Christianity by proper motives, and how would it be possible for them in their heathen ignorance to be impelled by such. By God's grace, however, I will not let this opportunity escape. The good seed of the Word shall be scattered as abundantly as possible, and God will give His blessing where it pleases Him. On this account he was in no hurry to celebrate baptisms, the first of which did not take place until after two years, and there were only two families. After 10 years Rhenius had 2,000 families with 7,500 souls in 244 villages; 64 Catechists instructed them, and in 62 schools 1,300 children were taught. Rhenius now divided the whole region into 10 districts, over each of which he placed a Catechist at the head of the rest. All the native Assistants came once a month to Palamcottah, gave an account of their work, were instructed in God's Word, were admonished and dismissed in God's name.

Rhenius carried on an extensive correspondence, and sent to his King Friederick William III of Prussia a report of the Mission. The King received this very kindly and sent to him the following letter:—

"*To Mr. Rhenius, Missionary.*

I was very glad to receive with your letters of the 2-9-1818, the New Testament in the Tamil and Telugoo languages, and the interesting Report of your Mission. I see from it that your endeavours to obey the command of the Saviour to spread abroad the Gospel have been rewarded with blessed results. With pleasure, therefore, I show to you the interest I feel in it, by informing you that I have made provision for a permanent assistance to the Mission School of this place. This medal I send you as a remembrance of me.

FRIEDERICH WILHELM."

BERLIN, 30*th Dec.* 1820.

The first fruit of the royal assistance to Missionary work, obtained in this way by means of Rhenius, was the education of Gützolf, who was afterwards celebrated in the Chinese Mission. A Count Dohna sent him a considerable present, with which Rhenius purchased a piece of land and founded a new Christian village, called in honor of the Count Dohnavoor. In it he also built a Church out of the Count's money, and to this day the village is inhabited entirely by Christians. The Rev. Schaffter who came to help Mr. Rhenius resided in Dohnavoor. Bernhard Schmid, who until then had been his faithful Assistant, was compelled on account of severe suffering in the head to leave the plains and withdraw to the Blue Hills. This Dr.

Bernhard Schmid has subsequently been reproached with inactivity as a Missionary. In Tinnevelly, however, he labored faithfully and remained in union of spirit with Rhenius until his death. Because his sufferings in the head were invisible, men judged by what they could see only, and judged falsely. (After spending 18 years in the plains he went to the Hills in 1835, but as even this cool climate was not sufficient to restore his health, he went to Europe, 1836. He returned, however, to India in 1845 and resided at Ootacamund where his leisure was employed in the study of Botany in which he made many important discoveries. He died at Calicut in 1857 at the advanced age of 70.) Rhenius also received a valuable Assistant in the shape of the Rev. Müller, who subsequently became his son-in-law. In this year, 1835, there were 3,275 families with 11,186 souls in 261 villages, under Christian instruction, but only 2,198 persons were baptized. Four German Missionaries, Rhenius, Schaffter, Müller and Lechler were at the head of the work, assisted by 120 Catechists. They had 107 schools with 2,882 children, and a High School for the training of Catechists and Teachers. Rhenius founded several Associations amongst the Christians, such as a Tract Association, a poor fund for the support of the widows of Catechists and Teachers and a philanthropic Association, called Dharma Sangam for the support of oppressed and persecuted Christians. This Association imposed upon itself the duty of purchasing land where persecuted Christians might take refuge and settle down. By means of the rent which the Christians afterwards paid for the land, this Association soon became self-supporting. It built houses for the Catechists and Teachers, and soon acquired a capital of Rs. 15,000. The other Associations also proved of great benefit and exist to the present day.

Besides these undertakings Rhenius was very active in literary matters. He wrote a great many tracts, which were printed and distributed by his Tract Association; and also compiled useful school books, and a Tamil Grammar, which to this day is a faithful guide in Tamil to the Missionary. He also translated the New Testament into Tamil, as he wished to have a more popular version than ours, translated by Fabricius, is. His wish, however, of making it popular led him into writing a paraphrase rather than a translation. In spite of this, his translation was used by many Missionaries and congregations, and especially in the south.

Rhenius, therefore, during his 15 years of labor in Tinnevelly, had brought about greater results than any other Missionary of modern times. Even the work of the Jesuit Xavier is not to be compared with that of Rhenius. Xavier went on baptizing until his arm was tired, and was incapable of giving to the people even a single address. But after only two years he declared his baptized converts to be too bad to be Christians, he forsook them and went away. Rhenius, however, first thoroughly instructed them, and founded Schools, Colleges and entirely new Christian villages. From within he raised the whole race by Evangelical Christianity and also from without by discipline, order and constitutional rules. Besides he remained at his post until his death, and by means of his writings he still speaks to his congregations, though dead. His Christians consider it a great honor to have been baptized by him. It is true they do not exclaim Saint Rhenius! (as the Papist do, Saint Xavier!) pray for us! but could such a prayer be of any use it would be more in accordance with common sense in the case of Rhenius whose life was spent among his Christians, than in that of Xavier, who considered his converts too bad, and forsook them.

In 1835, however, the incongruous position of an Evangelical Lutheran Christian in an English Society, which must always exist, and which had already led to misunderstanding, produced a regular rupture, and Rhenius fell out with his Society. The Church Missionary Society is very mild in regard to English Church matters, and Rhenius was even still milder in regard to Lutheran matters, indeed he was a regular Unionist. And if it were possible for conscientious Missionaries of one Church to work in conjunction with another Church, it must have been possible in this case. But nevertheless it came to be impossible. The way in which matters came to a rupture was as follows:

Rhenius had prepared with much care a number of Catechists and Teachers. Five or six of these he considered worthy of ordination and wished to place them as Pastors in the newly collected Congregations. Our old Missionaries had often done this and had frequently sent such Pastors to

Tinnevelly, who alone had kept together and led the work, during the 'dark times' of Tinnevelly when there was no Missionary there. The English Chaplain, Hough, gave the two last of the Pastors sent by our Lutheran Missionaries the highest testimony. The Society, therefore, had nothing to object against the ordination of Rhenius' pupils; nor did it, but demanded, and rightly from its stand-point, that the ordination should be carried out by the English Bishop. Rhenius would have preferred ordaining them himself as our old Missionaries had been in the habit of doing, but made no objections to their being ordained by the Bishop as long as he did not pledge them by the English confessions of faith with which the Candidates were for the most part unacquainted or when they were acquainted with them, were unable to subscribe. The Bishop, however, could, of course, only ordain according to the rules of his Church, and so nothing came of the whole ordination. The conscientious Rhenius then found it impossible to go on with his work and accordingly made to the Society three proposals; 1st, to go to England and discuss the matter personally; or 2ndly, to withdraw to Madras and engage in literary work; or 3rdly, to separate from the Society and work in conjunction with some other Mission Society in India. The Society chose the first of these proposals and invited him to a personal interview in London.

But nothing came of this arrangement and this was the reason. Mr. Harper, an English clergyman in Madras, editor of a religious newspaper and Secretary of the Missionary Committee, had brought out a little book on the Church, written with High Church opinions, and containing many assertions opposed not only to holy Writ, but also to Church history, and had challenged Rhenius to write a review of it which he promised to publish in his paper. Rhenius did so, for as Secretary to the Committee he was in a way Rhenius' superior. The review, however, by no means turned out to be what Mr. Harper had expected for Rhenius picked the little book mercilessly to pieces and proved so convincingly the untenability of the doctrine of the succession that there was nothing to be said in answer. Mr. Harper considered it, therefore, to be *best* not to publish this review, and not to say a word in answer. Rhenius quite honestly sent a copy of his review to the Church Missionary Society in London and they also sent no word in reply. Rhenius' opinion was known and no objection was made to it; indeed they even defended him against Dr. Wilson the Metropolitan at Calcutta who had wished to interfere in the Mission without knowing anything about it.

As, however, Mr. Harper would not publish the review of his book, Rhenius urged on by some of his friends, printed it himself in a separate pamphlet, and then, because he had *printed* his refutation of the doctrine of Episcopal Succession (not because he had *written* it) he was dismissed by the Society.

It is easy enough to dismiss a Missionary like Rhenius, but it is often difficult to bear the consequences. Legally the Society probably acted rightly in dismissing a Missionary who openly attacks its teachings; but it would have been wiser if they had at once forgotten the long-forgotten pamphlet.

The Society did not only dismiss him from its employ, but also removed him from Tinnevelly and took possession of all the stations, even of those which like Dohnavoor has been bought and built out of German money. When Rhenius and his fellow Missionaries, at the request of their Christians proposed to go on with his work unaided by the Society, the then Secretary Tinker who had come from Madras to take charge of the stations, informed them that the Society would certainly send out Missionaries and take forcible charge, even though Rhenius should remain. In order, therefore, to avoid dissensions and scandal, Rhenius expressed himself willing to go. But then his brethren Schaffter, Müller and Lechler, who fully agreed with Rhenius, and who were deeply wounded at the treatment he had received, declared that they too could not stop; and when the Madras Missions Committee wished them to sign a document "that they resigned all claim to any portion of the Tinnevelly Mission and to the souls who had been or who might be converted by means of their labors, and would quietly withdraw from Tinnevelly whenever the Committee might request them," they one and all resigned their appointment.

The Missionaries with their families now withdrew to Arcot, in order to commence a new Mission; and the whole

Tinnevelly Mission with its hundreds of villages and schools, with its thousands of Christians and catechumens and with its 120 Catechists, was given over to the charge of an English Missionary (Pettitt) who had only been two years in the country and who knew nothing at all of Tinnevelly. This was a crying injustice not only to the young Christian congregations, but also an injustice to the young Missionary whose inexperience only led him from one mistake into another.

Towards the end of June 1835, the brethren had left Tinnevelly, and already at the commencement of August or only six weeks after their departure, they were implored by 44 Catechists and congregations to return. At the end of August, 80 Catechists and 15 Seminarists addressed the Committee in Madras, describing their condition and begging for the restoration of their Pastors. Rhenius and his brethren received a copy of the Address, with an earnest request that they would not forsake them in their need, or otherwise they would be compelled to turn to some other Mission.

What was Rhenius to do? For the sake of peace, and in order not to lead the congregations astray, he had yielded, but now there was no peace, and confusion was becoming worse confounded. After consultation with his brethren and friends, he decided upon returning to Tinnevelly. In October he was again at his post and was received by his Christians with great delight. Schaffter, Müller and Lechler soon followed him.

Of course, the Society had its supporters and Mr. Pettitt even travelled about and nailed up the Churches of those Christians who adhered to Rhenius; he even closed the Church of Dohnavoor built with German money and threatened to bring those before a Court of law who should interfere with his nails. Rhenius, his brethren and the Christians bore all this with patience, they complained to no Court, but pursued their way quietly and increased abundantly. His friends in India, England, Germany and America helped him generously. He required nearly Rs. 25,000 annually and the Lord gave it him in abundance until his death. This unhappily followed in three years, on the 5th June 1838 in the 48th year of his age and in the 24th year of his unbroken Indian career.

'I am not well, the heat is very great.' These are the last words in his faithfully kept diary. His signature to an appeal to the English residents of Palamcottah to support the Bible Society, written on the morning of his death was the last stroke of his pen. After a short sickness he was seized with paralysis and fell asleep so softly that it was scarcely noticed.

"My judgment is with the Lord
And my work with my God"

is the inscription on his grave. It was not without tears that I stood by his last resting place.

His fellow Missionaries write of him:—"No one was ever more zealous in his duties than Mr. Rhenius was. They were not mere duties to him, but his food and his drink. In season and out of season he was always bent upon doing something useful. Time was very precious to him and each portion of his work had its allotted time. His patience and submission to the Divine Will were wonderful. No one ever saw him impatient or discontented. Whatever happened he accepted as a dispensation of God and submitted to it joyfully nor did he allow it to disturb the deep peace of his soul. When he received evil treatment he was in the habit less of thinking of himself than to lament the weakness of human nature, so that what to others would have been a severe trial of patience he seemed scarcely to feel." Newspapers also, which during his rupture with the Society had attacked him severely, now began to sing of his praise. The *Spectator* of 7th July 1838, writes:—

"Mr. Rhenius was no ordinary man; his talents were of a very high order, and had he chosen any other walk of life there is no doubt that he would have risen to eminence amongst men of talent and learning. But gifts like his directed without interruption towards one object; a piety so joyful and so sincere; unremitting diligence with a sound constitution of body, and powers of mind, so well directed, are able to accomplish great things, so that Mr. Rhenius though a simple Missionary has, in course of time, won a firm place in public opinion. There was a power of mind about him which exercised a great influence over all with whom he came in contact. We have learnt the power of his influence in several instances. Personal considerations never entered his thoughts and a wish for personal or family distinction, found no place in his noble bosom. He was a thoroughly disinterested character. In his many and valuable Tamil writings he has left to the young native Church of Southern India a rich legacy, but to his family he has left no other legacy than his name distinguished for humanity, piety, talent and usefulness," &c.

Other newspapers wrote to the same effect so that provision was made for his widow and six children. Nor did the Church Mission Society remain in the back ground, but paid to the widow her pension as if Rhenius had not been dismissed and pays it to this day. For to this day his widow lives and resides in Bangalore. For 35 years has she been a widow, and is still quite lively in spirits: to her and her children I am indebted for many a source of information which would otherwise have remained closed to me.

Rhenius was a diligent correspondent, and I cannot forbear giving at least one extract from one of his letters, which he wrote to a Missionary scarcely a year before his death, for these words of his are to-day worthy to be taken to heart and not by Missionaries only. To the question what was the reason that his work met with such great results, whilst that of others was fruitless, Rhenius replied: "Yea, Father, for thus it hath been pleasing to Thee, that is the answer!" and then he continues:—"If I am permitted to give a further explanation of the subject, that much depends upon the spirit in which the means are made use of. Many may plough, sow and water and yet with but little success, owing to want of power and skill. By spiritual power and skill I understand especially proper motives and reasons of action. These are love to Christ and to our fellow sinners, and a burning desire to save the latter from their sins and to glorify the former, and I must add: the carrying out this work as servants of our Lord Jesus Christ and according to his commandment without regard to others. But it is a fact that we can preach, and proclaim the Gospel, and be otherwise very diligent without being actuated by these spiritual motives or by only a little of them. We can regard our Missionary work as a duty which we are bound to perform towards men who provide us with our temporal wants. We can also be actuated by the feeling that it would be wicked to be idle in this work, and that we should be talked about if we were. In short, we may be very active in our duties though we regard it merely as an office among men, and one to maintain us in the world."

"I will not say that these motives and intentions are the only ones (I hope there are very few Missionaries who have no other but these), but these may at the same time be the chief motives whilst the proper motives are only secondary, so that in this respect we are more servants of men than of Christ, or endeavour to serve two masters. But, however active we may be in this way, the blessing from above will always be wanting. The Holy Ghost has not fully taken possession of us, and though we may preach and proclaim the Gospel, yet we do so without power. I really believe, my dear Brother, that in our time there is no want of plans and systems for spreading Christianity. We have enough of these, and in this respect no change is required. But I fear that there is much want of proper motives of the proper mainspring of action. There is a want of an Apostolical spirit, of heartfelt love to men, our fellow sinners, who have need of the same Saviour; of unqualified obedience to our Lord and Saviour; with regard to man of perfect simplicity and God-like sincerity in doing His will, cost it what it may; the firm resolve to follow His Word in our calling without human inventions; trust in His promises, and a wish only to increase the glory of God and the salvation of sinners. These, these are wanting and these wants need to be supplied."

"From what I have said, you will perceive that I do not so much find a want in the means and ways of spreading Christianity, but rather in the state of the Missionaries' hearts. We all want more spirituality, more personal sanctity, more real and vigorous trust in Christ, our Lord and Master in this great work; more constant living in it, morning and night, more faithful prayer for His blessing and guidance. And here, allow me to speak to you frankly as between you and me, I have often heard, that you are rich, that you have a house at————and money in the Bank. If this is true, I have no doubt you have acted from reasons of prudence in order to provide for a future day. But this is fitting for persons who do not serve Christ, not for us who know and serve an Almighty and All-sufficing God and Saviour. Is there not in this a want of faith in His care for us? and if this is so, if we cannot trust Him in regard to these minor things, of what nature will our faith be with reference to higher things? It can only be a very weak faith and must necessarily cast a great shade over our work in His vineyard. His commandment is: "Seek ye first for the Kingdom of God and His righteousness, and He will provide all such (minor) things." If the above rumour is true, I should like to say: " my dear Brother, sell everything and employ it on the poor heathens. Lay it all at the feet of Jesus Christ and turn to Him in perfect faith that He will provide for you and yours. In this way whilst honoring Him, He will again honor you and will make you a light which shall shine brightly, &c."

The Church Missionary Society did not get another Rhenius, but it has since then faithfully labored in the Tinnevelly field. At present it has in nine chief stations, 8 European Missionaries and 31 native Pastors, assisted by 206 Catechists. The number of Christians is about 27,000 in 471 congregations; above 11,000 catechumens are under instruction, and about 700 heathens were baptized during last year. The catechumens are made to wait several years for baptism. It has 377 schools with more than 11,000 children, and besides a boarding-school for girls, they have in Palamcottah a female Teacher's Seminary with above 100 pupils. These are educated so as to pass the Government Examinations and are then sent out as Teachers. Thirty have already been appointed to newly founded Girls Schools, and the Director of the Seminary hopes to be able to open 10 new schools every year and provide them with Teachers from this institution. These schools are especially intended for heathens, for, experience teaches that every superstition has a firmer hold among women than among men, and in India it is only too often the case that men who are willing to become Christians are kept back by their wives and allow themselves to be hindered, in order to avoid a family-scandal. From this Teacheress Institution we may, therefore, expect great good. An English woman, Sarah Tinker, gave a considerable sum of money towards it, and thus founded the Institution which now bears her name and is known as the " Sarah Tinker Institute." Would that German women would do the same for our Mission!

The handful of Christians which Rhenius had collected in Madras have kept firm also, and now numbers 711 souls. The number is, perhaps, trifling, but their mode of government is important. These 711 souls are divided—for they are scattered—into two native pastorates. Each of the two congregations chooses 2 delegates. These 4 delegates with the two native Pastors and the English Missionary (who also choose two assessors) form the "Native Church Council." This Native Church Council manages all the concerns of the congregations. The contributions of the congregations are paid into a common Fund called the Native Church Fund. The President (the Missionary) and the Secretary (one of the delegates) are the trustees. This Fund together with a grant-in-aid from the Society, which, however, yearly decreases, goes in payment of the salaries of the native Pastors, Catechists and Teachers. In the year 1868 when this arrangement was made, the grant-in-aid given by the Society amounted to Rs. 300 per mensem. In the following year it was Rs. 250; in 1870 only Rs. 200, and in 1872 only Rs. 170, whilst the contributions of both congregations amounted in this year to Rs. 1,549. The Society, therefore, has saved during the last five years, during which the congregation has been divided into native pastorates above Rs. 2,500.

It will be interesting to hear what the native community themselves think of this arrangement. One of the two native Pastors of these congregations writes as follows :—

"Although the native congregations should have native Pastors, I am of opinion that they should not be left entirely alone, until they are in a position to govern themselves. But at the same time the native congregations should be taught the great lesson of self-help, of self-action, and self-government, where that has not been done it should be done without delay. For otherwise the Missionary Societies would learn by sorrowful experience that this method is not only unsound but very expensive. The native congregation would cling to the Societies like creepers, and their increasing numbers would necessitate such outlays that at last it would be impossible to meet them. It is, therefore, of the greatest importance to educate our native congregations to a condition of independence, self-government and self-progress. This is also the opinion of the Rev. H. Venn, who for half a century has been the Honorary Secretary of the Church Missionary Society. In 1867, he writes to the Bishop of Jamaica :—' It may well be said that it is a recent discovery of Missionary science, that when the

Missionary is of another and higher race than his converts, he cannot undertake to be their *Pastor*. For although they may be bound to him by personal ties, yet if he continues to be their Pastor they will not form a vigorous native Church, but, as a rule, will remain in a state of dependence and make but little progress. The same congregations under competent native Pastors would be independent, and their religion would gain a more manly and homely form.'

In conclusion, it is clear that in order to make the native congregations independent, they must be brought as soon as possible to think and to act for themselves. A child will never learn to stand and walk alone if it is always kept in swaddling clothes. It is true that native congregations when left alone, will commit many a mistake and will stumble, but through these mistakes and falls they will learn how to walk in safety. The native congregation (at Madras) has reached its present condition by increasing its subscriptions and diminishing its expenditure, and we are not without hope that, in the course of time, we shall require no more help from the Society."

This is what a native Pastor writes, and his words as well as those of the late Mr. Venn, quoted by him are well worthy of note.

CHAPTER V.

THE MISSION OF THE ENGLISH AND AMERICAN (NON-CONFORMIST CHURCHES.)

The western ghauts slope down towards the south before they reach Cape Comorin the southernmost point of India. The land of the Tamulians which for the greater part is separated from Travancore by these mountains, continue its level plains towards the south-west coast, and thus forms the southernmost point of the kingdom of Travancore. The country, the people, and their conditions of life are here the same as in Tinnevelly. The simple, less cunning and more easily led Shanars turned here as in Tinnevelly in crowds towards Christianity. The Rev. Ringeltaube labored here from 1810, collected several congregations and built some little Churches in the shadow of the palm trees, which he himself planted. His name is still remembered. He was an industrious preacher, travelled much, but suffered much in his head and had to leave India. The London Missionary Society under which he worked sent their first Missionary there in 1818, and has since then faithfully continued Ringeltaube's work. The demon-worship to which all the Shanars are addicted seems to be still wilder here than in Tinnevelly. They have established "devil-dancers" or demon-priests, who dressed in a fantastic garb make enormous jumps and thus bring to the demon, worship and sacrifice. I will give a few examples of how this is done, and how in spite of all this Christianity still gains ground.

A woman had been for many years suffering from severe hysterical attacks. These were ascribed to the influence of a demon, but the only thing was that they did not exactly know which devil it was. The priests prescribed costly sacrifices, first for one demon and then for another, they made the wildest jumps, the husband spent his money and the wife kept her sickness. One day when the husband had to start on a long journey, the wife got so violent an attack, that she lay there like one dead. The best of the "devil-dancers" were at once summoned, and they made quite a respectable devils' noise, but the sick woman remained motionless. At last the priests could stand it no longer, and seized by rage, one of them caught hold of a knife, ran at the woman and shouted out: "Reveal thy name or I will cut thee to pieces!" another seized a fire-brand and exclaimed, "I will burn thee unless thou tellest thy name," (the name of the possessing devil). But still the sick woman remained motionless. So it went on till midnight, until at last the husband had had enough. He exclaimed: "Stop! it is sufficient. How can you drive out the devil when you do not even know his name. Get out of this! I will have nothing more to do with you. From henceforth I will join the Christians." He then gave his sick unconscious wife in the charge of some Christian neighbours and said: "If she dies during my absence, bury her after your fashion, I will have nothing more to do with the demons." The Christians nursed her, and the woman recovered. On his return the man believed and his whole house, and four other families who had been witnesses of what had happened, followed his examples.

Two of these families had between them a temple, in the middle of which was an image of the terrible Isakki. This abomination held a child between its teeth and another in its hands. They wished to destroy the idol, but nevertheless seemed to be restrained by fear. The Missionary was, therefore, invited and a large number of people also attended. After an address to the by-standers, Isakki was first of all knocked in pieces, the roof was then pulled down and, lastly, the walls were levelled to the ground, wherein the Missionary also helped. The ceremony concluded with an address and with prayer. But in the same night the wife of one of these new converts was seized with a violent attack of sickness. The villagers at once collected, and were, of course, of opinion that this was Isakki wreaking an awful vengeance. A devil-dancer who had served Isakki also came and shouted like a mad one: Now, I will destroy thee! Now, I will tear out thy vitals! The woman, however, in spite of all this recovered, upon which the devil-dancer called out: "It is true that Isakki seized her, but the prayers of the Christians have nailed her to the Murunkai-tree." In another village some Christians had, as a next-door neighbour, a bigoted 'devil-dancer' who often mocked them on account of their prayers and hymns, but who it seems also feared them. He also had a temple of his own in the middle of which was the powerful Pulaveshekaran mounted on a horse, with a crown on his head and a sword in his hand; by his side there were also other idols. This savage idol-worshipper had a son 12 years of age who became very ill. The ordinary sacrifices were made, but the boy became always weaker and weaker until at last he lost all consciousness. The heathens at once made a loud yelling, as is their custom when any one is about to die. In this extremity, the anxious father turned to his hated Christian neighbours and begged them to intercede for him, and added that in future he would no longer worship idols. The Christians prayed and by the grace of God the boy recovered. Thereupon the man gave over to the Missionary the different articles he had used in his demon-worship and begged him to come into his village and destroy the idol. The Missionary came and a number of people assembled in the house. After an address, the mighty Pulavashekaran was tumbled into the dust and the temple destroyed. A few days afterwards the man's wife sickened and all the villagers again thought that Pulaveshekaran was about to take a terrible revenge; the woman, however, recovered and the whole family were converted.

An old 'devil-dancer' had served his demons until his 60th year, when at last he was attacked with rheumatism and great pains in his limbs. The man then concluded that his demons were no good and turned to God. His wife, however, was even worse than Mrs. Job, she not only mocked him but left him as she herself would not become a Christian. The man, therefore, was left in a helpless state and was dependent upon the generosity of others. But his patient suffering conquered at last his bad wife and her children. They returned to him, were all converted and the old man's spirit became again young.

One must not suppose that this demon-worship is nothing more than ignorance and superstition. It is both, and a good deal more besides. Nor must one suppose that these demon-priests, devil-dancers, or whatever else they may choose to call themselves are nothing more than clever cheats—cheats they are—to be sure, but they are more than that, they are also cheated. After conversion they have frequently admitted that they have trembled body and soul through fear of these demons. Demon-worship has an awful power, not a life-giving one, but still a power; it is the dark power of death which controls their minds and not only those of the ignorant. I know many educated men, young men as well as old, who have received an English education and hold high Official appointments, but in spite of their knowledge they are still held in chains by this dark influence. Each soul that is rescued from this influence, whether he is a well educated Official or an unlettered laborer, is a work of the Almighty God and Lord of Life, Who alone is able to conquer the powerful prince of darkness and of death, and to take from him his prey. The man who denies this, knows nothing of heathendom.

The Gospel influence, however, is not only felt by the lower classes, but the higher ones also are not able to withstand it. Their time has not yet come, it is true, but it is approaching, one remarkable example I must cite: Two Catechists went together to preach and said something about Rama just as it occurred to them. A young Brahmin woman, scarcely grown up, listened to them and exclaimed: "What have you to do with the history of our good god Rama, ye preachers of Jesus? Speak of your own god and leave our Rama alone, lest by any chance you anger him and he devour you." Thereupon her old mother hurried out of the house and punished by thrusting in the mouth some moist earth which she had found near her waterpot, saying: You fool! what possesses you to talk like this? I know what our gods are. If a piece of stone gets into our mouths with our rice, we throw it away, but in the temple we fall down and worship a similar piece of stone. We tread upon one stone at our thresholds, and pray to another which has been cut by the mason. I agree with our poet who says:—

உள்ளதெய்வம் கல்லடா,	Ulla devam kallada,
உள்ளுவுந்தெய்வம் செம்படா,	Ullāvum devam sembada,
பின்னைதெய்வம் ஆருடா,	Pinnai devam ārada,
பேச அவ தூறடா.	Pēsa avaturada.

The god within is made of stone,
The one outside is brass alone,
Of him behind what is the name,
To tell it, is it then a shame.

This was what the Brahmin woman taught her daughter!

Understanding can go so far and can recognize a stone to be a stone, but it cannot go so far as to turn to the true God. This can only be brought about by the power and the grace of the Almighty God.

The number of Tamil Christians in Travancore consists at present of 27,000 souls in 240 congregations of whom, however, only 9,000 are baptized, as this rite is here often delayed for many years. Of Missionaries, however, there seem to be very few, for there are only six with ten native Pastors who are assisted by 18 'Evangelists' and 136 Catechists. The number of new conversions from the heathens is unfortunately not so great now as it was formerly, and one of the causes of this probably is the small number of Missionaries.

Besides this field the London Society has four other stations in Madras, Tripatore, Salem and Coimbatore, with some 2,000 adherents, of whom, however, only about 500 are 'Church Members.' On the other hand, it has in its Boys' Schools more than 1,000 pupils, and in its Girls' Schools more than 650.

The Wesleyan Methodists have, according to their Report for 1872, nine stations in Tamil land (south, Madras—north, Madras, St. Thomas' Mount, Negapatam, Manargudi, Malnattam, Trichinopoly, Trivalore, Caroor,) and 14 Missionaries supported by 8 Catechists. In all the nine stations there are 174 "full believing members of the Church" and 24 on probation. Their chief work lies in the schools. Here there are 2,700 pupils who, of course, are almost all heathens. Lately the Society has lost several Missionaries by death and others have been more or less prevented from work by sickness.

The Scotch Churches, the Established and the Free Church and especially the latter, are very diligent in the Tamil country, but are occupied almost exclusively in the higher schools for heathens. The work is in a certain degree one for the future. It is sufficient for the pulling down of the mighty fabric of heathenism, for he who has been instructed in a Mission school can never again like his forefathers believe thoroughly in idols, although for the sake of custom he may wear their marks on his forehead. Besides, he becomes acquainted with the Bible, and with it receives some historical acquaintance with Christianity. Now and then even a young man is converted and then employed in the schools as a teacher. In this way they have collected small congregations of a few hundred souls in the vicinity of the principal station, Madras. In the same degree that the number of converts is small, the number of pupils is large. In the Free Church Mission there are in 14 schools more than 2,600 pupils, of whom more than 900 are girls. The work is conducted by more than 150 teachers under able Scotch Missionaries, who with much self-denial conduct a Missionary work in a way which they believe to be effectual, nay, almost the only effectual method. The Missionaries remark in their Report: "All these tabulated results represent only a portion, and a very small portion of what is actually going on; there are higher fruits of our labor which cannot be calculated in an arithmetical manner. The development of character, the commencement of self-reliance and independent thought, the awakening of moral and religious feelings, the quiet and, perhaps, imperceptible influence of truth can be seen and felt by those who come in daily contact with the different classes. We cannot report any instances of conversion of the heart to God, but results of a lower, preparatory, but yet valuable kind are clear enough and resemble the faint streaks before the dawn of a brighter day in this part of India."

The shadow that has fallen on the school Missions of every kind during late years is the almost total absence of results in reference to conversions to God and gathering congregations. At the commencement, when these school Missions were founded, their effectiveness was judged by the number of the pupils, who by means of the instruction received in these schools, had been led to relinquish idolatry and turn to Christ, and the present Christians and ordained natives of these institutions date mostly from that time. As, however, for some years the Government have been giving grants-in-aid according to the results as tested by an Examination in mere secular subjects, and pay to the teachers as much as half their salary if they will teach secular subjects daily for six hours, and lastly, as upon passing the Government Examinations, depends not only the much-coveted distinction of B.A., but also the even-more-coveted appointment to some Government Office, and as in Government Examinations no attention is paid to religious subjects; everybody now strives to succeed in passing as large a number of boys as possible. It is natural, therefore, that, though with the best intentions, and though he be himself unaware of, or deny it, the Missionary allows Christian instruction to fall in the back ground and become a matter of secondary importance, and this is proved by the very marked difference between former years and the present ones. The institutions of these educational Missions among the Free Church Mission occupy the highest rank, and are, therefore, more training schools than Missionary ones. Lord Napier, when presiding at the Examination of the Central School of this Mission in Madras, made some sound and valuable remarks. He said to the Missionaries :—

"I thank you for your kind invitation which has placed me in a position to take a share in these proceedings. I regard this school with peculiar interest, and it causes me sincere pleasure to be a witness of its strivings and prosperity. If we look at the large number of the pupils at the various classes from which they are drawn, at the high attainments of the staff of teachers, and at the old and well founded reputation of this establishment, it would be difficult to over-estimate its value as a popular means of the moral and intellectual development of the country. It is certain that you render to the Government considerable service in a matter in which we take deep interest: It is certain that you bestow upon the people many and wide-spreading benefits. I congratulate the pupils on the successes which they have gained in the University Examinations, and I beg them earnestly to give by their diligence and obedience the only reward to their teachers which they can bestow upon them in return for a life of banishment, of labor and of self-denial."

Of American Missionary Societies there are two in the land of the Tamulians. The oldest is that of Madura which was founded in 1834. Madura is the next district north of Tinnevelly and the chief town of the same name is, doubtless, the finest town in South India. It has fine level broad streets, in part ornamented with palm trees; it is full of palaces and temples, and even now it can at once be seen that this was once the residence of mighty kings. This was the capital of the powerful Pandion kingdom from which ambassadors are said to have come to Rome to the Emperor Augustus. The palaces which remain are even to this day worthy of admiration, so much so that the Government is at present spending hundreds of thousands of Rupees in order to preserve them to posterity. During the last centuries the royal power was continually on the wane, but even one of these last Princes built a hall of pillars, that is said to have cost 10 millions of Rupees. In the middle of this hall, near the finest of the many fine pillars, stands the prince himself with his hands folded, on his left is his wife also with her hands folded, but with a hole in her stone hip. When I asked the meaning of this, the Judge who was my guide explained it as follows: This queen was a princess of the house of Tanjore and a very proud woman. When the Prince highly pleased with his really wonderful building, asked his wife: "Has your father anything like this?" She answered spitefully, "My father's cowshed is finer than that!" Thereupon the Prince drew his dagger and threw it at his wife, whom it struck in the hip and remained sticking there. As a remembrance of this she has been represented with a hole in her stone hip. The Prince may have been a little violent, but the haughty wife deserved correction, for neither in her father's palace which is still standing nor in his whole town, is there a hall to compare with this one.

The people also take an interest in restoring the mighty temples, and as much as Rs. 5,000 is often expended on a single granite pillar. Rich Tamulians take a pride in having been able to erect one or several pillars. I have nowhere seen idolatry with so much life in it as in Madura. The kings of Madura cultivated literature which here attained its highest prosperity. Even to this day the inhabitants of Madura boast that they speak the purest Tamil and they may be right. Madura—the sweet—with its palaces, tanks, palm groves, once seen is not easily forgotten. Ch. Fr. Schwartz who was so well acquainted with South India was also astonished when he saw Madura.

The finest and sweetest part of Madura, however, are the 139 congregations in 249 villages containing more than 7,000 Christians. The Missionaries have here the practical as well as proper principle of a congregational 'call.' Every congregation or, it may be, two or three small congregations combined invite some particular candidate, and promise according to their means his salary. The Missionaries then ordain and install the man 'called' and add so much as is indispensable out of the Mission funds for his subsistence, until the congregation is in a condition to pay him more. This is surely the best way to teach a congregation to be independent! At present no congregation gives less than one-fifth of their Pastors' salaries and many give as much as one-half. The salaries of the Pastors begin at very little and rise from Rs. 10 to Rs. 35 per month. Fourteen Native Pastors are already officiating, assisted by 113 Catechists and governed by 10 Missionaries. Experienced Catechists used to be ordained, being content with but little, and are more suitable to the village congregations than classically educated and inexperienced young man who look upon village life with contempt.

The Missionaries of Madura are also very busy in the spread of the written Word. In their last year, reported on, they had partly sold, and partly given away 138 Bibles, 177 New Testaments, 2,800 single Gospels and more than 24,000 Tracts. The Bible is held in high estimation even by many a heathen. There is a heathen Doctor there who always carries about a Bible, and when lately he was called in to attend for some time the Professor of Sanscrit at the pagoda, he not only gave him medicine daily, but also read him out every day something from the Bible. How many Christian Doctors would do the same ?

The Mission has also a Medical Missionary in whose charge is a Hospital, in which during the last year more than 14,000 patients were treated. Of course, to each of these patients the word of God was also read and preached.

The other American Mission is that of Arcot. In 1836 there came two Missionaries from Ceylon to Madras and founded two stations, and eventually a printing press which has done much good. These two Missionaries, Winslowe and Dr. Scudder, preached diligently and collected several Christians but never succeeded in getting together a respectable congregation. They were also (except in the beginning) only meagrely supported from America, and frequently thwarted, since Directors at a distance often know better what should be done than the Missionaries who are on the spot. Hence after the death of these two Missionaries, the Mission in Madras was given up. Dr. Scudder, however, had seven sons, all of whom became Missionaries, a case probably unprecedented. Six of these brave sons are still at their posts, two are Doctors of Theology and the remaining four Doctors of Medicine. These brothers founded in 1853 the Mission of Arcot with the chief stations of Arcot, Vellore, Chittoor and Arnee. As the majority also render medicinal aid, they find a ready access to the heathens. When they travel about and take their medicines with them, they have sometimes from 70 to 80 patients a day, to whom God's Word is administered in addition to medical treatment. In their Hospital at Arcot they have daily 150 patients. They travel about much and preach the Gospel in every village. If any one applies for religious instruction, they do not accept him, if it is in a place where as yet there are no Christians, unless there are at least three families prepared. They then send a Catechist who instructs the people, generally in the evening, since during the day they must work. At their first reception the catechumens have to make three pledges; 1, to avoid all idolatry ; 2, never to work on Sundays ; 3, to eat no meat of deceased cattle. The last condition often causes trouble, but is always firmly insisted upon, as indeed is necessary. All of the lower castes, the pariahs, and especially the chucklers or leather workers are only too fond of eating the flesh of deceased cattle. When Brahmins abhor all meat, and the other castes abhor beef, people who eat the carcases of dead cattle must be to them an abomination such as we can scarcely conceive. Even in Germany, in our days a flayer was so despised that no one would drink from the same glass he had drunk from, and yet they were never reproached with having eaten dead meat. The chucklers are not only the flayers of the country, but also the vultures. The slaughtering of living cattle is done by other persons, but they are the only ones who touch fallen cattle, they take off the skin, which they tan and manufacture into shoes, harness, &c., and then eat the carcase. It is with right, therefore, that our old Missionaries already protested strongly against this, and what has since been neglected is now earnestly remedied by the Arcot Missionaries. The instruction of their catechumens lasts generally for a year, and the little flock is then at once formed into a congregation. In 1871, they had already 18 congregations with 2,478 Christians who contributed Rs. 1,450 towards their own maintenance. In their schools, which are for Christian children only, there are 760 children and there is a Seminary for girls as well as one for boys.

These are the English and American Missions in Tamil land. The Baptists have also a so-called Mission but they only throw out their nets to catch Europeans and East Indians.

In the year 1860 there were 117 European Missionaries in the land of the Tamulians, 91,844 native Protestant Christians and 43 ordained Native Pastors. During the last 10 years the work has made a pleasing progress. There are now 104 Native Pastors in the Tamil country, on the other hand the number of European Missionaries has unfortunately been reduced by 35, for in 1871 there were only 82 Missionaries. The number of native Christians, however, has increased by 26,473 souls, so that the total number of native Protestant Christians is now 118,317. It cannot, therefore, be said that the Missionaries have labored in vain, or that the Lord has withheld His blessing. Blessed be His name and praise be to Him for the unspeakable mercy which He has hitherto shown to the Tamulians. May His grace be poured upon them even yet more and more abundantly, for there are still to each

Missionary more than 180,000 heathens! This is the state of things in the Tamil country, but in the rest of India it is even worse. What can a poor Missionary in a climate like that of India, with his many scattered handfuls of Christians, with schools and buildings to erect, do among so many heathens? Truly it is easy for those who "live at home at ease" to talk about the small results of the Mission, especially whilst they support it only slightly and pray for it lukewarmly. Those who pray earnestly that the Kingdom of God may come have, however, reason to thank Him for having heard their prayers, and to become for the future even more fervent in their prayers and more earnest in their work. The results of the Mission are great enough to lead us to expect still greater. They are not, however, large enough to warrant the folding of our hands laying them in our laps and doing nothing.

"Therefore, my dear Brethren, stand fast immoveable and increase in the work of the Lord, for ye know that your work is not fruitless before the Lord."

FINIS.